The Logic of Marx's Capital

SUNY Series in the Philosophy of the Social Sciences
Lenore Langsdorf, Editor

The Logic of Marx's Capital

REPLIES TO HEGELIAN CRITICISMS

Tony Smith

State University of New York Press

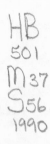

Published by
State University of New York Press, Albany

For information, address State University of New York
Press, State University Plaza, Albany, N.Y., 12246

Library of Congress Cataloging-in-Publication Data

Smith, Tony, 1951-
    The logic of Marx's Capital : replies to Hegelian criticisms / by
Tony Smith.
        p.   cm. — (SUNY series in the philosophy of the social
sciences)
    Includes bibliographical references.
    ISBN 0-7914-0267-3. — ISBN 0-7914-0268-1 (pbk.)
    1. Marx, Karl, 1818-1883.   Kapital.   I. Title.   II. Series.
HB501.M37S56   1990
335.4′1—dc20   89-21839
                                                                          CIP

10   9   8   7   6   5   4   3   2   1

Contents

v

CONTENTS

Introduction

One cannot simply assume that the world needs yet another book on Hegel and Marx. The Hegel-Marx connection has been explored at great length. There have been Marxist studies of Hegel's *Phenomenology*,[1] studies of Hegel's influence on the 1844 *Manuscripts* and other early writings of Marx,[2] comparisons of Hegel's philosophy of history with Marx's historical materialism,[3] discussions of how Marx formulated his theory of ideology in opposition to the Hegelian theory of consciousness,[4] criticisms of Hegel's *Philosophy of Right* from a Marxist standpoint,[5] and defenses of Hegel from these critiques.[6] There have been general comparisons of the role of dialectics in the two thinkers,[7] and studies of Hegel's influence on Marx's concept of science,[8] and on his concept of alienation.[9] However there is one central area that has yet to be explored adequately. This is the role of Hegelian dialectical logic in *Capital*.[10] Consideration of this issue opens three areas of investigation, areas to be explored in the present study. 1) How did Marx employ dialectical logic in his theory? 2) What purpose does it serve? 3) Did he get it right?

1) The importance of Hegel's *Logic* for an understanding of *Capital* has been stressed as long ago as an 1891 letter by Engels. But scholars thus far have examined sections from *Capital* in isolation.[11] No one has established in detail that *Capital* is a systematic theory of economic categories ordered according to a dialectical logic taken over from Hegel. Beginning with "commodity" and "value" at the start of Volume I and progressing step by step to the end of Volume III, I attempt to show precisely how Marx employed dialectical logic in the construction of his theory.

2) Although the full role of dialectical logic in *Capital* has not been adequately established previously, it has been widely accepted that Hegel's *Logic* did influence Marx in the writing of *Capital*. However the dominant view today is that the influence of Hegel on Marx was pernicious.[12] Thus far no one has attempted to answer this perspective in detail. My objective is to establish not just that Marx employed dialectical logic, but why he needed to do so.

ix

A dialectical theory of categories begins with an appropriation of the categories used in understanding a given object realm. It then proceeds to a systematic reconstruction of those categories, moving from the categories that are the simplest and most abstract and deriving categories that are progressively more complex and concrete. I shall show that this approach allowed Marx

> i) to clarify the categories used in contributions to empirical social science, so that these categories could be used in a reflective fashion (something that is not typically the case); ii) to propose a theory of fetishism, in which the appearances generated by concrete processes in capitalism are shown to mask capitalism's inner nature; iii) to assert strong claims of necessity, such as "capital of necessity involves exploitation" and "values of necessity underlie prices";[13] and finally iv) to ground revolutionary politics; revolutionary politics always keeps in mind the necessity of the transformation of fundamental structures; this presupposes that fundamental structures can be distinguished from those that are not fundamental, and dialectical logic enabled Marx to make this distinction.[14]

These four concerns form the core of Marx's position, and Marx used dialectical logic in each case. I argue that Marx's success in establishing his perspective thus stands or falls with his use of dialectical logic.

This, of course, is not to deny that in *Capital* and elsewhere Marx made numerous and profound contributions to economics, political science, sociology, history, anthropology, and so on, that can be considered independently of dialectical logic. But ignoring dialectical logic ignores the architectonic of *Capital*. It ignores what makes the work a whole, as opposed to an aggregate of separate empirical studies.

3) If we grant that Marx attempted to employ dialectical logic in *Capital*, the next question follows at once: did he get it right? A third objective of the present work is to evaluate objections that can be made against Marx regarding his use of dialectical reasoning. In the history of philosophy dialectical logic is most closely associated with Hegel. Objections to Marx that accept the general validity of dialectical theories, while rejecting the dialectical element in Marx's theory in specific, are almost exclusively made by Hegelians. Therefore I shall call this set of objections "Hegelian objections" throughout.

It would be pointless to defend Marx against imaginary strawmen and women. Fortunately it will be an easy matter to avoid this. Significant evaluations of Marx's theory from a Hegelian standpoint can be found in the writings of two contemporary philosophers. Klaus Hartmann's *Die Marxsche Theorie* is the most detailed critique of Marx from a Hegelian standpoint that has ever been written.[15] In the United States, Richard Dien Winfield's work, especially his recently published *The Just Economy*, supplements Hartmann in a number of important respects. No one has ever attempted to see if the forceful Hegelian criticisms of *Capital* proposed by Hartmann and Winfield can be answered. This is the third task I have set for myself. As I work through the progression of economic categories in *Capital* the relevant Hegelian objections are considered at each stage.

The book is divided into two parts. The first part consists of three chapters. Chapter I presents Hegel's dialectical methodology and the outline of his system. I discuss a number of passages that establish that Hegel's methodology involves a reconstruction of an object realm in thought, rather than any process of thought "creating" its object out of itself. Hegel did indulge in picture-thinking that suggests the latter. However within the context of Hegel's own philosophy such picture-thinking is clearly assigned to a prephilosophical level, a fact that many of his critics (including Marx) have failed to realize. The chapter concludes with a presentation of the logical levels of being, essence, and notion, and a brief discussion of how they are applied in Hegel's categorization of the socio-political realm. Chapter II turns to Marx. I show that Marx's often vehement rejection of "Hegelian" dialectical logic is actually directed against certain bastardized versions of it. I argue as well that dialectical logic is necessary to fulfill the essential tasks of historical materialism. The chapter concludes with a discussion of the ways in which Hegel's position *does* differ from Marx's. Having established that a dialectical logic taken over from Hegel is crucial for an understanding of *Capital*, I go on in Chapter III to offer a preliminary sketch of the main sorts of objections a Hegelian could make against Marx's use of dialectical logic.

In the second part of the book I present a reading of *Capital* as a systematic theory of economic categories constructed according to a dialectical logic. In Chapter IV, I consider the initial stage of the theory, the value form. Chapter V traces the dialectic of the simple commodity form and the progression through the three stages of the money form. Chapters VI and VII discuss the first category falling under the dialectic of the capital form, "capital in production." Chapter VI deals with the initial determinations of capital in production, "labor-power as a commodity" and "exploitation." Chapter VII examines "the production process proper," which is in turn broken down to "capital as principle of organization of the labor process," "capital as principle for the transformation of the labor process," and "the accumulation process." In Chapter VII the topic of Volume II of *Capital* is explored, the level of "capital in circulation." The main "categorial" determinations here are "simple reproduction," "surplus," and "expanded reproduction." Chapter IX turns to Volume III and the categories on the concrete level of many capitals. These categories fall under the heading of "capital in distribution." The distribution process that occurs within industrial capital is considered first. Here the topic of the transformation of values into cost-prices and prices of production arises. Next comes the distribution that results from the confrontation of industrial capital and effective demand. With this we move from the level of prices of production to the yet more concrete level of market prices. Finally there are the distribution processes uniting industrial captial with rent, bank capital, and so on.

In each stage of the presentation the content of each category and the transition from one category to the next are examined in terms of our three fundamental questions: How did Marx employ dialectical logic in his theory? What purpose does it serve? Did he get it right?

A first draft of this work was written while on leave at the University of Sussex. I would like to thank the members of the Radical Philosophers Hegel Reading Group for many valuable discussions, especially Chris Arthur, Joe McCarney, and Sean Sayers. The last draft was completed while attending a National Endowment for the Humanities seminar under the direction of John Elliott. I would also like to thank Dick Howard, Michael Löwy, Ernest Mandel, Lynn and Bryan Maddock, William McBride, the numerically ordered Smiths, Alan Wald, and my colleagues at Iowa State for the help and encouragement they have given me at different stages of this project. The work is dedicated to Rebecca Burke, my companion, my comrade, my wife.

PART ONE

Philosophical
Foundations

I

Hegel: Method and System

Anyone who has ever attempted to come to terms with Hegel will understand how impossible it is to cover major aspects of his thought in just a few pages. In this chapter the aim is simply to introduce provisionally some Hegelian motifs that will recur throughout the course of this study. I shall discuss Hegel's general method and the features of Hegel's system that are most relevant to the present work. The aim throughout is to present those aspects of Hegel's thought that help us understand Marx's theory. But different aspects of Hegel are important for different aspects of Marx. Hegel's *Phenomenology* is most important for an understanding of the theory of alienation in the 1844 *Manuscripts*;[1] the theory of history found in the *German Ideology* is defined in opposition to Hegel's unpublished lectures on the *Philosophy of History*,[2] and so on. The present work does not attempt a full-scale treatment of the intellectual relationship between the two thinkers. It is concerned only with Marx's economic theory as found especially in *Capital* and *The Theories of Surplus Value*. Yet more specifically, it is concerned only with the systematic dimensions of that theory. In this context a comparison with the systematic writings of Hegel's mature period — the *Logic*, the *Philosophy of Right*, the *Encyclopaedia* — is called for (although I shall refer to other works where relevant).

A. Hegel's Dialectical Method

The most direct approach to our subject matter is to state how Hegel's method works in a step by step fashion.

3

1. *The Starting Point*

For Hegel, "philosophy is its own time apprehended in thoughts. It is just as absurd to fancy that a philosophy can transcend its contemporary world as it is to fancy that an individual can overleap his own age."[3] This means that for Hegel the point of departure for the operation of his method is the immediately given experience at a particular historical juncture. But at first this immediate experience is not "apprehended." And so thought must proceed from that which is initially given onwards.

2. *The Stage of Appropriation*

What is "initially given"? This, of course, is an empirical matter. And so the next stage is an appropriation of the results of empirical studies. This empiricist moment in Hegel's methodology is often overlooked, but it is clearly stated in passages such as the following: "The knowledge of the particular is necessary. This particularity must be worked out on its own account; we must become acquainted with empirical nature, both with the physical and with the human... Without the working out of the empirical sciences on their own account, philosophy could not have reached further than with the ancients."[4]

The demand to become "acquainted with human nature" should be taken in the broadest possible sense. Hegel includes under it all areas of human endeavor, from the most mundane events of the everyday world to religious beliefs and the construction of metaphysical systems. But in Hegel's view it is not the philosopher's task to appropriate everything about everything, even if that were not a hopeless project. What is of interest to the philosopher is the fact that it is impossible to engage in discourse without employing categories, whether our discourse concerns metaphysics, the empirical sciences, religion, or events in the everyday world.[5] The philosophical appropriation of immediately given experience is an appropriation of categories. Usually we are content to employ categories in an unreflective fashion. But for Hegel the highest form of thought occurs when thought makes itself its own object. This occurs whenever our thinking considers the basic categories we employ in and of themselves, rather than in terms of their reference to specific objects of experience. For instance, we can assert that "This leaf is green" in a variety of different contexts for a variety of different purposes. But the highest expression of pure thought occurs when every other concern is bracketed out besides the explication of the pure categories employed in this assertion, categories such as "individuality" ("this"), and "existence" ("is").[6]

Before proceeding it is important to stress once again that these categories do not spring out of thin air. They are initially won in confrontation with the empirically given. The goal is not to "create" the world out of thought *ab nihilo*, but to *reconstruct* the intelligibility of the world, and this requires appropriating the fundamental categories that capture that intelligibility. As if in anticipation of the criticism that in his methodology thought generates its own content, Hegel writes: "In order that this science (i.e. Hegel's own theory) may come into existence, we must have the progression from the individual and particular to the universal — *an activity which is a reaction on the given material of empiricism in order to bring about its reconstruction. The demand of a priori knowledge, which seems to imply that the Idea should construct from itself, is thus a reconstruction only* . . . In consciousness it then adopts the attitude of having cut away the bridge from behind it; it appears to be free to launch forth in its ether only, and to develop without resistence to this medium; but it is another matter to attain to this ether and to development of it."[7]

3. *The Stage of Reconstruction*

At this point Hegel could have anticipated contemporary conceptual analysis and treated one or another individual category in isolation. Or he could have followed Aristotle and thrown out many different fundamental categories together more or less haphazardly, leaving future scholars to debate how they all fit together. Or he could have followed Kant and searched for some external schema to impose an order on the categories, as Kant did when he deduced his set of categories from the table of judgements. Instead Hegel attempted to provide an immanent ordering of the basic categories.

Many people believe that Hegel failed in this task. For instance Jon Elster writes that

> Hegel, in *The Science of Logic*, derived the various ontological categories from each other according to certain deductive principles which have resisted analysis to this day. The connection is neither that of causes to effect, not that of axiom to theorem, nor finally that of given fact to its condition of possibility. The "self-determination of the concept" appears to be nothing more than a loose *ex post* pattern imposed by Hegel on various phenomena that he found important.[8]

But Hegel's procedure is not really *ad hoc* at all. To see this we have first to consider what a category is. It is a principle (a universal) for unifying a manifold of some sort or other (different individuals, or particulars). A category thus articulates a structure with two poles, a pole of unity and a pole of differences. In Hegelian language this sort of structure, captured in some category, can be described as a unity of identity in difference, or as a reconciliation of universal and individuals. From this general notion of a category we can go on to derive three general types of categorial structures.

5

In one the moment of unity is stressed, with the moment of differences implicit. In another the moment of difference is emphasized, with the moment of unity now being only implicit. In a third both unity and differences are made explicit together. Hegel's next claim is that there is a systematic order immanently connecting these three categorial structures. A structure of unity in which differences are merely implicit is simpler than one in which these differences are explicitly introduced; and one in which both unity and differences are explicit is yet more complex still. Similarly, the first sort of structure is the most abstract, while the other structures are successively more concrete.

Yet another way of speaking about the immanent connections here is through the idea of a dialectical contradiction. Hegel's views on contradiction have been quite controversial.[9] But at least in the context of constructing a systematic theory of categories he appears to have meant something fairly straightforward.[10] If a category is in general a principle that unifies a manifold, then if a specific category only explicates the moment of unity, leaving the moment of difference implicit, then there is a "contradiction" between what it inherently is *qua* category (a unifier of a manifold) and what it is explicitly (the moment of unity alone). Overcoming this contradiction requires that the initial category be "negated" in the sense that a second category must be formulated that makes the moment of difference explicit. But when this is done the moment of difference will be emphasized at the cost of having the moment of unity made merely implicit. Once again there is a contradiction between what a category inherently is and what it is explicity. Overcoming this contradiction demands that the second sort of category also be negated, and replaced with a category in which both poles, unity and difference, are each made explicit simultaneously. Hegel is well aware that "contradiction" and "negation" are not being used here in the sense given to them in formal logic. Following a tradition that goes back to Plato, he asserts that in the above usage "contradiction" and "negation" are logical operators for ordering categories systematically, as opposed to logical operators for making formal inferences. The logic with which we are concerned here is *dialectical* logic.

It is interesting to note that in the culmination of Hegel's *Logic*, the section "The Absolute Idea," we do not find any reference to some special metaphysical entity. Instead we find a summary of dialectical method. It begins with a category of simple unity: "The beginning...content is an immediate, but an immediate that has the significance and form of *abstract universality*...it is a *simple* and a *universal*."[11] But when measured by what a category inherently is, this is inadequate: "Hence the beginning has for the method no other determinateness than that of being simple and universal;

6

this is itself the *determinateness* by reason of which it is deficient."[12] This deficiency can be overcome only if the moment of difference is made explicit. In this sense "the immediate of the beginning. . .is not merely the *simple,* but as *abstract* is already *posited* as infected with a *negation.*"[13] The "negation" of the simple unity is the moment of difference that it itself contains implicitly. With this we have "the emergence of *real difference.*"[14] Hegel states that the moment "by which the universal of the beginning of its own accord determines itself as the *other of itself,* is to be named the *dialectical* moment."[15] Or, again, "the dialectical moment. . .consists in positing in it the difference that it implicitly contains."[16] But this stage of difference is itself one-sided and partial, "therefore with it the dialectical moment consists in positing the *unity* that is contained in it."[17] When the stage of difference is dialectically negated, we once again have a category of unity, but now it is a complex unity, one that incorporates the moment of difference; it "is in general the unity of the first and second moments, of. . .the simple resulting from *sublation of difference.* . .This *result* is therefore the *truth.* It is *equally* immediacy *and* mediation."[18] Since a category of unity-in-difference on one level can itself prove to be a category of simple unity from a higher level perspective, thereby initiating another dialectical progression from unity through difference to unity-in-difference, we can construct a systematic theory of categories by employing the dialectical method. In this sort of theory we move in a step-by-step fashion from simple and abstract categories to those that are complex and concrete, with dialectical logic providing the warrant for each transition:

> The determinateness which was a result is itself, by virtue of the form of simplicity into which it was withdrawn, a fresh beginning; as this beginning is distinguished from its predecessor precisely by that determinateness, cognition rolls onwards from content to content. First of all, this advance is determined as beginning from simple determinatenesses, the succeeding ones becoming ever *richer and more concrete.* For the result contains its beginning and its course has enriched it by a fresh determinateness. . .at each stage of its further determination it raises the entire mass of its preceding content, and by its dialectical advance it not only does not lose anything or leave anything behind, but carries along with it all it has gained, and inwardly enriches and consolidates itself.[19]

At the conclusion of the linear progression of categories we once again arrive at the initial starting point. But it has now been apprehended in thought. If dialectical logic is rigorously adhered to, the move from one category to the next is not *ad hoc.* The linear progression from a category of immediate unity to one of difference, and from there to a category of unity-in-difference, is not a mere formal schema imposed by Hegel externally. It is instead "the absolute method...does not behave like external reflection but takes the determinate element from its own subject matter, since it is itself that subject matter's immanent principle and soul."[21] In this manner the object realm of experience has been reconstructed in thought.

B. Dialectical Logic and Materialist Ontology

Hegel is typically presented as an "idealist" whose dialectical method is so permeated by idealistic prejudices that it could not be taken over by materialists without severe alteration.[22] At times Marx himself inclined to this view. In the next chapter we shall discuss both where Marx was mistaken in his estimation of Hegel's idealism and the senses in which seeing Hegel as an idealist is justified. In the present section I shall discuss some of the ways Hegel's position is not as incompatible with a materialist perspective as may appear at first sight.

What is an idealist? Let us term "the real process" the total series of all events that have occurred, are occurring, or ever will occur in the world. The method considered in the previous section begins with an apprehension of this real process, moves to an appropriation of the fundamental categories implicit in that apprehension, and then orders those categories. This ordering can be termed "the process in thought," or "the logical process." The question of idealism arises when we try to connect the real process with the process of thought. From this perspective there are four related ways Hegel could be considered an idealist. First, Hegel could have identified the real process with the process of thought in the sense that each stage in the former corresponds to a stage in the latter. Second, he could have denied that the real process had any element in it that could not be reduced to a logical category in the process of thought. Third, Hegel could have asserted that the process of thought is not in any sense a function of the real process. Fourth, he could have held that some sort of idealistic supersubject is the ultimate foundation for the real process. Hegel has often been interpreted as being an idealist in each of these respects. These interpretations are, I believe, mistaken.

1. The Independence of the Real Process

For Hegel the systematic progression of categories follows an immanent logical ordering distinct from the order of events in immediate experience. "What we acquire...is a series of thought and another series of existent shapes of experience; to which I may add that the time order in which the latter actually appear is other than the logical order."[23] The converse, of course, holds as well: the historical progression in the real process is not reducible to the logical progression of categories within Hegel's system. For example, were the real material process reducible to a mere appearance of the logical process, then it would seem to follow that from a grasp of the latter one could extrapolate to the course which future real events must follow with logical necessity. But Hegel makes no such move. He instead acknowledges that the real process has its own pattern of future develop-ment, one irreducible to the pattern of logical development in the process of thought.[24]

2. Otherness in the Material Realm

For Hegel the independence of the materially given from thought is not merely a function of its following a distinct ordering. For Hegel there remains something "other" which separates the material realm from thought. In the real process there is an irreducible residue of contingency, a surd without an intelligibility to be grasped by thought, an element which cannot be reduced to logical categories. Hegel acknowledges a residue of the material, impenetrable by thought, at practically every stage of his system. It is found, to list just some examples, in the individual soul,[25] in the content of sensations,[26] in the workings of the market place[27], in the content of positive laws[28], in history,[29] etc. At points such as these, thought confronts "something other" than itself. Because Hegel acknowledges a contingency and accidentality in the real world that cannot be reduced to categories, he does not reduce the world to logical necessity. Its independence is guaranteed.

What are we to make of Hegel's often-repeated assertion of the unity of thought and being? Does this not imply a confused merger of real subjects (beings) with mere predicates (thought), and a denial of the independent reality of the former? Consider the following sentence: "This spiritual movement (i.e. the logical process). . .which. . .is the immanent develop-ment of the Notion, this movement is the absolute method of knowing and at the same time is the immanent soul of the content itself."[30] Phrases such as "spiritual movement," "the immanent development of the Notion," and "the absolute method of knowing" bring to mind a familiar Hegel, the object of countless polemics, the absolute idealist intent on reducing the real process to the thought process. But with the last clause we get a different picture. Thought, the dialectic of categories, is not claimed to be identical with the *whole* content, but only with its "soul." Hegel's project thus does not involve a reduction of real material things and events to categories. "This identity of being and thought is not however to be taken in a concrete sense, as if we could say that a stone, so far as it has being, is the same as a thinking man. *A concrete thing is always very different from the abstract category*

9

as such.''[31] In referring to the identity of thought and being, Hegel's point is that the ultimate intelligibility of these concrete things can only be grasped by means of thought determinations, in a categorial reconstruction of the given. This should be acceptable to anyone who accepts the validity claim that theoretical formulations (thought) can in principle capture what is true about their object (being). (As we shall see, in this sense Marxism too is committed to the identity of thought and being.)

3. The Dependence of the Thought Process on the Real Process

As we have seen above in the discussion of the starting point of theory, for Hegel philosophy is "its time apprehended in thoughts." The real process, which includes the process of history, asserts it independence from the thought process by providing the ultimate horizon within which the thought process is situated. Could there be any doubt, for example, that a "Hegelian" system constructed in Classical Greece or Medieval Europe would be radically different from what Hegel himself constructed in nineteenth-century Germany? Classical Greece, Hegel would point out, lacked the principle of subjectivity. Medieval Europe had that principle, but had no way of reconciling it with an Essence that it conceived as lying "Beyond." Any reconstruction of categories during those periods would differ drastically from Hegel's, in which — Hegel would insist — these problems had been overcome. Also we have already noted that in Hegel's view systematic philosophy cannot fully develop prior to the historical rise of the empirical sciences. These points show that the thought systems constructed in the history of philosophy cannot go beyond the level attained in a particular period of historical development. They are instead dependent upon the principles attained by their historical period. Thus the former (the logical process) does not at all negate the independence of the latter (the real process).

4. Idealistic Supersubjects and Picture-Thinking

Hegel makes a number of comments on the meta-theoretical level that seem to suggest that the movement of categories is the unfolding of a supersubject. This most peculiar sort of metaphysical entity is termed *Geist* (Spirit), The Absolute, The Idea, and at times it is also identified as God (e.g. when the contents of the *Logic* are described as God's thoughts prior to creation.[32]) This would be bad enough, but this Spirit is also said to bring about the real process, including both nature and the human world. From a materialist standpoint, here too there seems to be a confusion of real subjects and predicates. Whereas in reality thoughts are properties of real human subjects, here it seems that "Thought" or Spirit is hypostasized into a supersubject, while real humans are made into its predicates. Obviously such a topsy-turvy metaphysics is incompatible with a materialist ontology.[33]

There is no shortage of passages in Hegel that suggest this interpretation. However we must interpret Hegel's remarks within the context of his own system. A central tenet of this system is the distinction between *Vorstellung* and *Denken*.[34] *Vorstellung* may be translated as "imaginative representation" or "picture-thinking." In it a concept is conveyed through the aid of an image. This eases comprehension of the concept, but at the cost of introducing extraneous elements that may prove misleading. For a full grasp of the concept it must be considered as a pure thought determination. All extraneous images must be removed, just as the comprehension of a circle demands an understanding of its mathematical definition that goes beyond any imaginable picture of a circle. This is why for Hegel religion, consisting of picture-thoughts, must be placed on a systematically lower level than philosophy, even though both share the same content.

This distinction is clear enough, but Hegel muddled things considerably by continually resorting to picture-thoughts within his own systematic philosophy. When he writes that Absolute Spirit is self-acting and productive, creating the realm of nature and human spirit, he is indulging in picture-thinking, in imaginative representations that on his own terms belong on a prephilosophical level. He no doubt thought that this rhetorical device would ease his (mostly Christian) audience into his system, since he identified this Absolute with the Christian God. He assumed that his audiences would then learn how to translate such pictures into their proper philosophical import.

What is the philosophical notion Hegel is attempting to convey with his talk of a self-generating Absolute? The content of philosophy, i.e. the series of determinations that makes up the process of thought, has two dimensions to it. First, as discussed previously, this content is initially appropriated from the real process and then reconstructed in thought so as to capture the intelligibility of that real process. In this sense the content of philosophy is most definitely *not* self-generated; it depends upon the real process. But, second, the series of determinations is characterized by certain logical connections that can only be brought out in the process of thought. The transitions from one category to the next are immanently justified in terms of the objective content of each category; in this sense the transitions are "self-acting." Once all the extraneous pictures have been weeded out, "Absolute Spirit's productive activity" means that in the process of thought "the content (is) objectively and intrinsically determined, and (hence) self-acting and productive"[35] in this sense.

Consider the following passage from *The Philosophy of Spirit*: "This development (i.e. Hegel's categorial reconstruction) brings forth a succession of shapes; *these, it is true, must be specified empirically*, but in the philosophical treatment cannot remain externally juxtaposed, but must be

11

known as the corresponding expression of a necessary series of specific Notions, and they are of interest to philosophy only in so far as they express such a series of Notions."[36] Insofar as the succession of shapes "must be specified empirically" the content refers to a real process ontologically distinct from the logical process. But insofar as the content expresses "a necessary series of specific Notions" then it simultaneously involves an element that is not given in the real process. "Self-generating Absolute" is a quite extravagant term used to bring out this component of necessity.

"Absolute Spirit", then, is not a metaphysical supersubject. There are only thinkers in Hegel's ontology, flesh and blood men and women. There is no entity "Thought" separate from them. But these thinkers have two dimensions. On the one hand thinking could trace subjective psychological associations, or associations based on real processes that are objective but contingent. In so far as we think of necessary connections, however, then we are operating on a different level, which Hegel extravagantly termed that of the "Absolute." In other words, the opposition here is not between an "Absolute" hypostasized supersubject and real human subects. It is instead between real human subjects who grasp the "objectively and intrinsically determined content" of categories and real human subjects who content themselves with whatever thought associations they find most psychologically plausible or given in contingent experience. This is why when we finally come to the section on the Absolute in Hegel's Logic we do not find a supersubject. Instead Hegel discusses a method that in principle any thinker can follow in order to derive necessary connections among categories.

Finally, there is all the God-talk in Hegel that seems to suggest that Hegel accepted an idealistic metaphysical entity. Hegel does use the term "God" continually in his philosophical writings, and he obviously hopes his Christian audience will accept the orthodoxy of his usage. But when we read his philosophy of religion we discover that at the highest stage of religion "God" does not refer to some father figure somewhere beyond, nor to some filial figure dead long ago. At the highest stage of Hegel's philosophy of religion we find instead the spirit that binds together the human community. From a metaphysical standpoint this spirit is not some sort of separately exising entity distinct from the human community. It is instead an ultimate principle of unity immanent within that community.[37] This is no more inherently idealist than the solidarity that may bind the oppressed together.

In summary, Hegel often did talk of Spirit in terms that suggest a supersubject. The metaphysics involved in such picture-thinking is indeed incompatible with a materialist ontology. But on Hegel's own terms such talk properly has no place within a strictly philosophical framework.

Philosophically such talk refers to the claim that the content of the theory unfolds immanently. As we shall see below, Marx too made this sort of claim.

The conclusion of this section is that Hegel's dialectical methodology is not as antithetical to materialist considerations as is often thought. As we shall see in the next chapter there are good reasons to contrast Hegel's "idealism" with Marx's "materialism." But they do not involve the fundamental method whereby Hegel constructed his dialectical theory.

It has been somewhat artifical to discuss Hegel's method in abstraction from the content of his system. After all, it is one of his central tenets that method and content *cannot* be separated. We now must try to incorporate the content of Hegel's system into our discussion.

C. System

1. The Logic

Hegel's system is a reconstruction of the real process (the object realm) in thought, in order to capture its inner intelligibility. It does this by taking the fundamental determinations of the object realm and then noting that these categories define structures that are either structures of simple unity, or of difference, or of unity-in-difference. These structures can then be systematically ordered such that a linear progression of categories is constructed that moves in a step-by-step fashion from simple and abstract determinations to categories that are complex and concrete. The positing and overcoming of dialectical contradictions is the motor of this movement. We can begin to flesh out the content of this system by distinguishing the three main categorial regions: the logical, the natural, and the spiritual. The most distinctive feature of the logical realm is that categorial structures falling here are ultimately structures of simple unity, or in Hegel's own language "the distinctive feature of the logical Idea is immediate, simple being-within-self."[38] This means that here we find a series of principles considered in themselves, apart from any real embodiments they may have in the natural or spiritual realms. In other words, for Hegel the realm of the logical refers to a systematic ordering of pure (formal) ontological structures.

Although the region of the logical as a whole is characterized by simple unity, reconstructing this region in thought is a matter of explicating a dialectic of basic ontological structures. Within the logical realm there are three fundamental sorts of structures. The first is described with the category of being (*Sein*). This is a category of simple unity because the basic structure here is one of an aggregate of isolated and self-contained entities,

13

each of which is treated as a simple unity in itself.

X X X X X

Hegel argues that this one-tiered ontology is quite impoverished. Each isolated entity is supposedly a complete unity in itself. But each is confronted with others "outside" it, and would not be what it is without those others. An adequate determination of an entity requires an acknowledgement of its necessary interconnection with other entities. It must be acknowledged that there are principles which underlie the different units, connecting them together. In this manner a two-tiered ontology is formed, a more complex ontological structure with two poles. The first is the pole of the different unities or beings. The second pole is that of the essence (*Wesen*) that subsumes those separate beings under common principles.

$$- \overset{\displaystyle \overset{\frown}{\text{Essence}} \leftarrow}{\underset{\displaystyle \overset{\downarrow}{\text{X X X X X}}}{\vert \text{---} \vert}} -$$

Although the essence pole does unite different unities under it, the dominant characteristic of this structure is the difference between the two poles. This difference can be expressed in a number of ways. The essence pole can claim a priority that reduces the realm of beings to its mere appearances. Or the essence pole, the moment of unity, could be relatively extrinsic to the beings, such that the unity tends to break down and fragment.

In the final section, the notion (*Begriff*), Hegel introduces categories that allow for a mediation between these two levels, a unity-in-difference in which each pole remains distinct from the other while being reconciled within a structured totality. Differences here are no longer "swallowed up" by the pole of unity, or unity is no longer unstable and constantly in danger of fragmenting, the twin dangers within essence sturctures. Instead different individuals retain their autonomy within a unity strong enough to maintain them. The categories on the level of *Begriff* thus allow us to describe a complex ontological structure characterized by a reciprocal affirmation of different individuals within a common unity. This unity is both distinct from and united with the individuals. A notion structure is characterized by a harmonious reconciliation between universal and individual.

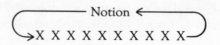

2. The Realphilosophie

The remainder of Hegel's system, which reconstructs the natural and the spiritual realms in thought, is termed by Hegel *Realphilosophie*. Here we have a progression of structures in which categorial-ontological forms discussed in the *Logic* have what can be termed "real embodiments."

This last phrase requires some comment. As we have seen, Hegel allows for an irreducible contingency in the world. In his language, the "actual" must be distinguished from the merely "existent." In existence there are always a plurality of contingent factors. These are the concern of ordinary life and of the empirical sciences. But the philosopher is not concerned with the great number of variations possible in existence. In Hegel's view the philosopher's task is to grasp the inner nature of things. Only those individual existences that measure up to their nature count as "actual" in Hegel's sense of the term.[39] Thus we cannot discover the actual by simply noting what is given in existence. Instead we must formulate pure types in thought. Such thought constructs are *categories*. These categories of *Realphilosophie* are constructed with the aid of the pure categories taken from the *Logic*. In this sense they are "real embodiments" of the latter.

In this work I shall not be concerned with the natural realm beyond simply noting that for Hegel it is characterized in terms of difference or "externality." In contrast, in a reconstruction in thought of the spiritual realm the structures defined will be ones of unity-in-difference. This means that they are structures which in principle allow for a reconciliation between universal and individual. But this reconciliation can occur to a greater or lesser extent, and so we can trace a dialectic of the basic forms of the spiritual realm. Since Hegel defines freedom in terms of this reconciliation, the stages of the dialectic moving from the less adequate spiritual forms to more adequate ones are steps in the "liberation" of spirit: "The several steps of this activity, on each of which , with their semblance of being, it is the function of the finite mind to linger, and through which it has to pass, are steps in its liberration. In the full truth of that liberation is given the identification of the three stages—finding a world presupposed before us, generating a world as our own creation, and gaining freedom from it and in it."[40] These three stages are termed by Hegel subjective spirit, objective spirit, and absolute spirit, respectively.

Since our main interest is the influence of Hegel on *Capital*, the level of objective spirit is where we must focus. This is the section of the philosophy of spirit where Hegel presents his theory of institutions. Here too any attempt at completeness is out of the question. Instead I shall stress only the categories of "right," "civil society," and "state." Since these categories are fairly familiar, the account can be brief.[41]

On the level of abstract *right*, with its subcategories of private property, contract, and right and wrong, we have a structure articulated wherein isolated individual wills have relations to specific objects and come into external relationships with each other in order to exchange these objects in contracts. Each individual claims to be independent and self-sufficient. We clearly have here a real embodiment of *Seinslogik*, a structure of social ontology that can be made intelligible in terms of Hegel's category of being. The breakdown of this stage consists precisely in the fact that in this structure each individual unity is necessarily connected to others and would not be what it is were it without these others. There is no property, for instance, without the acknowledgement of others. And yet these others remain external to the unity of the individual. This is a dialectical contradiction of the sort discussed above. We therefore have systematic motivation to make a transition to a higher level unity which can incorporate these differences within it. This brings us to the level of *morality*, where a moral code unifies the many different subjects standing under it. Here the different individual subjects do acknowledge their mediation under a moral system that unites them. In this sense the moral system is their essence. With this formulation of the moral community we have passed from the level of *Sein* to that of *Wesen*. However a new structural problem arises now. The unifying essential pole, the moral system, proves unable to hold the individual within its unity. Each individual subject can formulate his or her own interpretation of morality. This threatens to fragment the moral community into a mere aggregate of individuals. This would count as a retreat back to a social ontology based on a *Seinslogik*. If this is to be avoided, we must move to a new categorial level where a unity is articulated that is more substantive, i.e. that can prevent this fragmentation of the community. This can be done only if the different individuals are unified within institutions. The next level of categories, *ethical life (Sittlichkeit)*, includes the family, civil society, and the state. These are all institutional structures within which different individuals are united in a substantial fashion. The move from morality to ethical life thus roughly (but good enough for our purposes) maps the transition from *Wesen* to *Begriff*, from essence to notion.

Skipping over Hegel's discussion of the family, civil society is a unity wherein different individuals are explicitly united in a division of labor in which each one, in working for himself,[42] in reality is working for *all*. The institutional working of the market in a socially wide system of reciprocal need satisfaction unites the different individuals in a more stable fashion than shared allegiance to a moral code could ever do. But in civil society the unity and difference poles are not fully in harmony. On the one hand the unity operates in a blind fashion over the individuals through the laws of the market. On the other hand the different individuals and groups are only externally connected, being primarily concerned with their own private interests. These tensions in the structure of civil society lead Hegel to the category of the state. Here the unity of the community is consciously articulated in the sovereign, and the mechanisms of political association and citizenship educate the individual to concern for and participation[43] within the social whole. In this manner Hegel believes that within the institutional form of the modern state different individual citizens can in principle consciously affirm their unity within the political community.[44]

At this point three brief comments are in order. Each introduces a central theme of the following study. First, it is important to stress one final time that Hegel's system provides an immanent progression of categories. One category of necessity leads to another through the positing and overcoming of dialectical contradictions. The theory does not tell the story of any real historical subject maintaining its continuity in a historical process evolving from abstract right through civil society to the state. Instead we have a *logical* progression. Structurally, the unity that is civil society incorporates true differences with it, and thus is a more advanced structure than that of the isolated individual wills on the level of abstract right. But it fails to unify these differences adequately. Dialectical logic thus necessitates a new structure, captured in a new categorial determination, in which unity and difference are united in a deeper fashion. The transition to the state thus is a logical one accomplished in the process of thought rather than in a real historical process, although it is claimed that this reconstruction of socio-political categories begins with an appropriation of the real process and culminates with a grasp of the inner nature of that real process.

Second, categorial theories of this sort are by no means value free. They inherently have a normative, practical component. When a structure from the realm of *Realphilosophie* is interpreted in terms of a categorial structure taken from the *Logic*, this necessarily involves an evaluation of it. To the extent that the categorial structures of being (*Sein*) or of essence (*Wesen*) are applicable to it, the evaluation must ultimately be negative. In so far as it is a real embodiment of a notion (*Begriff*) structure, the evaluation must be affirmative. On the level of spirit the earlier categories fix structures within which relatively simpler and more abstract forms of freedom are possible, while within the structures that can be grasped in notion terms, more complex and concrete forms of freedom are in principle possible.[45]

Third, the categorization (and therefore the evaluation) of a stage in the *Realphilosophie* is a quite complex matter. There is no one-to-one correspondence between a category in the *Logic* and one in the *Realphilosophie*. In so far

17

as "civil society" is part of the spiritual realm, as opposed to the logical or the natural realms, it is a structure of unity-in-difference where categories on the level of the notion are applicable. But in so far as it is on the level of objective spirit, categories of essence are applicable, since according to Hegel no ultimately satisfactory reconciliation of unity and difference, universal and individual, is possible prior to the level of absolute spirit. However within the realm of objective spirit "civil society" is a determination on the level of ethical life (*Sittlichkeit*) as opposed to abstract right and morality. As such it is a structure to which notion categories are applicable. But relative to the state it contains a stress on particularity (private self-interest) that cannot be integrated seamlessly with the unified community. In this emphasis on the element of difference, civil society attains only a relative universality, and essence (*Wesen*) categories are in order.

Unfortunately there is not space to go into Hegel's system in any more detail. For our purposes it is sufficient at this point to have won a rough idea of what a category is, of Hegel's concept of "contradiction" and dialectical transition, of the role of material considerations in Hegel's theory, and of the outlines of Hegel's system. It is now time to establish that all this has some relevance to Marx's masterwork.

II

Dialectical Logic in Marx's Work

Ultimately the only way to show that *Capital* is a theory of categories ordered according to a dialectical logic taken over from Hegel is to go through *Capital* step by step. This will be done in the second part of this work. In the present chapter some provisional arguments for this will be presented. Two sorts of arguments will be made. The first is negative and indirect in form. I shall consider six reasons for Marx's often vehement rejection of dialectical theories of categories, and show that they do not apply to dialectical logic as presented by a charitably interpreted Hegel. In this context I also shall discuss four interpretations of *Capital* that deny the Hegelian elements of the theory. I shall argue that there are central aspects of the work that they cannot account for. Next, some more positive and direct reasons to think Marx took over dialectical logic from Hegel will be examined. I shall argue both that this is consistent with Marx's own methodological remarks and that dialectical logic is profoundly bound up with three central features of Marx's position. This does not mean, however, that we can simply conflate Hegel and Marx. The chapter concludes with a discussion of three fundamental ways in which Marx's position differs from Hegel's.

A. Indirect Arguments for Reading "Capital" in Terms of Hegelian Dialectical Logic

1. Marx's Critique of Categorial Theories

It seems as if the thesis that Hegel's *Logic* is relevant to an understanding of *Capital* can be thoroughly refuted simply by quoting Marx's own comments on Hegelian logic. Throughout all his writings attacks on Hegel's

19

theory are found. His hostility to this sort of theory seems constant, clear, and unequivocal. He presented six distinct arguments to justify this hostility. However when we look more closely it turns out that Marx rejected bastardized versions of dialectical theories of categories, and not the sort of theory presented by Hegel. I shall now consider each objection in turn. Certain features of Marx's thought that will be established in later chapters will be assumed provisionally here.

a) *Thought as self-generating*
b) *Thought as creating the real*

The first two objections Marx made against Hegel's approach can be considered together. Marx himself connects them when he writes "Hegel fell into the illusion of conceiving the real as the product of thought concentrating itself, probing its own depths, and unfolding itself out of itself, by itself."[1] On this interpretation, thought in Hegel's view generates its own content out of itself ("unfolding itself out of itself, by itself"). Somehow at the end of this process the real emerges "as the product of thought."[2] Both of these theses are incompatible with Marx's materialist standpoint, in which the real process is prior to and independent of the thought process, and in which the thought process derives its content from the real process.

Turning to the first objection, for Hegel the ordering of categories must commence only *after* a long and arduous appropriation of the given object realm. One can hardly present a categorial reconstruction without having first appropriated what is to be reconstructed. This, of course, does not imply that in practice Hegel himself always met this demand adequately. But in principle, as was stressed in Chapter I, Hegel's method includes both a stage of appropriation and one of reconstruction. Marx's account here leaves out the first part of Hegel's method, where the theorist must appropriate the content of the real process in order first to derive the categories that will later be systematically reconstructed.[3] As we shall see in section IIB below, Marx himself granted the necessity of distinguishing these two stages of dialectical method and he acknowledged that in his own writings the latter part is found. He also admitted that if the stage of reconstruction is looked at in isolation the very same criticisms he made against Hegel could be turned against himself: "Of course the method of presentation must differ in form from that of inquiry. The latter has to appropriate the material in detail, to analyse its different forms of development, to trace out their inner connexion. Only after this work is done, can the actual movement be adequately described. If this is done successfully, if the life of the subject-matter is ideally reflected as in a mirror, then it may appear as if we had before us a mere a priori construction."[4] The distinction Marx made here between the "method of presentation" and "the life of the subject-matter" is *precisely the same* as Hegel's distinction between "the immanent development of the Notion" and "the immanent soul of the content itself." The former "ideally reflects as in a mirror" the latter.

Regarding the second objection, the phrase "creating the world" was a picture-thought for Hegel, a *Vorstellung*, that has no place on the level of categorial thinking. The point of systematic theory is to reconstruct the world in thought, to capture its intelligibility. This does not imply, of course, that in practice Hegel himself always refrained from indulging in picture-thinking. Marx's criticism of passages where Hegel is guilty of this indulgence would be thoroughly justified if those passages were to be taken literally. But when one understands the cognitive status picture-thinking has for Hegel, one realizes that these passages are *not* to be taken literally. We shall return to this point in section f.

c) *Movement in thought as opposed to historical movement*

Proudhon can be taken as typical of someone who wished to construct a theory of economic categories along Hegelian lines. Marx rejected his theory in the following sarcastic terms: "Economists express the relations of bourgeois production. . . M. Proudhon, taking these relations for principles, categories, abstract thoughts, has merely to put into *order* these thoughts . . . The economists' material is the active, energetic life of man; M. Proudhon's material is the dogmas of the economists. But the moment we cease to pursue the historical movement of production relations, of which the categories are but the theoretical expression, the moment we want to see in these categories no more than ideas, spontaneous thoughts, independent of relations, we are forced to attribute the origin of these thoughts to the movements of pure reason."[5]

This partly repeats the first objection: in dialectical theories of categories a la Proudhon (or Hegel) thought is seen as self-generating ("we. . .attribute the origin of these thoughts to the movement of pure reason"). The new objection here is that categorial theories are to be rejected because they tend to follow an order different from the order in "the historical movement of production relations."

The problem with this objection is that Marx himself insisted that the process of thought does not merely echo the unfolding of the real process: "It would be unfeasible and wrong to let the economic categories follow one another in the same sequence as that in which they were historically decisive."[6] The model presented at the beginning of *Capital*, for example, does not represent some stage of simple commodity production historically prior to industrial capitalism. There has not existed in history

21

any such stage. The model at the beginning of *Captial* is instead a thought construct won by abstracting from generalized commodity production all but its simplest elements. Marx, proceeding systematically to progressively more concrete and complex elements, then reconstructed the inner logic of this mode of production. This systematic ordering follows its own immanent progression, from "value" through "money," "production of capital," and "circulation of captial," to "distribution of capital," to name the most important stages in the process from simple and abstract determinations to complex and concrete categories. As we shall see repeatedly in Part Two, this ordering is distinct from that whereby one phase of history replaces another. In real history, for example, there is no temporal separation between the production of capital and its distribution.[7]

It is certainly true that Marx's references in *Capital* to real historical processes (the primitive accumulation of capital in England, the intertwining of the history of class struggle and of technology, etc.) went far beyond anything to be found in Hegel. Hegel's historical references are mostly disgressions from his systematic ordering of categories. These comments are found for the most part not in the text itself, but rather in notes taken from Hegel's lectures and added to the text under the heading "additions." In contrast, the approach Marx employed in *Capital* may be termed "structural-genetic" or "logico-historical," in the sense that systematic considerations of the logical progression of thought are indissolvably mixed with historical considerations.[8] However in principle there is no contradiction between integrating a vast amount of historical material and constructing a theory in which categories are ordered logically and not historically.

Interestingly, the polemic against Proudhon actually further substantiates the view that Marx's theory should be read as a systematic ordering of categories. Proudhon proposed an ordering proceeding from the division of labor, through machinery, to competition. In his comments Marx does not reject the project of providing a systematic derivation of economic categories. What he objected to was that "M. Proudhon is presenting the order in which economic categories are arranged inside his head. I would not be hard pressed to prove that this arrangement is the arrangement of a very disorganized head."[9] Marx then went on to correct Proudhon, arguing, for instance, that "machinery" must be derived from "the war between employers and workers" and international competition, rather than from the division of labor. It turns out that the problem is not with the theoretical project of ordering categories systematically, but with Proudhon's execution of that project.

d) Categories as ideal

An especially vehement rejection of categorial thinking can be found in

Marx's *Notes on Wagner*. Here Marx insisted that "In the first place I do not start out from 'concepts' hence do not start out from 'the concept of value'... What I start out from is that simplest social form in which the labour-product is presented in contemporary society, and this is the 'commodity'."[10] This passage is often read as a rejection of Hegelian theories of categories on the grounds that by starting with 'concepts' these theories are inherently idealist. The true starting point for thought must instead be a concrete material object, such as the commodity.

The problem with this view is that the 'commodity' with which Marx began is *not* by any means a concrete material thing. Concretely, in generalized commodity production material commodities are generally produced within a capital/wage labor social relation that directly or indirectly involves bank capital and the state as well; they always appear with market prices attached to them that more or less deviate from their prices of production, which in turn deviate more or less from their values; when exchanged concrete commodities lead to a profit that generally diverges from the surplus value "contained" in them, and so on. Not one of these features holds for 'the commodity' Marx began with. This is a category, a thought construct, and not a concrete material thing. In this sense it is in principle as "ideal" as the thought constructs found in Hegel.

The problem with Wagner (and other of Hegel's epigone) is not that he employed concepts, but the sort of concepts employed. Wagner's method anticipated twentieth-century, ordinary language analysis. He considered the different uses of a term in everyday speech and then selected out the usage that is most prevalent as the key to grasping the meaning of the term. The dominant usage of the concept "value" has to do with use-values, and so Wagner concluded that this is the crucial element in the meaning of the term. Of course this was not Hegel's procedure. For Hegel the task of theory is to reconstruct the intelligibility of a given realm, and there is no reason whatsoever to assume that concepts as used in everyday speech will be adequate to this task.[11] When Marx rejected this methodology it was not the Hegelian approach that he rejected.

e) Logical division of concepts is external to the objects

The *Notes on Wagner* also include another objection to categorial theories. Marx insisted that this "method...has nothing in common with the academic German method of connecting concepts"[12] and that "I do not start from 'concepts' and hence do not start from the 'concept' of value, and therefore do not have to 'divide' the latter in any way." The phrase "academic German method of connecting concepts" has been taken to refer to the dialectical logic Hegel used to motivate moves from one category to another. Supposedly this leads to a division of concepts that remains external to the object being considered. This method should thus be rejected. But Wagner's method for deriving concepts in fact has little to do with Hegel's approach.

After Wagner extrapolated his most general concept from everyday speech, he then treated it as a genus. Other concepts fall under it as its species, and the task of theory is to trace the logical connections between a genus and its species. "Value" as use-value is for Wagner a genus under which various species of value are derived through the method of division that Marx referred to in the above passage.

Hegel's rejection of this approach was not less emphatic than Marx's own: "Because a principle of self-determination is lacking, the laws for this business of division can only consist of formal, empty rules that lead to nothing."[13] And Hegel's rejection was based on the same factors that motivated Marx. Division into genera and species remains external to the object being investigated: "This unsystematic procedure, which sometimes adopts a determinateness as essential moment of the genus and then either subordinates the particulars to it or excludes them from it, and sometimes starts with the particular and in grouping it lets itself again be guided by some other determinateness, gives the appearance of the play of caprice to which it is left to decide which part or which side of the concrete it will fix on and use as its principle of arrangement. . . . Thus it happens that in one series of natural objects marks stand out as very characteristic and essential that in others become inconspicuous and purposeless, so that it becomes impossible to adhere to a principle of division of this kind."[14] For Hegel, when the fundamental determinations of an object realm are reconstructed in a systematic progression moving from categories of simple unity and of difference to ones of unity-in-difference, the "soul of the content itself" is captured; this is not the case with onceptual divisions moving from genus to species. In the *Notes on Wagner* it is the latter, not the former, that Marx rejected. This will be discussed further in considering the final objection.

f) Reification of universals

The last reason Marx gave for rejecting categorial theories is that they involve a reification of universals. Concepts seem to be granted a type of metaphysical reality distinct from that of the instances under them. In this context Marx's insistence that he began with a real existent, the commodity, and not with a universal concept has considerable force. It is a plea for materialism and a rejection of conceptual realism.

This objection is presented most forcefully in the following passage from *The Holy Family*, which claims to capture "the mystery of *speculative*, or *Hegelian construction*":

24

If from real apples, pears, strawberries and almonds I form the general idea "Fruit," if I go further and *imagine* that my abstract idea "Fruit," derived from real fruit, is an entity existing outside me, is indeed the *true* essence of the pear, the apple, etc., then—in the *language of speculative* philosophy—I am declaring that "Fruit" is the "Substance" of the pear, the apple, the almond, etc.... (for) the speculative philosopher... "*the Fruit*" is not dead, undifferentiated, motionless, but a living, self-differentiating, moving essence... The different ordinary fruits are different manifestations of the life of the "*one* Fruit"; they are crystallisations of "*the* Fruit" itself... What is delightful in this speculation is to rediscover all the real fruits there, but as fruits which have a higher mystical significance, which have grown out of the ether of your brain and not out of the material earth, which are incarnations of "*the* Fruit" of the *Absolute Subject*... In each of them "*the* Fruit" realises itself by *degrees* and *necessarily* progresses, for instance from its existence as a raisin to its existence as an almond."[15]

Once again, Marx's point is valid. But once again the point does not apply to Hegel himself.

We have already considered the interpretation that Hegel's method essentially involves some supersubject termed "Thought" that somehow is self-generating and creates the world a priori out of itself. What is new here is the view that Hegel's method commits him to an indefinite number of such supersubjects. Marx claimed that for Hegel each and every universal term captures a speculative supersubject. To call this a "reification" of universals is actually far too weak. On this view Hegel treats universals not just as things but as persons! Marx is certainly correct to reject this quite bizarre view. But did Hegel really hold it?

Universals do play a special role in Hegel's thought. But not just any universal will do. For example, a "ground" is a type of universal in that it is an explanatory principle underlying a number of different consequences. Regarding this type of universal Hegel writes, "No ground suffices as mere ground; because it is yet void of a content objectively and intrinsically determined, and is therefore not self-acting and productive." There is no reification or personification of this sort of universal. It does not "act." In contrast, "A content thus objectively and intrinsically determined, *and hence self-acting*, will hereafter come before us as the notion."[16]

There is certainly some rather odd language use going on here. To call a second sort of universal, the notion, "self-acting" does seem to reify and personalize it. But if we look closer Hegel is not really saying anything odd here at all. For Hegel, to say that a universal is "self-acting" simply means that its content is "objectively and intrinsically determined." This is indeed a most unfortunate use of action language. But when the signification Hegel grants to this language is grasped, we can see that he is not committed to a reification or personalization of universals. Whenever there is a logical progression from a category of unity to one of difference, and from there to a category of unity-in-difference, this progression forms a content that is "objectively and intrinsically determined." Hegel would then say that in this case a special sort of universal is involved, one that is "self-acting."[17] But it does not "act" in any ordinary sense of the term. With this language Hegel was simply trying to capture the unity of the progression in which the three categories are united while remaining distinct.

Within the level of objective spirit the move from abstract right through morality to ethical life forms a single progression that in Hegel's view is objectively and intrinsically determined. Hegel introduced the term "will" to bring out this moment of unity. This is thus a special sort of universal, a notion. This does not make "will" into some separate sort of thing that undergoes some existential process taking it through three developmental stages. Categorial reconstruction is not metaphysical mythology. A Hegelian universal like "will" does not have a separate metaphysical status. It is a principle for grasping the intelligibility of the real, not a separate sort of really existing thing. A rejection of conceptual reification is thus not a rejection of the dialectical logic used by Hegel in his categorial theory. At most it is a rejection of Hegel's extravagant language.

Finally, the relationship of "will' to "abstract right," "morality," and "ethical life" is unlike the relation of "fruit" to "apples," "pears," "raisins," and so on. The latter is an example of the genus/species relation, and we have already seen that Hegel's dialectical method is not concerned with this relation. There is no immanent principle connecting species that would allow us to order them systematically according to a dialectical logic. One would be extremely hard pressed to find anything in Hegel's work as silly as suggesting there is some sort of systematic order progressing from "raisin" to "almond." And even if one could find an example of this, the most it would show is that Hegel failed in a particular application of the dialectical method, and not that that method is inherently flawed.

2. Some Alternative Interpretations of "Capital"

One indirect way of establishing the plausibility of reading *Capital* as a dialectical theory of categories in the Hegelian sense is to show that Marx's criticisms of categorial theories do not apply to Hegel's own use of dialectical logic. Another approach, also indirect in form, is to show the shortcomings in various interpretations of *Capital* that leave out the Hegelian dimension. The reading of *Capital* as a dialectical theory of categories is the only one that fulfills a basic canon for any interpretation of the work. This canon is quite obvious. And yet other interpretations, however illuminating they are in many respects, fail to meet it. It is simply this: an interpretation of *Capital* must be able to account for the main features of the work as a whole, all three volumes. In this section I shall consider three recent interpretations that fail to meet this canon. Then an interpretation that has a certain "classic" status in the Marxist tradition will be discussed.

a) "Capital" as a theory of natural necessity

Scott Meikle has recently proposed an interesting Aristotlean reading of Marx.[18] The forms discussed in *Capital* are forms in process, forms that unfold with a natural necessity. These forms consist of a potentiality that will of necessity develop in a certain direction as long as no external circumstance interfers. Just as an acorn must of natural necessity develop into an oak unless this is prevented by an outside force, so the elementary form of value—direct barter in which the value of one commodity is represented in the bodily form of another—must of natural necessity eventually develop into the money form, and then into the capital form.

This reading fails on two grounds. First, in a natural process of development the starting point is both a concrete entity and earlier in time than the end point. However in the passage already quoted in section A.1.d, Marx insisted, "What I start out from is the simplest social form in which the labour-product is presented in contemporary society." The phrase "simplest social form" informs us that Marx's starting point is an abstract structure rather than a concrete entity. And for Marx this form is no less a feature of contemporary society than the more concrete forms derived at the conclusion of his theory. This suggests that the relationship between the initial stages of the theory and the concluding stages is logical rather than temporal. (I shall return to this last point in section d below).

The second difficulty with Meikle's reading is that it fails to account for *Capital* as a whole. Consider the transition from the logically last determination of Volume I, "expanded accumulation,"[19] to the first new determination of Volume II, "simple reproduction." There exists no natural process in which the latter results from the natural development of the former. In fact in "nature," i.e., the developmental tendencies of concretely functioning capitalist systems, simple reproduction tends to *undermine* the possibility of expanded accumulation. A similar point holds for an example from Volume III, the relationship between "cost prices" and "market prices." In the actual functioning of capitalist systems cost prices never appear. Only market prices are given "naturally." How then could the latter arise out of the former according to a natural necessity? We are left with only two choices. Either entire chunks of *Capital*, perhaps the greater portion, must be abandoned on the grounds that Marx somehow made amazingly obvious errors in his estimation of the chains of natural necessity. Or we must look for another sort of reason for Marx to have so strongly insisted on ordering expanded accumulation prior to simple reproduction, and cost prices prior to market prices. Reading *Capital* in dialectical terms provides that reason. The necessity involved in these moves is a logical rather than natural necessity. (On the topic of logical necessity in Marx see section B.1.c and B.2.b of the present chapter and section A.3 of Chapter III).

b) "Capital" as a theory of material practices

This interpretation has recently been articulately defended by W.A. Suchting. He has developed it in the course of an extended polemic against the view that Marx constructed a dialectic of concepts. In Suchting's view Marx merely "flirted" with Hegel's terminology. The dialectic of production and consumption, for example, is described by Marx as a unity of opposites. For Hegel this would mean that they are unconditionally and essentially connected. But for Marx the unity is "a thoroughly conditional one by virtue of their being aspects of a material-social process."[20] The dialectical mediation of exchange-value and use-value also "is in the final analysis a material-practical one."[21] Likewise in the move from the elementary form of value to the money form "there is no real question of some sort of inherent dialectic of the value-form, some conceptual *vis insita* constituted by the contradictory character of the commodity, some immanent unfolding of the concept of value as it exists implicitly in the simple value-form." Instead "how the practice actually develops. . . is in no way deducible from the nature of the value-form. It can be known about only from a study of the practice itself as this proceeds under specific material conditions."[22]

The stress on material practice is not in itself mistaken by any means. But the view that this stress automatically rules out a dialectic of concepts *is* mistaken. First of all, how do we account for transitions like that from expanded accumulation to simple reproduction? There is no "material-social process" that connects these two determinations. Or how are we to understand the unity-in-opposition connecting Division I and Division II in Marx's schema of reproduction? These schema have been explicitly constructed with the aid of unrealistic assumptions, assumptions that no "material-social process" has *ever* held to (for instance, that surplus value can be reinvested only in the Division in which it was produced). This proves that these schema are thought constructs, categories, on a relatively high level of abstraction, and not at all descriptions of concrete material-social processes.

Suchting does admit once that in Marx, "there are, of course, 'necessary' connections between the elements of certain thought-objects constituted for the purpose of understanding real phases of actual capitalist systems."[23] Despite the inverted commas, the supposed incompatibility of Hegel and Marx is in effect given up with this admission, a point Suchting does not wish to concede. And so the point is not developed further, or even mentioned again. Suchting does not give a single example of such a "necessary connection" in Marx, and he denies that it is present in one of the more obvious places where it is, the dialectic of the commodity and money forms. He writes, "In the third section of the first chapter Marx sets up the conceptual-theoretical apparatus for the analysis of the commodity and of money, displaying the various possible value forms, from the simplest to that of money, without any attempt to show how one was connected with the next, except in the most formal way."[24] If there were no inherent, necessary, essential connection between the elementary form of commodity exchange and the money form, if this were merely a "formal" connection, Marx could not have dismissed as impossible in principle Proudhon's claim that we could abolish money while retaining commodity exchange. Yet he did precisely that, something that cannot be accounted for from Suchting's perspective.

c) *Capital as an empirical theory*

Among mainstream social scientists it is quite common to find *Capital* dismissed on the grounds that any contamination with Hegelian dialectics leaves a theory empirically worthless.[25] It is therefore hardly surprising that those who insist that Marx did make a great contribution to empirical social science in *Capital* have been led to deny a Hegelian dimension to this work.

There is certainly much in *Capital* that can be read as straighforward empirical theory. The sections on the length of the working day, the struggles at the point of production, the history of ground rent, can all be easily accounted for on this interpretation. Unfortunately, however, there is much that this reading cannot account for. Most importantly, it cannot account for the underlying thread that makes *Capital* a whole, rather than an aggregate of separate empirical studies. Within the confines of empirical social science alone there is no way to account for the systematic transition from expanded accumulation to simple reproduction, to repeat the example given above. Either Marx was mistaken in thinking that his theory formed a systematic whole, or we must attempt to account for what makes it a systematic whole, its architectonic. The latter pushes us once again back in the direction of dialectical logic.

In any empirical study categories will be employed. There is no choice about this. The only choice is whether those categories will be employed in an unreflective fashion, or whether they will be considered in and for themselves *qua* categories. Empirical social scientists typically take the first option, considering basic categories only in so far as they have empirical applications. Hegel took the second option. *Marx combined the two*. *Capital* includes numerous empirical studies that remain of interest to historians and social scientist today, studies that Hegelian philosophers would never undertake. But Marx felt that categories ought not to be employed in an unreflective fashion in these empirical studies. And this requires that they be considered in abstraction from any specific empirical application. Marx learned from Hegel that when fundamental categories are so considered, they have immanent systematic connections with each other. Tracing out the immanent systematic connections among categories allows us to employ these categories in a reflective fashion when we later turn to empirical investigations. That Marx constructed a categorial theory in *Capital* is no cause for shame from the standpoint of a commitment to empirical studies. For it is in no sense designed to replace such studies. It complements such studies by making those who undertake them reflect upon the conceptual tools they employ.

Social categories define fundamental social structures. A dialectical analysis of these categories can uncover basic structural tendencies in these structures. But structural tendencies are just that, tendencies. One cannot derive a concrete empirical process from a set of structural tendencies no matter how complete that set might be. Empirical studies will always be required. A full account of Marx's work would have to evaluate his contribution to various empirical disciplines, and not be limited to his systematic ordering of economic categories, as is the present work (although the line between categorial analysis and empirical studies is often not hard and fast, as we shall see repeatedly in the course of this study).

d) "Capital" as a logico-historical theory

In section A.1.c it was asserted that Marx employed a "logico-historical" method in the sense that at each stage in the logical progression of economic categories Marx incorporated extensive historical remarks. However among Marxists the term has generally been taken in a quite different sense, in which it connotes that Marx's ordering of categories presents an ideal type of historical stages, a logic of history that captures the dialectically necessary sequence in which history must unfold. The first two interpretations considered above can be taken as variants of this reading of *Capital*. This reading can also be found in Meek, in Howard and King, and in many many others as well.[26] But most damaging for my reading of *Capital* is the undeniable fact that it can be found in Marx as well.

Marx himself, after all, insisted that he had merely "coquetted" with Hegelian language in the book.[27] This is usually taken to mean that Marx abandoned the nonhistorical dimension of Hegel's method. In the "Afterword" to the second German edition he discussed the methodology he employed in *Capital*. In the course of the discussion he quoted with unreserved approval the following passage from a Russian review: "The one thing which is of moment to Marx, is to find the law of phenomena... the law of their development, i.e. of their transition from one form into another, from one series of connexions into a different one...Marx only troubles himself about one thing: to show, by rigid scientific investigation, the necessity of successive determinate orders of social conditions...Most important of all is the rigid analysis of the series of successions, of the sequences and concatenations in which the different stages of such an evolution present themselves." Marx commented, "Whilst the writer pictures what he takes to be actually my method, in this striking and (as far as concerns my own application of it) generous way, what else is he picturing but the dialectical method?"[28] Further, there are places in the main text where Marx went to great lengths to present his theory as an evolutionary logic of development in history, for example in the discussion of the different stages of the money form, the advance from manufacturing to big industry, and so on.

This is all quite incompatible with dialectical method understood as a systematic (nonhistorical) categorial progression. If the canon by which interpretations of *Capital* are to be judged is that they must account for the main features of the work, then it would seem that a systematic reading of the book must be rejected in favor of the logico-historical reading. But this latter reading has problems of its own. For one thing there is Marx's already-quoted comment in the *Grundrisse* that "It would be unfeasible and wrong to let the economic categories follow one another in the same sequence as that in which they were historically decisive." How can we put these apparently disparate views together?

At this point some commentators have proposed that Marx's position underwent a transformation. His earlier economic writings (*Grundrisse*, *Critique of Political Economy*) were constructed along Hegelian lines, employing a systematic dialectical logic that he later abandoned when it came time to write *Capital*.[29] This view fails to take into account the many places in *Capital* where a logico-historical reading breaks down. Some of these were mentioned in sections a) and b); others will be discussed in Part Two. It also fails to take into account Marx's insistence that in *Capital* he did not present "a general historico-philosophical theory.[30] A logico-historical

31

theory claiming to present the necessary dialectical development in history would certainly be that sort of theory.

Another, more plausible, interpretation is that Marx was thoroughly confused methodologically. Elements of a systematic dialectical logic similar to Hegel's coexist alongside elements of an evolutionary historical logic closer to Darwin. This is the position Hans-Georg Backhaus ultimately arrived at in his series of significant articles.[31]

This interpretation cannot be refuted at this point. In Part Two I shall show that from beginning to end Capital follows a systematic dialectical logic that betrays no sign of methodological ambiguity. This still leaves the question of why Marx at times endorsed a nonsystematic reading. My own conjecture is that this must be seen in the light of the public response to the publication of A Critique of Political Economy and the first edition of Volume I of Capital. In the history of the socialist movement, no works have ever been as eagerly anticipated. However it is also the case that few works have ever been greeted with more disappointment. Marx himself had assimilated systematic dialectics, and he gave himself a refresher course on Hegel's Logic just prior to writing these works.[32] But the reading public had changed, and the audience Marx wanted to reach could not penetrate his Hegelian approach to ordering economic categories.

At this point Marx had two options. In subsequent editions of Capital he could have anticipated Lenin's famous aphorism and insisted that no one could fully understand his work without a prior understanding of Hegel's Logic.[33] If he had taken this tack Capital would surely have remained a significant work in intellectual history. But it is doubtful it would have attained world historical significance. And so he took the second option. He downplayed the systematic nature of the theory and stressed the much more accessible historical components of the work.

He could do this without bad faith for three reasons. First, the book does contain historical theses and illustrations that can immensely profit those who lack all knowledge of Hegel and have no interest in the logic that generates a systematic theory of categories. Second, as we have seen, Marx had a metaphysical reading of Hegel. He took Hegel's retreats into the realm of Vorstellungen literally. For instance he interpreted Hegel's "absolute" as a metaphysical supersubject that generated itself out of itself, while overlooking those passages where Hegel asserted that philosophy is "its own time apprehended in thoughts." If this (uncharitable) interpretation is granted, then Marx would have been quite correct to contrast the historical starting point of his own theory to Hegel's position. Finally, the ultimate purpose of Marx's theory is to contribute to historical change. In this sense his position is historical in a sense that Hegel's is not, since Hegel's ultimate purpose is to reconcile us to the rationality of the present.

All of these considerations are cogent. They may also have encouraged Engels to downplay the systematic element in *Capital* when it came time for him to edit the second and third volumes after Marx's death. As we shall see in Part Two of the present work, however, none of these considerations changes the fact that a dialectical logic taken over from Hegel provides the architectonic of *Capital*. None of them changes the fact that the stages in the dialectical progression are derived systematically rather than historically. And none of them changes the fact that the ordering of the categories in *Captial* is as rigorously systematic as that found in the *Grundrisse* or *The Critique of Political Economy*.

Of course these four examples do not provide an exhaustive list of all the possible readings of *Capital*. Nor does the response to them conclusively establish the legitimacy of a categorial reading. I have simply tried to make the latter sort of reading plausible to those most inclined to dismiss it, those who stress (quite correctly) that issues of natural necessity, material practice, empirical research, and historical development were of great importance to Marx. But the plausibility of this reading can be established more directly (if still provisionally) as well.

B. Direct Arguments for Reading *"Capital"* in Terms of Dialectical Logic

The importance of Hegelian dialectical logic for an understanding of *Capital* can be established directly in two ways. First, a great number of Marx's own methodological remarks confirm this. Second, there are three tasks Marx set for his theory that dialectical logic is uniquely capable of fulfilling.

1. *Marx's Own Methodological Remarks*

When Marx's methodology is examined, it has three stages. They correspond precisely to the stages outlined by Hegel (see Chapter I, section A).

a) The starting point

In Marx's methodological reflections the starting point for theory building is the real process, "the real and concrete" as given in experience. But as immediately experienced it is not possible to have more than a "chaotic conception of the whole" of this experience.[34] Hence there is a need to proceed to the theorizing of that experience. This corresponds exactly to Hegel's dictum that "philosophy is its own time apprehended in thoughts."

b) *The stage of appropriation*

The second stage of Marx's method is to begin an analysis of the uncomprehended experience through an appropriation of the categories used to make that experience intelligible. In the case of *Capital* the object of experience Marx wished to comprehend was the capitalist mode of production. And so the relevant categories to appropriate are those of everyday experience in this mode of production and the concepts employed by political economists in their attempts to understand that mode of production scientifically. This appropriation is not a haphazard one; already there is a systematic intention at work. This intention is expressed in the fact that the concepts are worked through with the goal of reaching those which are simplest and most abstract (such as "commodity," "use-value," "exchange-value," etc.) From "a chaotic conception of the whole," Marx writes, "I would then, by means of further determination, move analytically towards ever more simple concepts, from the imagined concrete towards ever thinner abstractions until I had arrived at the simplest determinations."[35] This corresponds precisely to Hegel's second stage.

c) *The stage of reconstruction*

Having arrived at the "simplest determinations," Marx continues as follows: "From there the journey would have to be retraced until I had finally arrived at the (concrete), but this time not as the chaotic conception of a whole, but as a rich totality of many determinations and relations."[36] This involves a systematic reconstruction of the categories appropriated in stage b (supplemented where necessary), a progression from the simplest and most abstract determinations to the most complex and concrete ones. At the conclusion, the intelligibility of the initially given concrete will have been grasped by thought in a systematic fashion:

> The concrete is concrete because it is the concentration of many determinations hence unity of the diverse. It appears in the process of thinking, therefore, as a process of concentration, as a result, not as a point of departure, even though it is the point of departure in reality and hence also the point of departure for observation and conception. Along the first path the full conception was evaporated to yield an abstract determination; along the second, the abstract determinations lead towards a reproduction of the concrete by way of thought.[37]

This is precisely the thrust of Hegel's approach as well. For Marx too this "second path," the linear reconstruction in thought, does not follow the subjective psychological associations of the theorist. Nor does it follow associations based on objective, but contingent, connections. In moving from abstract categories to concrete ones in a step-by-step fashion the connections are, in Hegel's language, "intrinsically and objectively determined." In Marx's language the goal is to trace "the intrinsic connection existing between economic categories or the obscure structure of the bourgeois economic system...(to) fathom the inner connection, the physiology, so to speak, of the bourgeois system."[38] *This is nothing more than the Hegelian goal of reconstructing the world in thought through working out a systematic theory of categories.* By tracing the "intrinsic connections existing between economic categories" the object realm is reconstructed in thought, the object realm here being the bourgeois system.

Marx's commitment to a dialectical ordering of economic categories comes out quite forcefully in his criticism of earlier economic theories. Adam Smith's theory is to be rejected because he did not distinguish determinations on a abstract level ("value" and "surplus value") from those on a concrete level ("price" and "profit"): "These two concepts of his run counter to one another in his work, naively, without his being aware of the contradiction."[39] With Ricardo the two levels are distinguished. But he makes two fundamental errors. First, in his specification of the abstract level he lets concrete considerations intrude: "He must be reproached for not going far enough, for not carrying his abstraction to completion, for instance, when he analyses the *value* of the commodity, he at once allows himself to be influenced by consideration of all kinds of concrete conditions."[40] Second, he and his followers treat the law of value, an abstract determination, as if it held directly on the level of concretion. In other words, they skip over the intermediate categorial links connecting the abstract level with the concrete level:

> Ricardo's method is as follows: He begins with the determination of the magnitude of the value of the commodity by labour-time and then *examines* whether the other economic relations and categories *contradict* this determination of value or to what extent they modify it. . . This inadequacy (of method) not only shows itself in the method of presentation (in a formal sense) but leads to erroneous results because it omits some essential links and *directly* seeks to prove the congruity of the economic categories with one another.[41]

The alternative theoretical approach, applied by Marx in *Capital*, presents the development of the various categories in their proper systematic order:

> With Ricardo the one-sidedness arises also from the fact that in general he wants to show that the various economic categories or relationships *do not contradict the theory of value*, instead of on the contrary *developing* them together with their apparent contradictions out of this basis or presenting the development of this basis itself.[42]

2. Need for Independence of the Thought Process

In Chapter I Hegel's stress on the independence of the thought process could be granted at once. The controversial point was whether his "idealism" led him to deny the independence of the real process from thought. Just the reverse holds with Marx. No one would consider questioning whether Marx insisted on the autonomy of real material processes. But dialectical logic necessarily involves granting a considerable independence to the thought process. Is this compatible with Marx's materialism? I shall argue that dialectical logic is not merely compatible with Marx's materialist ontology. It is a crucial feature of historical materialism. The independence of the thought process provided by dialectical logic was an essential part of Marx's attempt 1) to overcome various illusions; 2) to assert certain theoretical claims of necessity; and 3) to ground revolutionary politics theoretically. With this in mind the point can be put even stronger. Marx, like Hegel, not only granted an independence to the thought process. He granted it a certain priority as well.

a) Overcoming illusions

An insistence on the priority of the real process (and a corresponding rejection of Hegelian dialectical theories of categories) sounds, at first hearing, the proper position for a materialist to take. But if Marx had adhered to this position, *Capital* would never have been written and historical materialism would never have arisen. For it is a central thesis of Marx's position that in capitalism the real process necessarily generates appearances which are illusionary:

> These same circumstances (independent of the mind, but influencing it), which compel the producers to sell their products as *commodities*—circumstances which differentiate one form of social production from another—provide their products with an exchange-value which (also in their mind) is independent of their use-value. Their "mind," their consciousness, may be completely ignorant of, unaware of the existence of, what in fact determines the value of their products or their products as values. They are placed in relationships which determine their thinking but they may not know it. Anyone can use money as money without necessarily understanding what money is. *Economic categories are reflected in the mind in a very distorted fashion.*[43]

For example, those immersed within the real process inevitably consider "price" and "supply and demand" fundamental economic categories, see the wage contract as a free exchange of equivalents, see "capital" as a productive factor in its own right, and so on. Empirical sciences which do not call into question the priority of the real process make such appearances the first principles of their theories. The result is what Marx termed "vulgar

36

economics," not historical materialism. *The intelligibility of the concrete and material can only be grasped through asserting the priority of the thought process over how the concrete and material is given in appearances.* The concrete and material has a depth level underlying its surface level of appearances. The task of thought is first to pierce through the appearances to that depth level (the level of "value" as measured by labor-time rather than "price," where exploitation is discovered within the wage contract, where only labor counts as productive of value, and so on) and then to proceed to the mediations that connect the depth level with the given appearances. To fulfill this task it is not sufficient for thought to assert its independence; it must assert its *primacy* over the appearances generated by the real process. A dialectical reconstruction of categories allows for this. In this there is no difference in principle between Hegel and Marx. Both assert that it is only in thought, in theorizing, that the intelligibility of the world can be grasped.

b) Theoretical claims of necessity

Most of the claims we make about the world are contingent, and are warranted if and only if certain contingent processes can be observed in the world. However much observation may be theory dependent, such assertions are dependent upon real material processes in a relatively direct fashion. But there are some sorts of statements that are not meant to be contingent in this sense, and that therefore cannot have their validity established through a (relatively) straightforward reference to the world.

Consider the difference between the assertion "The owner of this plant exploits these workers" and the statement "captial inherently involves the exploitation of labor." The validity of the first assertion depends on a variety of contingent facts about the world: the plant is owned by this person rather than another; it continues operating rather than going out of business; it has these workers rather than those; and so on. The validity of the second assertion depends on there being capital and labor, and this may be historically contingent. But once capital and labor are given, the relationship of "exploitation" is claimed to hold of necessity, irrespective of specific contingent facts about the world. A theory that wishes to establish a claim of this latter sort must therefore be of a different type than one in which the former sort of claim is made. The goal of the latter sort of theory is still to say something true about the world. But mere observation of the world does not establish necessary connections. One cannot jump from statements of the form "This capitalist exploits those laborers," no matter how many, to the assertion that "capital necessarily exploits labor." A different sort of argument is needed.

The defenders of neoclassical economics do not believe that this different sort of argument can be provided. They hold that exploitation is a thoroughly contingent matter that occurs only in the more or less exceptional cases where a factor of production is not compensated for its productive contribution. In this sense capital too can (contingently) be "exploited." Marx did not hold that the connection between captial and the exploitation of wage labor was true tautologically. But as we shall see in Chapter VI, he did insist that it is necessarily the case that there is a dominant structural tendency for those who control capital to exploit those who do not. As a result Marx held that there is a systematic and necessary connection (and thus a logical connection, in the sense of dialectical logic) between the categories "capital" and "exploitation." The underlying intention behind Hegel's extravagant language of "self-acting" thought was precisely to defend claims of this sort regarding the systematic and necessary connections among categories. Far from being hostile in principle to Hegel here, Marxists should attempt to formulate nonmystifying expressions to capture what he was trying to express. Formulating necessary categorial connections demands that some measure of independence from real processes be granted to the process of thought.

In conclusion, it is true that Hegel stressed the logical necessity that he felt characterized the ordering of categories constituting his system. It is also true that Marx stressed the independence of the material realm from thought. But each thinker's position also embodies the point stressed by the other. Hegel, like Marx, thematized the "otherness" of the material realm. And Marx's theory, like Hegel's, includes claims of systematic necessity (for instance, the conceptual connection between "capital" and "exploitation," or the logical necessity with which the category "value" precedes the category "price"). It therefore is mistaken to contrast Marx's "materialism" to Hegel's "idealism" based upon how the real process is related to the thought process in their work. Marx's need for dialectical logic was no less than Hegel's.

c) *Revolutionary politics*

Revolutionary politics can be defined in two ways: i) revolutionary politics are always oriented to the long term goal of changing the fundamental structures of society (however necessary it is to be concerned with transitional goals here and now[44]); and ii) revolutionary politics against capitalism involve the claim that the fundamental structures to be changed are inherently and necessarily exploitative. In contrast, the reformist is one who is concerned with changing less than fundamental structures, and/or one who feels that the fundamental structures can be made nonexploitative if they are tinkered with in the right way. On both points a theoretical grounding of the revolutionary perspective requires dialectical logic.

38

i) Revolutionary transformations attack the fundamental structures of a social system. But the distinction between fundamental and nonfundamental structures can only be adequately worked out within a systematic categorial theory. Some feel that measures such as tinkering with monopoly rents through increased state regulations, or regulating closely the transactions of financial capital, and so on, constitute a radical step towards socialism. A revolutionary Marxist, in contrast, holds that only a move away from the commodity form, the money form, the captial/wage labor relation, truly counts as a revolutionary transformation to socialism. The theoretical basis for the Marxist position is found in *Capital*. In so far as the commodity form, the money form, and the capital/wage labor relation are abstract categories serving as principles for the derivation of further categories in a reconstruction of the capitalist mode of production, they articulate structures and structural tendencies that define that system. This implies that transforming other tendencies, thematized in the systematic reconstruction by later, more concrete, categories, leaves the heart of that system intact. Without dialectical logic establishing this connection—a connection which is, by the way, verified practically in the continuous failure of regulations regarding monopoly profits and bank transactions to significantly transform the capitalist system—conscious revolutionary action guided by theory would be impossible. Directionless, ad hoc, spontaneous, and ultimately useless reactions would be the only response to capital. A dialectical theory of categories is a condition of the possibility of conscious revolutionary transformation (which, of course, is not to say that it is a sufficient condition).

ii) The theoretical point made in section b) has practical implications. Severing the connection between Hegel's dialectical logic and *Capital* comes at the cost of undercutting Marx's attempt to provide a foundation for the rejection of liberal reformist practice. The liberal reformist argues that the shortcomings in generalized commodity exchange are not inherent in the value form itself. They are due only to contingent conditions. The reformist argues that if only these conditions could be changed (through state regulations, nonadversarial work relations, or whatever) then in principle these shortcomings would be overcome. In contrast, Marx's position was that the problems lie with the value-form itself, and not with any set of specific conditions. Only the revolutionary transformation of that form can adequately address the shortcomings. To justify this position theoretically Marx had to establish that phenomena such as exploitation and crises are inherent in and necessarily connected to the value form. An examination of specific conditions alone does not provide a basis for asserting necessary and essential connections of the sort required. Dialectical logic does, for it allowed Marx to deduce the categories of "exploitation" and "crises" from those of "value" and "capital."

Postscript

This chapter should not end with the impression that the positions of Hegel and Marx can simply be conflated. There are three important areas in which Hegel's "idealism" can legitimately be contrasted with Marx's "materialism." Since these areas are well known, they can be presented briefly here.

First, for Hegel the coherence of a categorial theory was both a necessary and a sufficient condition for its validity. For Marx, it is a necessary condition only. For Hegel, a thought system can account for its own validity within itself. This explains the circular structure of his system, in which the last category supposedly validates the choice of the first, just as when given the first, the last ultimately follows. Marx rejects this idealistic theory of verification, i.e. a verification, that never leaves the sphere of ideas. His alternative is a verification through material praxis: "the question whether objective truth can be attributed to human thinking is not a question of theory but is a practical question. Man must prove the truth, i.e., the reality and power, the this-worldliness of his thinking in practice."[45]

A second contrast involves the content of their theories regarding human history. Hegel grants an explanatory primacy in history to systems of ideas. Specifically, it is the introduction of religious world views which first initiates a new stage in world history. Religious principles are then subsequently incorporated in legal, social, economic, and political institutions. It was, for example, Christianity which introduced the principle of the modern world: "the consciousness (that persons are free) arose first in religion, the inmost region of Spirit; but to introduce the principle into the various relations of the actual world, involves a more extensive program than its simple implementation; a problem whose solution and application require a severe and lengthened process of culture. In proof of this we may note that slavery did not cease immediately on the reception of Christianity. Still less did liberty predominate in States; or Governments and Constitutions adopt a rational organization, or recognize freedom as their basis. That application of the principle of political relations; the thorough moulding and interpenetration of the constitution of society by it, is a process identical with history itself."[46] And, yet more explicitly, "States and Laws are nothing else than Religion manifesting itself in the relations of the actual world."[47] In Marx's theory of history, systems of ideas such as religious

40

world views do not have this primacy in historical explanation. Cultural phenomena have no more than a relative autonomy from material socio-economic processes: "This conception of history thus relies on expounding the real process of production—starting from the material production of life itself—and to comprehending the from of intercourse connected with and created by this mode of production, i.e., civil society in its various stages, as the basis of all history; describing it in its action as the state, and also explaining how all the different theoretical products and forms of consciousness, religion, philosophy, morality, etc., etc., arise from it, and tracing the process of their formation from that basis; thus the whole thing can, of course, be depicted in tis totality (and therefore, too, the reciprocal action of these various sides on one another)."[48]

The third area in which Hegel's idealism is opposed to Marx's materialism involves the question of the autonomy of individuals. This is a topic that will concern us throughout the present work. At this point it can simply be asserted that the common principles employed by Hegel and Marx commit them both to advocating a social system within which universal and individual are united in their difference, i.e. a society in which the priority of the community does not lead to a sacrifice of the autonomy of individuals. In logical terms, both seek a set of institutions that can be properly categorized using categories from the level of the notion (*Begriff*). Hegel alone, however, feels that the autonomy of the individual in principle can be preserved within the modern capitalist system. In his model of that system Hegel includes certain features to guarantee this: individual rights to property, the individual child's right to education, the individual's right to free speech and to various other civil rights such as a fair and public trial by peers according to public laws, etc.[49] Hegel is therefore intellectually reconciled with the modern capitalist state. His attitude towards it is the contemplative ("idealistic") one of appreciating its inner rationality.[50]

For Marx, the measures listed by Hegel are totally incapable of guaranteeing the autonomy of individuals within the political community. As long as the society is subject to the imperatives of capital accumulation, measures like property rights instead allow the exploitation of one class over another. This exploitation both negates the individual autonomy of the members of the exploited classes and prevents a true universal, one incorporating the interests of all, from being articualted. Marx's theory therefore culminates with a call to praxis which transforms the material conditions so as to create a material reality in which the universal (the community) is truly united with the autonomy of the individuals within it. This call to material praxis is the third and most important area in which Marx defends a materialism not to be found in Hegel.

41

We shall return to some of these themes later. For now it is enough to have established what Marx himself stressed and what Lenin well knew: an understanding of Hegel's *Logic* is central to a full grasp of Marx's theory. *Captial* is a dialectical theory in the sense first worked out by Hegel. But what does this mean exactly? And how does Marx's theory fare when measured by this standard?[51]

III

Hegelian Readings of "Capital"

In this chapter I first consider three different ways *Capital* could be read as a dialectical theory of economic categories. Two of these possibilities are dismissed. Once the third option has been introduced, it immediately leads to a number of questions regarding Marx's success in constructing a dialectical theory. Objections made to Marx's theory from this perspective may be termed "Hegelian" objections. I list three sorts of Hegelian objections that will occupy us in the remainder of this study.

A. Alternative Readings of "Capital" as a Dialectical Theory

In the first two chapters I have argued that the methodology Marx employed in *Capital* is a dialectical one taken over from Hegel. But there are at least three ways in which this could be the case. The results of the first two chapters can be further clarified by considering each in turn.

1. *Capital and Essence*

It has often been noticed that in *Capital* Marx especially employed terms taken from the second level of Hegel's *Logic*, the level of essence (*Wesen*). In fact it might seem that the whole book is structured by the contrast between a level of underlying essence and a level of appearances or manifestations of that essence. The beginning of *Capital* captured the essence, or "inner nature" of this mode of production, capital in general. Then in Volume III Marx traced how this essence appears on the concrete level of many capitals. This reading is presented by Krahl, among others.[1]

43

An understanding of Hegel's dialectic of essence is indeed crucial for a adequate reading of *Capital*. This point will be seen again and again in the course of this study. However as it is presented by Krahl and others this reading misses a central feature of the theory in *Capital*, which we may term its "linearity." *Capital* does not just examine the dialectic of a single categorial structure, moving from its essence to its appearances. It is instead a linear progression from one essence structure to the next. Consider structures of social relations defined by the categories of "value," and "capital" in Volume I. Each of these forms a distinct essence structure, and each has its own distinct form of appearance. "Value" is manifested in "exchange-value," while "capital" is manifested in investment funds, means of production, purchased labor-power, stored inventory, and funds received from sales. The contrast between essence and appearance can help us understand each structure. But it is not sufficient if we want to understand the dialectical logic of the transition from one structure to the next.

2. *Capital as Mapping One-to-One with the Logic*

A second reading of *Capital* that takes its start from Hegel's *Logic* is able to provide an account for the linear progression in *Capital*. it does so by mapping the dialectical progression of categories found in Hegel's *Logic* to the sequence of categories in *Capital*. if we assume that Hegel has provided sufficient motivation for the transitions in the *Logic*, and that the categories of *Capital* map those of the *Logic*, then the linear progression in *Capital* has its justification in terms of dialectical logic already provided for it. This reading of *Capital* takes its inspiration from Engels' remark that the move from "commodity" to "capital" maps that from "being" to "essence" in Hegel's *Logic*.[2] Rüdiger Bubner has presented a more fleshed-out version of this reading.[3] However the most detailed reading of *Capital* from this perspective by far is found in an early paper by Richard Winfield.[4]

However helpful this approach may be in illuminating specific transitions in *Capital*, there are a number of reasons to think that it ultimately is not adequate. For one thing, Marx was among the most generous of all authors when it came to crediting his sources. He freely admitted his debt to Hegel's *Logic* and its method. But he nowhere even hinted that he derived the specific content of his theory through taking a category from the *Logic* and directly translating it into an economic category. If anything remotely like this had been his procedure, somewhere or other he most likely would have mentioned it.

Perhaps even more telling is the fact that Hegel himself rejected the claim that the categories of the *Logic* can directly map onto sections of the *Realphilosophie*. The precise relationship between the two is disputed, but what is not in dispute is that it is a much more subtle relationship than any sort of one-to-one correspondence. For example, a relatively early category in the ordering making up the *Realphilosophie* may be a real embodiment of a relatively advanced categorial structure from the *Logic*. Similarly a late category in the *Realphilosophie* may be a real embodiment of a fairly early category in the *Logic*.[5]

Finally, even if Hegel did hold that the *Logic* provided a ready-made key to unlock the categorial ordering within a specific object realm, it is hardly plausible to assert that Marx held this view. It is impossible to see how this procedure could be made compatible with Marx's own vehement and unequivocal rejection of those like Proudhon who believed that dialectical logic provides a key that can unlock the secret of a given object realm, thereby saving one from the arduous task of appropriating that realm in its specificity.

    3. Capital as the immanent Unfolding of the Subject Matter

The third manner of interpreting *Capital* as a dialectical theory is the one that will be defended in the remainder of the present work. A dialectical theory that is to avoid the criticisms Marx made of such theories must begin with an appropriation of its subject matter. Both the categories employed and the logical connection among those categories must be specific to that subject matter. Reading *Capital* as a dialectical theory is a matter of grasping this specificity of categories and their connections. The logic of the content must be allowed to develop itself immanently within the theory. This approach is consistent with both Marx's comments regarding the importance of re-reading the *Logic* prior to writing *Captial, and* with Marx's consistent rejection of the attempt to impose a logical ordering on an object realm externally.

Prior to undertaking a detailed reading of *Capital* from this perspective, what can be said about this sort of theory? There are a number of conditions a theory of categories must fulfill if it is to capture adequately the immanent unfolding of the subject matter. Just as one can make general statements regarding the conditions theories of mathematical physics must fulfill if they are to count as successful cases of that sort of theory (for example, they must be coherently formulated in terms of post-Euclidean geometry), so one can make general statements regarding the conditions dialectical theories of categories must fulfill if they are to count as successful cases of this quite different sort of theory. In this context three conditions can be mentioned.

The first has to do with *the starting point* of the theory. This must be the simplest and most abstract category, the one from which the remaining categories of the theory can be derived. For the theory to capture the immanent intelligibility of its object, this starting point must be the most

45

abstract and simplest determination immanent to that object.

The second condition involves *the linear progression* of the theory. The transition from one category to the next must be based on the content of the specific categories. At first it seems as if this forbids any general remarks on how transitions are motivated. If they must be immanent to the content of the specific categories, then it would seem that no general remarks are in order. However this is not the case. There are both general features of categories and general patterns of categorial transitions. A category is in general a principle unifying a manifold. As we saw in Chapter I, we can derive from this three specific sorts of categorial structures. Some categories will stress the moment of unifying. Ohters will stress manifoldness, difference. Still others will articulate a more or less precarious balance between the two. These are the only possibilities. And since the most fundamental categories define the most basic ontological structures,[6] basic ontological structures can also be characterized either in terms of unity, difference, or unity-in-difference.

When it comes to the systematic connections among categories, if our aim is to order from the simplest to the most complex, then categories (and the ontological structures they define) of simple unity must be ordered prior to those of difference, and those of unity-in-difference must follow the latter. If this is not done dialectical logic breaks down. Any dialectical theory of categories will include a number of sequences from unity through difference to unity-in-difference, each on its own level of relative abstractness/concreteness. An immanent unfolding of the subject matter demands that the various fundamental structures in the object realm receive their proper place in this systematic ordering. Any specific transition must have its systematic motivation in terms of this architectonic. Convincing reasons must be provided explaining why a category of unity must necessarily lead to a category of difference, and why a determination of difference must give way to one of unity-in-difference.

Third, there is the question of *the general categorial/ontological framework* used throughout the theory. Hegel's *Logic* may not contain all possible fundamental categories and basic ontological structures. But it certainly contains the most comprehensive set ever derived. Whether theorists interpreting a given object realm are aware of it or not, the odds are great that their theories will be constructed with the help of specific fundamental categories (and will imply specific ontological structures) that can be found in the *Logic*. Marx is no exception to this point. When he defined the categories "commodity," "money," "capital," and so on, he did so in terms of a specific categorial framework found in Hegel's *Logic*, one taken from the level of essence (*Wesen*). For his theory to capture the immanent

46

unfolding of its object realm, then, this categorial framework (and the social ontology it imples) must capture the truth of the specific object realm.

Capital is a wonderfully rich work, with many different sorts of theories included within it. Whole chunks of it are devoted to historical studies, others are treatises in sociology, political science, economics, and so on. But the work is not just an aggregate of distinct bits. It forms a unity, and this unity stems from the fact that, whatever else it is, Capital is also a systematic theory of categories. Despite all the profound differences that separate Marx and Hegel, Capital nonetheless can be termed a "Hegelian" theory from this perspective. To count as a successful case of this unique sort of theory the three conditions just listed must be fulfilled. Therefore any criticism of Capital that is based not so much on its historical, economic, political, or sociological claims (although these may all be relevant to a considerable extent), but on its failure to fulfill these three conditions, may be termed "Hegelian" objections. The main Hegeliam objections can now be stated in a preliminary manner.

B. The Main Hegelian Objections to "Capital"

This section is fairly abstract, and may prove difficult for readers not already familiar with categorial theories in general or Capital in specific. However before proceeding to a detailed reading of Capital as a categorial theory it seems useful to catelogue the main sorts of Hegelian objections that will be confronted in the course of that reading. A case can be made that Capital fails to fulfill the three conditions required for a systematic theory of categories to count as successful. This case has been made most forcefully by Klaus Hartmann, upon whose work the following is based.[7]

I. The Starting Point

A truly dialectical theory begins with a given totality of experience that is initially uncomprehended. The theoretician then analyzes that totality into its simplest determinations, the most abstract categories applicable to that experience. The theory will then proceed to reconstruct the given totality through moving to ever more complex and concrete determinations. The choice of the initial categories is thus obviously of crucial significance for the theory as a whole. For a Hegelian the crucial question here is whether this starting point has been adequately formulated in Capital. It may be argued that Marx did not begin with the simplest and most abstract categories immanent within the capitalist mode of production. His true starting point is instead a model of species-being that has been arbitrarily inserted into the theory. Marx wished to attain a negative result, a critique of capitalism. To arrive at this result he needed a negative starting

47

point. Contrasting the essential features of commodity exchange with the extraneously introduced model of species-being gave him the negative starting point he desired. In this manner Marx both begged the question and betrayed the proper procedure for dialectical categorial reconstruction.

Another aspect of this is that a dialectical theory should be on the level of thought determinations, of pure categorial thinking. The model of species-being seems to merely on the level of *Vorstellungen*, of picture-thoughts or imaginative representations. Neither logical analyses nor logical transitions can be won from mere picture-thoughts. Rather than being the suitable starting point for a dialectical theory, a theory beginning with picture-thoughts can proceed arbitrarily, following the subjective inclinations if its author.

2. The Linear Progression

The second area of dispute involves the *linearity* of the theory in *Capital*. Under this heading four specific Hegelian objections can be mentioned.

a) In the linear progression of a dialectical theory the transition from one category to the next must be logically justified in terms of thought. If it is, then it is possible that the results of the theory may have the universality and necessity that is sought. However if the transitions are based merely on what appears intuitively plausible, then the results are as contingent as the intuitions to which appeal is made. From an orthodox Hegelian standpoint it can be questioned whether Marx consistently adhered to strict categorial analysis and the logical derivation of one stage of the theory from the preceeding one. Instead, at crucial transitions throughout the work Marx seems to have resorted to picture-thoughts, or stories. He seems to have hoped that this made the transitions plausible and that his readers would not notice that no dialectical justification for the transitions had been given. A quid pro quo appears to operate at places like this, in which picture-thoughts taken from imagination or history are supposed to do the work that only a logical analysis of categories can do.

For example, it might be thought that the transition from the commodity-money-commodity circuit (C-M-C) to money as an end in itself (M-C-M) is not made through an immanent categorial analysis of the former. Instead we are asked to imagine how the psychological disposition of greed can lead to hoarding. Or later in Volume I the notion of relative surplus value is discussed in terms of a lengthy presentation of struggles in the factory in nineteenth-century England. This story provides Marx's account with some intuitive plausibility. But an orthodox Hegelian would point out that a strictly dialectical theory has no place for such contingent historical matters.

b) A Marxist might grant that there are places in *Capital* where the transition to a subsequent category is not fully motivated by the categorial analysis of the preceding category. And it might also be granted that at such places Marx does often insert historical discussions. This does not necessarily imply, however, that these references to history are meant to do the work of justifying a logical transition. In such cases the justification might be instead that the theory must go further if it is to fulfill its objective and provide us with a systematic ordering of the categories that make the capitalist mode of production intelligible. It would be easy enough to show that in Hegel's theory too there are numerous places where the theoretical motivation for moving to a category comes not so much from the conceptual analysis of the preceding determination, but rather from the project of reconstructing the given totality.

If this sort of justification for Marx's systematic ordering were allowed, it might provide a way to deal with transitions subject to the previous objection. For instance, even if it should turn out to be the case that it is not possible to give a direct justification for the move to money as an end in itself, this move may still be warranted by the need to account for capitalism, the given totality that is to be comprehended. Remaining at C-M-C doesn't further this endeavor, while moving to M-C-M does. This, and not any story about hoarding, justifies the transition.

A second Hegelian objection to Marx's linear progression attempts to undercut this sort of defense. It is true that in Hegel's systematic theories transitions are justified in a "backwards" as well as in a "forwards" direction. The forwards justification is the immanent move from one category to the next, justified in terms of moving from categories of immediate unity through categories incorporating differences to categories balancing unity and difference together, proceeding until the given experience has been reconstructed in thought. The second sort of justification proposed for Hegelian theory stems from the claim that this theory moves to higher and higher syntheses, to results that are **truer** than what has gone before. In the Hegelian view the culmination of Hegel's theory in a true form to be affirmed provides a backwards grounding for the earlier categories leading up to it. If the theory culminates in a stage that is true "for itself," i.e. concretely and actually, then this shows that an earlier stage leading up to it must have been true "in itself," i.e. abstractly and potentially.[8]

Marx's theory is not affirmative in this sense. The earliest categories of *Capital* are part of a critique of capitalism and this negative standpoint is maintained throughout. But in a critical theory with a negative result no backwards justification of earlier stages is possible. If this is the case, then all the weight must fall on the forwards justification. Therefore in cases where this fails, where the categorial analysis of an earlier stage by itself is not enough to warrant a dialectical transition, only *ad hoc* transitions are possible. In these cases transitions can be made due to the subjective intentions of the author to get to the particular results he or she wants. Such transitions are not grounded immanently within the theory itself.

c) The linear progression in systematic dialectical theories is supposed to move from abstract categories to concrete ones. If this progression is to be theoretically sound, the abstract stages of the theory must truly be abstract. The theorist cannot take a number of simultaneously coexisting concrete factors and arbitrarily select one of them to serve as an abstract principle for the explanation of the others. However at crucial points in *Capital* it appears that Marx followed precisely this procedure. For instance labor (variable capital) and raw materials, machinery, etc., (constant capital) are concretely coexisting factors of production. Yet at the beginning of Volume I Marx sets constant capital equal to zero, concentrating on variable captial alone, which he explicates in terms of the labor theory of value. He subsequently uses this theory to derive constant capital. There is an appearance of a dialectical progression here, from an abstract principle to a concrete that is explained by that principle. But for an orthodox Hegelian this appearance is unjustified. It stems from the fact that constant capital, which must be presupposed at the start, has been arbitrarily abstracted from at the beginning.

Another example of this sort of move may be mentioned. In the intial stages of the theory the inner nature of capital is defined in terms of the unrestricted drive to accumulate surplus value. Issues connected with the realization of surplus value (i.e. questions regarding effective demand for the commodities put up for sale) are put off until later, more concrete, stages of the theory have been reached. If unrestricted accumulation is held to be part of the "inner nature" of Capital on the abstract level, then realization difficulties can easily be derived. Thus Marx appears to offer here an a priori argument for realization crises being immanent within capital. But this seems to rest on how the theory has been constructed, and not at all on the inner nature of capital. Concretely the concern for accumulation and a concern for realization are simultaneously coexisting in the nature of capital. It was therefore artifical for Marx to have ignored the latter when he constructed his abstract notion of captial. The argument for an immanent tendency to realization crises rests exclusively on this illicit abstraction, which is then used to explain concrete capitalism.

d) Finally, besides the mistake of separating concretely coexisting factors and treating some as abstract principles for the explanation of others, there is an opposite sort of error that also must be avoided in systematic categorial theories. Just as the concrete ought not to be treated as if it were abstract, so too the abstract ought not to be treated as if it were

50

concrete. Abstract stages of a dialectical theory cannot be assumed to have a real continuity with concrete stages. If it is assumed that an abstract stage is really operative on the concrete level, then it may be possible to derive certain conclusions. However the justification for these conclusions will rest on the theoretical confusion of abstract and concrete levels, and not on the inner nature of the object being investigated.

There are a number of places where it appears that Marx was guilty of this error. In Volume I of *Capital* Marx introduced "the law of value." In Volume III Marx insisted that this law continues to hold on the concrete stages of the theory. But how could value considerations be operating on the concrete level? To assert a real existential continuity such that value (or "the law of value") as a category is still applicable on the concrete level of prices and profits seems to misunderstand how linear categorial reconstructions work. But this seems to be precisely what Marx did. Concrete categories are derived from abstract ones. But once this derivation has taken place the earlier determinations no longer play the central role in categorial descriptions. Marx appears to have failed to grasp this essential feature of dialectial theories.

3. The Categorial-Ontological Framework

The final area of disagreement regards Marx's use of what a Hegelian would term *Wesenslogik*, the logic of essence.[9] In many ways this is the most significant issue of all. What is at stake here is the basic categorial structure that is most applicable to capitalism.

Let us recall what is meant by an essence structure. Hegel described it in the following terms: "In essence...the determinateness is not a simple immediacy but is present only as *posited* by essence itself; it is not free, but present only as *connected* with its unity."[10] This conveys the idea that an individual moment ("the determinateness") within an essence structure is thoroughly subordinate to the essence lording over it (it "is present only as posited by essence itself"). It is, in brief, "not free." Contrast this with the following passages taken from the introduction to the section of ethical life (*Sittlichkeit*). These passages convey that the stage of ethical life can be seen as a real embodiment of notion categories.

> Ethical life is the Idea of freedom in that on the one hand it is the good become alive—the good endowed in self-consciousness with knowing and willing and actualized by self-conscious action—while on the other hand self-consciousness has in the ethical realm its absolute foundation and the end which actuates its effort. Thus ethical life is the concept of freedom developed into the existing world and the nature of self-consciousness...The objective ethical order...is substance made concrete by subjectivity as infinite form...The ethical order is freedom or the absolute will as what is objective.[11]

51

—Because the substance is the absolute unity of individuality and universality of freedom, it follows that the actuality and action of each individual to keep and to take care of his own being, while it is on one hand conditioned by the pre-supposed total in whose complex alone the exists, is on the other a transition into a universal product.[12]

The difference between a notion structure and an essence structure is the difference between an ontological structure in which freedom is fully acknowledged and one in which it is not.

In Hegel's system the determinations of generalized commodity exchange fall under the category "civil society." I have already noted that grasping this category in the terms of Hegel's Logic is a complex matter. In so far as it falls in the philosophy of spirit as opposed to the philosophy of nature, it is on the level of Begriff. In so far as within the philosophy of spirit it is on the level of objective spirit, as opposed to subjective spirit or absolute spirit, Wesen categories are appropriate. It is also on the level of Wesen in so far as it represents only a relative universal as compared to the more concrete universal of the state. But in so far as it is alongside the family and the state on the level of ethical life, it can be interpreted in Begriff terms.

To the extent that Hegel described civil society in essence terms, he anticipated Marx to a remarkable degree. But any attempt to conflate their views on the nature of civil society would be totally implausible.[13] For Hegel civil society is "overdetermined" in that it can also be described in notion categories[14], whereas nothing similar can be said of Marx. The passages quoted above from the introduction to the section of ethical life are meant to apply to generalized commodity exchange, a part of ethical life in Hegel's view. In terms of the opposition between Hegel and Marx on the categorization of civil society, the crucial fact is that Hegel insisted that the structure of civil society institutionalizes a reconciliation between universal and individual. This reconciliation includes the moment of freedom. As a result Hegel sees civil society as a set of institutions necessary for the objective social embodiment of freedom. There are no other socio-economic institutions that better institutionalize freedom. This emphasizes the sense in which civil society is categorizable in Begriff terms.

In contrast, for Marx civil society sets an alien force over and against individuals. The problem is not one of affirming self-consciously a reconciliation between individual and community that has already taken place. The task instead is to grasp the power objective forms like "commodity," "money," and "capital" have over individuals, preventing such a reconciliation. In other words, Marx emphasized the sense in which civil society is categorizable in essence terms. Individuals within it are "not free, but present only as connected" with a unity imposed upon them by capital. (What is more, this unity is not even stable according to Marx. Marx's theory of crisis is meant to show that the unity imposed by capital accumulation breaks down without alleviating subjugation to the capital form. As we saw in the discussion of the concept of *Wesen* in Chapter I, the inability to unify in a stable fashion is also a characteristic of an essence structure.)

More specifically, there are three main areas where Marx insisted that capitalism is a structure whose social ontology is best grasped in terms of the categories of essence . . . and where the orthodox Hegelian insists otherwise.

a) Marx's employment of a *Wesenslogik* occurs already in the initial categories of commodity and money. Marx saw the commodity as abstract labor in an alienated form, as a fetish that stands over and against human agents, as a thing which takes on the characteristics of a subject while reducing true human subjects to things which are its moments. In contrast, when Hegel explicated the category of commodity he found that it involves a notion of reciprocal need satisfaction. Through commodities different individuals are mediated together in a system of needs forming a dynamic unity-in-difference.

This gives Hegelians an argument for asseting that *Capital* rests upon a *petitio*. Anything derived from the negative starting point of commodity fetishism, i.e. of an inhuman thing operating as a subject over human agents who are reduced to thing status, is bound to be negative too. Once the phenomena had been initially categorized in terms taken from the level of *Wesen* it was easy enough for Marx to propose his critiques. But for an orthodox Hegelian these critiques do not follow from the immanent nature of commodity production. They can be traced to an arbitrary categorization made by Marx to get to the negative results he wished to obtain. The debate regarding the proper categorization of the money form follows the same line of thought.

b) Marx derived the capital form from the commodity and money forms. In his theory, capital is also categorized with terms taken from the second level of Hegel's *Logic*. Capital is treated as an essence that subsumes laborers, consumers, and even individual capitalists under it as "moments," of its circuit, moving from investment capital (M), through productive capital and the production process, to capital in the form of produced inventory, and then to realized capital (money after sales). It is capital that is the subject of phenomena within the capitalist mode of production, whereas the activity of real human subjects is treated as corresponding to the inner nature of capital. This is an essence structure, as described in Hegel's *Logic*. Here too once the phenomena had been categorized in this fashion it was easy enough for Marx to formulate his critiques. But here too there is an alternative categorization that employs terms taken from the level of *Begriff*. For the orthodox Hegelian, the capital and labor relation and the capital and consumer relation can both be treated in positive terms as forming a unity-in-difference of reciprocity. Rather than a total control of one side over against the other, each side is a co-principle needing the other side with which it is mediated. Likewise the orthodox Hegelian holds out the structural possibility for coordination among different individual capitalists, rather than their necessarily being condemned to follow the dictates of the "inner nature of capital" whatever the forseeable costs to their own interests might be.

c) The final issue in the controversy regarding *Wesenslogik* is in many respects the most important. The orthodox Hegelian stresses that civil society, belonging on the level of *Sittlichkeit*, is a universal, a unity-in-difference that may be categorized in terms of a *Begriffslogik*. But it is only a relative universal. Hegelians agree with Marxists to the extent that for Hegelians too the moment of difference, of antagonism among particular interests, received special stress in the unity-in-difference of civil society. But for the orthodox Hegelian there is a higher categorial level than that of civil society, a more affirmative social form, a higher universality, the *state*. Marx, by defining the state as ultimately the defender of capitalist interests, refuses to grant this. As a result, Hegelians argue, Marx cannot account for forms of state legislation that go against both the short- and long-term interests of capital. Whatever imbalances may exist in principle on the socio-economic level between capital and labor, capital and consumers, and among individual capitalists, can in principle be corrected through workers'- rights legislation, consumer-rights legislation, and the coordination of investment on the level of the state. The state is a distinct type of institution with the telos of reconciling whatever antagonisms persist on the level of civil society.

Once again the issue here is categorial rather than empirical. Whether any given capitalist state has successfully reconciled its particular interests within a higher universal is irrelevant when one discusses the nature of the state in general. For a Hegelian the ultimate reason for why a *Wesenslogik* is inadequate for a reconstruction of the capitalist mode of production is that this does not allow one to grasp the fact that, in principle, the state attains a universal reconciliation compatible with that mode of production.

At this point it is time to ask the prosecution to rest. These Hegelian objections regarding the starting point, the linear progression of Marx's theory in *Capital*, and the fundamental categorial structure employed, will orient the reading of that work that follows in Part Two.

54

PART TWO

The Systematic Ordering

IV

The Value Form

Marx's theory is a critical theory. It attempts to present a systematic critique of the capitalist mode of production. Marx claims that this critique is not to be accomplished through reference to some external standard. Beginning from the earliest categories and proceeding, it is instead to emerge through the reconstruction of the categories that constitute the intelligibility of this mode of production.[1] The selection of the initial determinations is thus extremely important for the theory as a whole. As we have seen in the previous chapter (section B.3), one objection that has been made against Marx from an orthodox Hegelian standpoint is that Marx's selection of the starting point was not made on dialectical grounds. Rather it was made in order to get to the results which he wished to obtain. The interpretation of *Capital* upon which this objection is based is presented in the first section of this chapter. In the following section the objection is developed in detail. I then present an alternative reading of the beginning of *Capital*, and propose replies to the criticisms of Marx that have been considered.

A. A Standard Reading of the First Sections of "Capital"

The reading presented in this section is fairly widespread. For our purposes what is of importance is that it is accepted among the leading Hegelian critics of Marx.

Marx began *Capital* with the category "commodity." But in a logical sense this is not the simplest and most abstract determination of the capitalist mode of production. Commodities have two distinct aspects,

57

"use-value" and "exchange-value." Starting from these factors we can trace two distinct paths to prior principles underlying the category "commodity." Let us begin with use-value first. Use-values are produced when qualitatively different forms of concrete labor combine with the productive power of nature. Concrete labor transforms the raw materials of nature so that they can meet the needs of those who consume them. Ultimately the production of commodities *qua* use-values, like all production, rests on labor as the ontological-anthropological ground of the produced use-values.

Marx here appropriated the theory of objectification Hegel developed in the *Phenomenology of Spirit*, giving it an anthropological twist. Intrinsic to the human essence is the collective activity of objectifying that essence through cooperative concrete labor. This is part of the human "species-being." From this perspective, then, the species-being model seems to provide the ultimate starting point of Marx's theory. This model provides a standard that explains the condition of the possibility of any economy in terms of creative human labor.

However this is only half of the story. For Marx also traced a second move from the "commodity" to logically prior determinations. This begins with the commodity *qua* exchange-value. At first two commodities are produced by two separate producers. In so far as one commodity is exchanged for another, the two commodities are made commensurable. They are reduced to some common feature in terms of which they can be compared. Marx termed this common feature "value." This feature common to both cannot involve their use-values, since as use-values they may not share any qualities at all. Marx believed that after eliminating all other candidates the fact that both are produced by labor is all that remains. But since the two different concrete labors may very well be qualitatively distinct and incommensurable, the labor common to the two commodities must be a nonconcrete type of labor, abstract labor. Abstract labor is therefore the measure of the value of the commodities. From this perspective abstract labor seems to provide the logical starting point of Marx's ordering of economic categories.

However the true starting point of Marx's theory on this reading is neither the species-being model nor the category of abstract labor. It is both taken together, with the former providing the standard upon which the critique of the latter is based. Compared to the (positive) anthropological model of species-being in which creative human labor objectifies itself in its objects, abstract labor appears as a thoroughly alienated (negative) type of labor in a number of different regards. Instead of being part of a collective activity, labor under commodity production is undertaken in isolation from that of other commodity producers. Instead of cooperating together in a common project, the only common features agents share in the commodity process is the fact that each has invested a comparable amount of abstract labor time in the products. Instead of forming a true social community, these isolated producers are brought together only through the subsequent exchange of commodities. In this sense the commodity seems to stand over and above the isolated producers. In the terms of Hegel's *Logic* the commodity appears as an essence, subordinating labor under it (even though the true social ontology here, captured in the species-being model, is the exact reverse of this). This is the phenomenon Marx termed the "fetishism of commodities."

Abstract labor is interpreted here as a negative (alienated, fetishized) social form in comparison with the anthropological model of species-being. This is the starting point in the reconstruction of the capitalist mode of production proposed by Marx. Subsequent determinations will be systematically derived from this starting point. Being derived from a negative form, they too will fix in thought negative structures to be critiqued. As the various forms of commodities, money, and capital are derived from abstract labor and exchange value, both reification and fetishization worsen. Negative economic forms take on even more power over human subjects. In explaining how these forms are derived from exchange-value Marx therefore attempts to explain immanently why they are to be critiqued.[2]

B. Hegelian Objections to the Initial Categories in "Capital"

Beginning with Böhm-Bawerk a great number of specifically economic objections to the above perspective have been proposed. In the present work, however, our concern is with objections that stem primarily from Marx's employment of dialectical logic (although, of course, considerations of the economic content of his theory will often prove necessary). There are four specific objections to be considered that involve questions of dialectical reasoning. They culminate in the claim that Marx's theory rests upon a petitio.

1. The Species-Being Model

A number of problems emerge in Marx's alleged anthropological model from a Hegelian perspective. First, the species-being model is a picture-thought (*Vorstellung*). It is not a pure category of thought, but an image of anthropological activity in which nonalienated producers objectify their human essence in a harmonious process of cooperation. Such pictures have no place in a dialectical ordering of pure categories. Second, the model of species-being presupposes that a number of different categorial determinations cannot be operating at once. In the species-being model labor can only be social, it cannot be private as well as social. In short, it allows no element of difference: "In the case of species-being everything is total and universal . . . undifferentiated, abstract. And so opposition, particularization, differentiation . . . is avoided. This is the model that underlies the critique of commodity fetishism."[3] But in reality labor that is undertaken privately in a commodity economy may simultaneously serve others with whom the laborer has no direct personal relationship. As Hegel insisted, the relationship may be positive without face-to-face direct contact taking place.[4] Third, the standard being used to evaluate economic structures is not introduced immanently in the course of the categorial progression, as would occur in a truly dialectical theory. Instead the species-being model is introduced from outside the development of the economic theory proper.

These problems undermine Marx's attempt to derive a critical theory without begging the question. Marx's theory seems *necessarily* incapable of grasping the positive, affirmative dimensions of the given economic structure. Within the context of an economic dialectic proper there is no reason to introduce an anthropological model of undifferentiated species-being, unless it is to get to the results Marx wished to obtain.

2. An *Illicit* Abstraction

Böhm-Bawerk argued that the move from "exchange-value" to "value" measured by abstract labor was not sufficiently justified.[5] Marx supposed that the exchange of two qualitatively distinct use-values required that they share a common feature, abstract labor. But there are a number of other features shared by exchanged commodities. They are all objects of utility that are desired to some extent or another. They are all scarce objects to some extent or another. In fact, *more* commodities have these features in common than abstract labor. Some things become commodities *without* being produced by labor, as long as some people desire them and they are scarce enough (e.g. found objects, objects made in totally automated production processes, etc.).[6] Marx provided no grounds for preferring his "common feature" to these other ones.

Böhm-Bawerk was a great enemy of dialectical theories. But his objection can be reformulated so that it points to a failure on Marx's part to employ dialectics. From the standpoint of dialectical logic we may ask what a formal abstraction such as "abstract labor" is doing in a supposedly dialectical theory in the first place. A systematic reconstruction in thought of a given realm cannot be won through the procedure of formally abstracting a common feature of the objects in that realm. Hegel has shown that this approach will *always* run into the difficulty pointed out by Böhm-Bawerk: one formal abstraction is as good (or as bad) as another. Hegel made this point in the discussion of the category of "ground": "Various grounds may be alleged for the same sum of fact."[7]

3. The Neglect of Use-Value

Besides the theoretical difficulties involved with the species-being model and with the notion of abstract labor, there is a further difficulty stemming from the way Marx separated use-value and exchange-value. On the present reading, Marx's initial analysis proceeds along distinct tracks. One path starts from the notion of use-value and goes back to the species-being model, and the other begins with the notion of exchange-value and goes back to value created by abstract labor. The two strands meet only when the former is externally applied to the latter as a standard of criticism. Thus any mediation of use-value and exchange-value is ruled out a priori. More specifically, exchange-value is theorized as if it were unconnected with demand. In this manner Marx reinforced the negative results he wished to obtain. If we view the commodity exclusively under the heading of exchange-value, then it may indeed appear merely as a thing standing over aginst us, as a fetish. Its mediating role in uniting the community is lost. A truly dialectical theory, however, would seek an affirmative synthesis of exchange-value and use-value. It would not insist on defining each in isolation from the other.

4. The Assumption of a Wesenslogik

Marx saw the commodity as an alienated form, as a fetish that stands over against human agents, as a thing that takes on the characteristics of a subject while true human subjects are reduced to being its moments. In contrast, when Hegel explicated the category of commodity exchange he found that it involves a notion of reciprocal need satisfaction. Through commodities different individuals are mediated together in a system of needs forming a dynamic unity-in-difference. Thus in the Philosophy of Right "civil society" falls on the level of Sittlichkeit, ethical life, the stage of social ontology where categories taken from the level of Begriff are appropriate.

This gives Hegelians a further argument for asserting that Capital rests upon a petitio. Anything derived from the negative starting point of commodity fetishism, where an inhuman thing operates as a subject over human agents who are reduced to thing status, is bound to be negative too. Once the phenomena have been initially categorized in terms taken from the level of Wesen, it is easy enough for Marx to propose his criticisms. But for a Hegelian these criticisms do not follow from the immanent nature of commodity production. They follow instead from the arbitrary categorization made by Marx to get the negative results he wished to obtain. The fact that subsequent forms in the dialectical progression articulate structures in which human subjects are alienated follows only because concepts such as

61

demand, consumption, and use-value have not been incorporated in the initial principle from which the remainder of the theory is derived. From a negative principle only negative results follow; this proves nothing if there is no good reason to accept a merely negative principle at the beginning. In Hegelian terms, Marx's interpretation is locked into a *Wesenslogik*. Starting with the analysis of commodities onward, the nonhuman side (commodities, money, capital) holds sway over human subjects: "The commodity sphere...lies on the *other* side, namely that of the objective essence as subject over against humans as subjects."[8]

Before proposing replies to these four points it is first necessary to introduce a different reading of the beginning of *Capital*.

C. An Alternative Reading

Consider the first paragraph of *Capital*: "The wealth of those societies in which the capitalist mode of production prevails, presents itself as 'an immense accumulation of commodities', its unit being a single commodity. Our investigation must therefore begin with the analysis of a commodity."[9] Two things are to be noted here. The obvious point is that Marx asserted that in some sense his theory begins with the commodity. The not-so-obvious point is that before turning to this beginning Marx has already specified both the general region and the specific region of which the commodity is the first determination. The general region is that of modes of social production. The specific region is that of the capitalist form of social production. On my reading the fundamental purpose of the first section of Chapter One of *Capital* is to explicate the relationships connecting a) the general realm of social production; b) a specific mode of social production; and c) the category that is the first determination of that specific mode. This is analogous to the relationships connecting "will," "abstract right," and "possession" in Hegel's *Philosophy of Right*. "Will" defines the general region of objective spirit, "abstract right" is a specific region within the realm of objective spirit, and "possession" is the initial determination of that specific region.

Let us attempt to push this parallel further. For Hegel the principle for ordering specific regions of objective spirit is immanent to the determination that defines this realm in general, i.e. "will." For Hegel the will is first and foremost free. And so the different forms within which will is embodied can be immanently ordered according to the level of freedom attained.[10] In an exactly parallel fashion "social production" is inherently social and inherently concerned with productivity. This provides an immanent standard for ordering different forms of social production. The different forms can be immanently ordered according to the degree of sociality and the level of productivity that they institutionalize.

Let us take sociality first. Sociality can be either direct or indirect, and either restricted or unrestricted. From a formal standpoint this gives four logical possibilities. Restricted and indirect sociality is exemplified in artisan or guild production. Sociality here is indirect in the sense that labor is undertaken by isolated *private* producers and is only subsequently established as social when the commodities produced by the artisans are sold. It is restricted in that traditional codes restrict the types of artisan labor that are performed, the relation between master, apprentice, and journeyman, and so on. In Marx's view this type of production should not be counted as a form of social production in the full sense. Instead it is a subordinate type that exists within the context of more dominant forms. (In Western Europe, for example, artisan production was of relatively limited importance in the feudal period, and when it did gain in importance it proved inherently unstable and led to capitalism.)

This leaves three other logical possibilities: direct and restricted sociality, indirect and unrestricted sociality, and direct and unrestricted socialty. From a dialectical perspective, these structures can be systematically ordered moving from the simplest to the most complex; from a form of simple unity, to one of difference, to one of unity-in-difference.

Forms of social production that have direct and restricted sociality are forms of simple unity from the present theoretical perspective. All historical examples of precapitalist forms of production can be grouped together under this heading, including kinship societies, slave societies, feudal societies, societies based on patriarchal production within peasant households, and so on. The social relations here are both immediately given and restricted to traditional roles. Regarding the directly social feudal structures, for instance, Marx wrote in Chapter One of *Capital*: "No matter, then, what we may think of the parts played by the different classes of people themselves in this society, the social relations between individuals in the performance of their labour, appear at all events as their own mutual personal relations, and are not disguised under the shape of social relations between the products of labour."[11] Similarly, patriarchal peasant production is "common or directly associated labour," i.e. directly social: "The labour-power of each individual, by its very nature, operates in this case merely as a definite portion of the whole labour power of the family."[12] The restrictedness in this last example is described by Marx as follows: "This mode of production pre-supposes parcelling of the soil, and scattering of the other means of production, so also it excludes co-operation, division of labour within each separate process of production, the control over, and the

63

productive application of the forces of Nature by society, and the free development of the social productive powers. It is compatible only with a system of production, and a society, moving within narrow and more or less primitive bounds."[13]

In section D.2 we shall see that Marx defined the capitalist mode of production as a form of indirect and unrestricted sociality. In section D.4 and throughout the course of this work we shall see that for Marx this form is characterized by the moment of difference, of fragmentation, of alienation and exploitation, of antagonism, of alien forces with which individuals cannot ulitmately be reconciled. Because of this Marx insisted that this sphere be described with categories taken from Hegel's level of essence (Wesen).

Finally, a form of direct and unrestricted sociality is a structure of unity-in-difference. This would be "a community of free individuals, carrying out their work with the means of production in common, in which the labour-power of all the different individuals is consciously applied as the combined labour-power of the community."[14] This is the socialist form of production, which Marx described with categories taken from Hegel's level of the notion (Begriff). Only now is a reconcilation of universal (the community) and individual attained.

When we examine the aspect of productivity we do not need to adjust this ordering. The different stages of sociality overlap with an ordering in terms of advances in productive capacity. The form of direct and restricted sociality does not institutionalize technical advance. Institutionalized technical advance requires some amount of social experimentation, and societies bound by fixed and traditional social roles do not generally encourage this experimentation. The capitalist form does institutionalize technological change, as does the socialist form. But the former according to Marx does so in an alien fashion, manifested in socio-economic crises, while the latter does not.

This ordering has subtle correspondences with the ordering given in history. Later stages in the systematic ordering occur later historically as well, but Marx is well aware that not every instance of an earlier historical stage gives way to a stage that is later from a systematic standpoint. These stages must be seen a a rational reconstruction of history.

Obviously this aspect of Marx's theory could be the subject of a study of its own.[15] However the present work, like Capital itself, is concerned primarily with the capitalist mode of production in specific, and not with the general ordering of the various forms of social production. And so it is time to turn to the objections mentioned in the previous section.

64

D. Responses to the Hegelian Objections

1) The Category of "Social Production" Versus the Species-Being Model

The first Hegelian objection had to do with the species-being model Marx allegedly presupposed at the beginning of *Capital*. But on my alternative reading Marx did not move from the commodity to any species-being model. Instead we have the following chain, to be read from left to right:

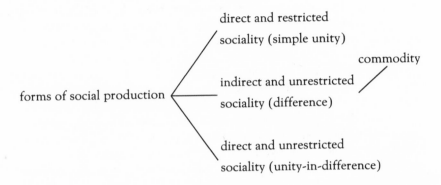

forms of social production

direct and restricted sociality (simple unity)

indirect and unrestricted sociality (difference)

direct and unrestricted sociality (unity-in-difference)

commodity

Once this is grasped the three problems considered in connection with "species-being" lose their force. These were that the starting point of *Captial* is a picture-thought, that this picture excludes any possibility of difference, and that it provides a standard for critique that is external to its object.

First, just as Hegel could describe "will" in general terms prior to considering the forms within which it is embodied,[16] so too Marx could discuss "social production" independently of the specific forms of social production. And just as the former could be done without resorting to some dialectically illegitimate picture-thought, so too could the latter. In all forms of social production humans cooperate in transforming nature. But this cannot be pictured. The reader is invited to attempt to imagine a social division of labor that is not within the serf form, or the slave from, or the commodity form, or the socialist form, or some other specific social form. It cannot be done. The notion of "social production" is only determinate enough to define a general region of investigation, an object realm to be reconstructed in thought. Unlike the model described in section B.1 above, it is not determinate enough to be pictured in imagination. It thus cannot be ruled out as a starting point for a dialectical theory of categories. In fact every systematic theory of categories demands some such concept at the beginning.

Second, the concrete universal "social production" does not refer to a pure human community where all categorial differences and all differences among persons and groups have been eliminated. It simply defines a region to be investigated. There is a difference between a category that stands in need of further determination and a category that excludes determination. "Social production" is a category of the former sort, which stands in need of determination through a systematic ordering of the various forms of social production. There is nothing in Marx of the latter sort. It cannot be said that Marx is against real subjects simultaneously having more than one categorial determination. All social labor done by real human subjects *always* (except in extreme Robinson Crusoe cases) unites individual and social determinations, *whatever* the mode of production might be. If forms of commodity fetishism are to be criticized and a model of socialism defended, this is not due to the former uniting different categorial determinations while the latter does not. And if forms overcoming class differences are to be affirmed, this is in no way due to an overcoming of difference as such. Even under socialism there is no guarantee that proposals regarding production and consumption decisions will automatically cohere in a simple and direct fashion. Differences of opinion on these matters will persist, and socio-political mechanisms for resolving these differences must be institutionalized. Institutional mechanisms such as the election of all officials and the unrestricted right of recall which Marx advocated *presuppose* that differences will arise between the delegated and those who delegate. Otherwise such procedures would have no point. Marx did have a positive model of social production. But it is one of associated workers councils, and this model does not exclude differences within it.[17] The model described in section B.1 pictures a romantic utopia that has no place at all in Marx's theory, neither at its starting point nor at its conclusion.

Third, if the notion of social production is too indeterminate to do anything more than fix a general region of investigation, then it is also too indeterminate to serve as an external normative standard for evaluating specific forms of social production. This does not mean that there is not a normative dimension to the starting point of *Capital*. But the normative component is immanent to the object realm being investigated and not external to it. An evaluation of a specific form does not rest on an external comparison with any ahistorical normative model. It rests instead upon the immanent analysis of the form itself, i.e. upon its place in the systematic ordering. The notion of sociality and productivity are immanent standards for ordering different forms of social production. The capitalist mode of production is an advance over forms characterized by direct and restricted sociality and low levels of productivity. However it was Marx's contention that indirect and unrestricted sociality necessarily involves alienation and exploitation. And it was his contention that the advances in productivity within this form are necessarily connected with crises. In the terms of dialectical logic, this is why the capitalist mode of production represents a stage of difference, where essence (Wesen) categories are applicable. And so in a systematic ordering the capitalist mode of production must be ranked below a form of social production that overcomes this alienation and exploitation, and allows for productivity advances that avoid crises. In the terms of dialectical logic it must be ranked below a form of social production representing a stage of unity-in-difference, where notion (Begriff) categories are applicable. In this manner Marx provided an immanent critique of the capitalist mode of production. There is no place here for an externally imposed contrast with an ahistorical model of species-being.

2) "Value" as a Form of Social Production,
vs. "Value" as a Formal Abstraction,

A second Hegelian objection to the beginning of Capital called into question the procedure Marx appeared to use when he explicated "value" in terms of "abstract labor." Marx seems to have asserted that "abstract labor" is the sole common characteristic of different commodities. But it is not. The process of formal abstraction reveals a whole series of other characteristics that commodities have in common. Further, some of these other characteristics hold for all commodities. In contrast, some sorts of commodities—found objects, objects produced in a possible future of total automation—are produced without any labor, abstract or otherwise. And, finally, the very procedure of formal abstraction is completely out of place in a dialectical theory.

If we examine Section I of Chapter I alone it may appear that Marx began with commodities and arrived at abstract labor as the substance of value through a process of formal abstraction. But the first four sections of Chapter I must be considered together. If section 4 is taken into account the initial moves in Capital appear quite different. For section 4 is where Marx emphatically insisted that the object of his investigation is a specific form of social production, and this provides the key to understanding the role played by the concepts of value and abstract labor in his theory.

There are indeed a variety of factors common to commodities. Hence as a formal abstraction the move from "commodities" to "abstract labor" is no more warranted than a formal derivation of any of a variety of common features. If Marx's argument rested on such a formal abstraction alone it

67

would indeed be inadequate. But that is not the whole story. Out of the variety of formal abstractions capturing features common to commodities with exchange-value, priority must be given to that which best distinguishes from other types of social productions the social division of labor within which commodity exchange occurs. After all, the theoretical purpose of the initial categories is to define the region to be investigated. Marx believed that this is accomplished best through the category value, defined in terms of abstract labor. In other words, *the foremost function of the labor theory of value is to define the capitalist mode of production in contrast to other forms of social production:* "The value-form of the product of labour is not only the most abstract, but is also the most universal form, taken by the product in bourgeois production, and stamps the production as a particular species of social production."[18] Abstract labor is the fundamental category used to explicate the notion of the value form, a form of indirect and unrestricted sociality allowing for advanced production. Its initial function in the theory is to set off a specific form of production from all others, so that the theory can then proceed to a reconstruction of the determinations that make this specific mode intelligible.

What then distinguishes the value form of production from others? Marx is unambiguous here. The value form is one where labor is only indirectly social:

> As a general rule, articles of utility become commodities only because they are the products of labour of private individuals or groups of individuals who carry on their work independently of each other. The sum total of all the labor of these private individuals forms the aggregate labour of society. Since the producers do not come into social contact with each other until they exchange their productions, the specific social character of each producer's labour does not show itself except in the act of exchange. In other words, the labour of the individual asserts itself as a part of the labour of society, only by means of the relations which the act of exchange establishes directly between the products, and indirectly, through them, between the producers. To the latter, therefore, the relations connecting the labour of one individual with that of the rest appear, not as direct social relations between individuals at work, but as...social relations between things.[19]

Marx also held that this form of social production was characterized by unrestricted sociality, in that it systematically unites different communities on an ever-widening scale, breaking down all fixed and traditional social roles.[20] But for our purpose it is the indirect aspect of this sociality that is to be stressed. For the immediately social forms of social production, as well as for the socialist form, labor in its concrete shape is directly social labor.

68

Those laboring provide for the satisfaction of social needs directly, whether these social needs are established by tradition or by democratic agreement among the producers. Under the value form, in contrast, concrete labor is done by private individual units of production.[21] This means that these units produce with the hope, rather than the assurance, that the labor they perform will turn out to be socially required.[22] Within this form, labor becomes social only when the product of one privatized act of concrete labor is successfully exchanged for that of another. Under the value form there is thus a clear distinction between "private labor" and "private labor that has proven to be social," i.e. that has produced a commodity with value. Now all concrete labor falls under the former category; when it is concretely performed it has not yet proven itself to be social. Therefore we must introduce a distinct term for the labor that falls under the latter category: "abstract labor."

Of course there are not two ontologically separate types of labor here. Instead we have the same instance of labor under two distinct descriptions. *Qua* privately undertaken, labor is concrete; *qua* shown to be social, to have produced a product with "value," the same labor is to be taken as abstract.

We may now turn to the specific Hegelian objections that arose here. We may begin with the objection that a formal abstraction has no place in a dialectical theory. This is correct. But it is not true that the concept of abstract labor is a formal abstraction.

Formal abstractions have two characteristics that are of significance in this context. First, they rest upon a subjective cognitive process in which the theorist selects a feature common to the phenomena under consideration. Second, the common feature may not have anything whatsoever to do with the inner nature of the phenomena being examined. The notion of abstract labor is not won through a formal cognitive process of abstracting a common feature shared by all commodities. It emerges instead from the social process of commodity exchange, a real process that is independent of the subjective cognitive acts of the theorist.[23] And abstract labor is an abstraction that uncovers the essential determination of the object realm under investigation. It captures the intrinsic specificity of a particular form of social production. For both of these reasons abstract labor must be considered as a "real abstraction" rather than as a merely formal abstraction.

Next there is the accusation that Marx ignored the fact that all commodities share a number of common characteristics that have nothing to do with labor, such as being objects of utility, objects of demand, and so on. It is true enough that commodities share these features. But these common features do not help to define a specific form of social production. Unlike "abstract labor" they are universal features characterizing goods and

69

services in *all* forms of social production. Marx's justification for not stressing these features follows at once from the simple fact that his concern was to investigate a specific form of social production.

This allows us to reply to the objection that some commodities also possess an exchange-value without any labor being put into their production at all. Found objects are found within *all* forms of social production. If in his category of "value" Marx downplayed the notion of "abstract labor" in order to accomodate the fact that found objects can have exchange-value as commodities, then the category would fail to do the required work of distinguishing one form of social production from others. Finally the fact that we can imagine a system of commodity exchange based on totally automated production in which labor plays no part whatsoever also fails to undermine Marx's labor theory of value. For in a world where *all* production was completely robotized we obviously would no longer be dealing with a form of *social* production at all. The fact that a category meant to define a specific form of social production fails to hold when we are no longer talking of social production hardly counts as an objection to that category!

Marx's labor theory of value is perhaps *the* most controversial category in Marx's theory. But from one perspective it is a quite straightforward notion. Organizing social production through privately performed, and therefore only indirectly social, labor is clearly distinct from organizing it so that labor is directly social. The notions of "value" and "abstract labor" are simply terms employed to distinguish the former structure from the latter. The obvious justification of this categorization was behind Marx's impatient reply to critics of the labor theory of value:

> All the gossip about the necessity of proving the concept of value is based only on the most complete ignorance, as much of the problem under discussion as of the scientific method. Every child knows that any nation which stopped work—I will not say for one year—but just for a couple of weeks, would die. And every child knows that the volume of products corresponding to the various needs calls for various and quantitatively determined amounts of total social labour. It is self-evident that this *necessity* of the *division* of social labour in certain proportions is not all negated by the *specific form* of social production, but can only alter its *mode of appearance*. Natural laws can never be negated. Only the *form* in which those laws are applied can be altered in historically different situations. And the form in which this proportional division of labour asserts itself as a *private exchange* of the individual products of labour, is precisely the exchange-value of those products.[24]

We have examined the notions of "value" and "abstract labor" solely in terms of their role in defining a specific form of social production. Marx also gave these notions a second function in his theory, that of serving as a quantitative measure for the exchange-values of commodities. On the present level of abstraction, commodities are exchanged according to the socially necessary abstract labor they contain. The further development of the theory affects both dimensions of value theory. "Value" is a category that needs to be developed dialectically. This means that there are a number of structures that manifest the value form, and the categories defining these structures must be systematically ordered from the simplest and most abstract to the more complex and concrete. The second dimension, calculating "value" as the quantitative measure of commodity exchange, also becomes progressively more complex as the theory moves from the abstract to the concrete level. Value theory as the dialectical derivation of social forms, and value theory as the quantitative measure of commodities proceed together. The latter aspect of the theory has been examined repeatedly by economists, and controversies still rage today.[25] In contrast, the former aspect of the theory has been relatively neglected.[26]

The main concern of the present study is the systematic ordering of the determinations of the value form. But on a number of occasions I shall note places where the quantitative dimension of value theory has been misunderstood by economists due to a failure to connect it with the qualitative (categorial) aspect of the theory. One example can be mentioned at once. Many mathematical economists have conflated Marx's notion of value with Ricardo's. For Ricardo "value" is defined in terms of embodied labor time, a notion that holds in *all* forms of social production. But only concrete labor can be "embodied." Abstract labor, labor specific to one type of social production, is labor which has proven to be socially necessary. Not all embodied labor proves to be socially necessary. Measuring the magnitude of embodied labor is a relatively straightforward procedure of simply summing up the direct and indirect labor inputs. Measuring the magnitude of abstract labor is inherently a much more complex matter.[27]

3. The Dialectical Unity of Use-Value and Exchange-Value

The third Hegelian objection accused Marx of formulating a negative or critical concept of the commodity by considering exchange-value in abstraction from use-value. When the role the commodity plays in meeting social needs is ignored, then of course the commodity appears as an alien thing standing over against the social community. But this view, the objection continues, is not based on the inner nature of the commodity itself. It is based instead on Marx's undialectical separation of use-value and exchange-value.

The objection misses its mark. In the simplest structure defining the value form, the value underlying exchange-value captures a moment of unity shared by commodities, and the distinct use-values of the commodities

71

express a moment of difference. If either moment is separated from the other this structure collapses at once. Marx did not make this mistake. The abstract labor that is relevant to value theory is by definition *socially necessary* abstract labor. Socially necessary labor is that which has produced commodities for which there is consumer demand. Goods and services which have no use-value have no exchange-value. In an altogether typical passage Marx writes, "Nothing can have value, without being an object of utility."[28] Familiarity with such passages makes the conclusion of Michio Morishima inevitable: "On the basis of the evidence I believe that Marx would have accepted the marginal utility theory of consumer's demands if it had become known to him."[29] If use-values are not put to one side in Marx's account, and if use-values are what is of interest to the consumers of commodities, then Marx's account also connects producers and consumers. For Marx the commodity thus *does* serve a mediating role in uniting the community, *contra* the supposition of the objection.[30]

A Hegelian would reply by saying that if Marx had truly seen the unity of exchange-value and use-value he would not have criticized the value form as inherently involving fetishism. Instead he would have affirmed it as a structure within which the needs and wants of a plurality of individuals are mediated together through commodity exchange. For orthodox Hegelians social relations mediated by commodities constitute a concrete universal, a positive form (even if they still require a yet more concrete universal, the state). With this we have clearly moved to the fourth Hegelian objection, which calls into question the fundamental categorial structure Marx employed in discussing the value form.

4. The Value Form and Wesenslogik

Marx was by no means the first to articulate the value form. We find the same structure defined by Hegel. Whenever two commodity owners contract together to exchange,

> there is put into the thing or performance a distinction between its immediate specific *quality* and its substantial being or *value*, meaning by value the quantitative terms into which that qualitative feature has been translated. One piece of property is thus made comparable with another, and may be made equivalent to a thing which is (in quality) wholly heterogeneous. It is thus treated in general as an abstract, universal thing or commodity.[31]

For Marx as well, two commodities that are qualitatively distinct use-values may somehow be made equivalent in exchange: "The valid exchange-values of a given commodity express something equal; secondly, exchange-value, generally, is only the mode of expression, the phenomenal form, of something contained in it, yet distinguishable from it."[32] This unifying

72

principle is also termed by Marx "value": "The common substance that manifests itself in the exchange-value of commodities, whenever they are exchanged, is their value. The progress of our investigation will show that exchange-value is the only form in which the value of commodities can manifest itself or be expressed."[33]

How should this value form be categorized? And since this categorization is not value free (so to speak), we must also ask how the value form should be evaluated. Should the value form be interpreted in terms taken from the second level of Hegel's *Logic*, the level of Essence (*Wesen*)? Essence categories are appropriate whenever we have structures in which a) individuals are united rather than being a mere aggregate of entities in only external relation (this distinguishes the level of *Wesen* from that of *Sein*); and b) there is no "reconciliation of universal and individual," that is, the unity is one imposed upon those individuals, one in which the full autonomy, the self-conscious freedom, of the individuals is not allowed to develop (this distinguishes the level of *Wesen* from that of *Begriff*). It is far too early to resolve this issue conclusively. The full categorization of the value form depends to a large extent on what sort of structures are later derived from it in the systematic progression of the theory. At this stage we can only i) point out some parallels in the positions taken by Hegel and Marx, ii) mention the main area of disagreement, and iii) offer a preliminary evaluation of their respective arguments.

i) Hegel clearly grasped many of the limits of the value form later pointed out by Marx. Hegel was no Lockean in his evaluation of societies of generalized commodity exchange. In Hegel we find critical concepts later discussed at length by Marx—for instance the reserve army of the unemployed and the systematic tendency to overproduction crises—explicitly derived from the value form.[34] Hegel did not see market societies as the ultimate sphere of freedom. From this perspective civil society is on the level of *Wesen*.

And just as Hegel appreciated some negative features of the value form, so did Marx acknowledge its positive features. Marx granted that the value form defines a structure of reciprocity and mediation. Each different individual engaging in exchange to satisfy his or her needs contributes to the satisfaction of the needs of others within a unified system of needs.[35] Further, Marx agreed that in some relevant respects self-consciousness and freedom are operative here. The where, when, and what of the exchange are based upon mutual consent, with each partner attaining the particular ends of his or her choice through realizing and respecting the choices of other. In this sense Marx's analysis of the value form suggests terms taken from the level of the notion.

73

ii) Despite recognizing the limits of civil society Hegel insisted that there is still a sense in which a *Begriffslogik* categorizes it. And despite recognizing the freedom allowed in generalized commodity exchange, Marx insisted that only a *Wesenslogik* adequately comprehends this sphere. This is more than a mere difference of emphasis. It is the difference between affirming a set of institutions and not affirming it. Hegel insisted that the institutions of market society provide a necessary moment of freedom. In commodity exchange reciprocal need satisfaction is accomplished through the free agreement of the contracting parties. Hegel also insisted that there is no alternative set of specifically socio-economic institutions that would allow for more freedom. And any respect in which the value form fails to attain the full level of the notion can be overcome through the intervention of the state, a higher level universal.

Marx disagreed. He rejected the view that a state that incorporates generalized commodity exchange can in principle overcome the structural contradictions in the latter (See Chapter X below). And he rejected the view that generalized commodity exchange considered in itself provides an institutional structure allowing for the greatest degree of freedom possible on the socio-economic level.

This disagreement stems from the fact that while Hegel and Marx both acknowledged the same *form* of value they had different views regarding the *substance* of value. For Hegel the substances of value is the free and mutual agreement of the partners who contract to exchange, which he terms "the stipulation."[36]

Richard Winfield brings out this all important dimension in a significant recent paper: "If individuals act towards one another so that how and what they will is determined solely in reciprocity with how and what others will, they will all exercise an autonomy whose specific character completely derives from their freely entered relationship."[37] In economic terms for Hegel "what provide the minimal institution of freedom in which interests are reciprocally realized are none other than commodity relations."[38] Winfield spells out the implications of this view with admirable clarity. Regarding the quality that makes two traded commodities possess an equivalent exchangeability he writes, "What is of crucial importance is that Hegel recognizes that this quality is something neither intrinsic to the natural qualities of the exchanged commodities, nor rooted in a psychological estimation of them, nor determined by anything preceding the mutually agreed exchange act setting them in their actual relation of equivalence. The voluntary bilateral character of commodity exchange requires that this be so, since what makes two commodities exchangeable is the concurring decisions of their respective owners, who, being independent

74

individuals in the market, need not be swayed by any particular external factors, nor conform to any stipulated model of 'economic rationality'. The only constraint they face is the necessity of reaching agreement with other commodity owners, who themselves act under the same condition of having to accomodate the needs of others in order to satisfy their own."[39]

In contrast, for Marx the substance of value is not the ungrounded free will of the exchanging partners. It is abstract labor. The wills of the exchanging partners are regulated by socially necessary labor time. This regulation is enforced through relations among commodities. In this manner the different individual wills are united, so a *Seinslogik* is not appropriate. But the unity is imposed upon those individuals. It is not one in which the autonomy, the self-conscious freedom, of these individuals can be fully realised. And so Marx employed *Wesen* categories here, and not those taken from Hegel's level of the *Begriff*: "The social character of activity, as well as the social form of the product, and the share of individuals in production here appear as something alien and objective, confronting the individuals, not as their relations to one another, but as their subordination to relations which subsist independently of them and which arise out of collisions between mutually indifferent individuals. The general exchange of activities and products, which has become a vital condition for each individual—their mutal interconnection—here appears as something alien to them, autonomous as a thing."[40]

As a consistent Hegelian Winfield rejects Marx's account, insisting that freedom, not abstract labor, is the substance of value: "Any labor theory of value that determines the exchange values of commodities by the conditions of their production misconstrues commodity relations by ignoring that every commodity exchange is determined by the free mutual agreement of the exchange partners. It is precisely this reciprocal freedom constitutive of commodity exchange that makes it poposible for non-produced items, such as labor power and land, to have exchange value as much as any product—so long as some individual agrees to trade another commodity for them. Consequently, when prescriptive economics turns to exchange value as it arises in commodity exchange, what it addresses is a relation of commodities in general rather than something specific to the particular class of commodities comprising products. Hegel understands this, and therefore properly analyses commodity exchange prior to and independently of his consideration of commodity production."[41] Consequently Marx's fetishism analysis, in which "the commodity" is seen as an essence standing over against human subjects, must be rejected: "When individuals enter into an exchange, they interact not as the subjects of things that rule their lives, but as masters of commodities—utilizing them as subordinate means to satisfy

75

their civil needs, and thereby exercise the honored freedom of achieving those particular ends of their own which advance the interests of others."[42]

iii) This debate will concern us throughout the present study. In the present context four points can be briefly presented in response to the Hegelian position defended by Winfield. First, Marx was certainly aware that nonproduced items such as land and other found objects could be exchanged (*contra* Winfield, labor power *is* produced; see Chapter VI). But for Marx the price of land is a function of the rent it may yield, which in turn depends on the power of land ownership to force a redistribution of some of the surplus value produced by abstract labor into its own pocket (see Chapter IX). Nowhere does Winfield—or Hegel—attempt to come to grips with this theory. As for found objects, one could see them as a counterexample to Marx's theory only if one thoroughly misunderstood the object of that theory. To repeat: Marx's goal was to reconstruct in thought a specific form of social production. The isolated and random exchange of found objects hardly counts as form of social production. For a society of commodity exchange as a whole, such exchange will always be marginal. In formulating a category meant to capture the basic intelligibility of this society it is legitimate to initially abstract from such marginal phenomena (Marx discussed commodities that have a price without having value in Volume III).

Second, it follows from what has just been said that it is *not* "proper" to analyze commodity exchange "prior to and independently of" commodity production. Commodity exchange *when instituted on a society-wide basis* must presuppose commodity production. And society-wide commodity exchange is precisely what is to be reconstructed in thought.

Third, when Winfield writes of exchangers that "the only constraint they face is the necessity of reaching agreement with other commodity owners" this is, of course, simply not the case. If agreements generally fixed exchange-values at a level below that of the cost of producing the commodities, exchange would soon cease. Winfield is aware of this, but believes that it does not undermine the thesis that "equivalent exchange-value is actually determined by the common resolve of these individuals to exchange them."[43] This is because "factors of production can only determine the minimum price that must be met if the product is to be sold without a loss in relation to the cost of its manufacture."[44] Once again Winfield has overlooked that the object of inquiry is not a random act of exchange, but a form characterizing an entire social order. In any given act of exchange the "common resolve" of the exchangers may lead to goods and services having exchange-values that wildly diverge from production costs. But for commodity exchange on a society-wide basis this cannot be the case.

If the exchange-value is far above the production costs of a commodity, this will eventually lead others to produce it and offer it at a lower exchange-value. As a result, in a society-wide system of exchange, exchange-values will generally fluctuate within relatively narrow limits. These limits are not determined by "common resolve," but by the objective material facts of production.

Fourth, however much freedom commodity exchangers retain, within the value form they are not free to put out of play structural tendencies built into the value form. Three structural tendencies can be mentioned: a) the neglect of certain social needs, b) the waste of some social labor, and c) the disregard of certain social costs.

a) Only those needs for which there is *effective* demand are taken into account in commodity exchange. All other social needs are in principle excluded, whether they are needs for public goods to be enjoyed by the community as a whole, or needs that individuals lacking sufficient purchasing power may have for consumption goods. For those who will the satisfaction of these social needs the value form operates as an external force systematically preventing that will from being fulfilled. b) Under the value form private labor becomes validated as social labor only in the eventual sale of a commodity product. But within this form there is no guarantee that the private labor undertaken will in fact be validated as social labor. If there is not any subsequent sale, the labor is wasted from the standpoint of society. Individuals who freely will to engage in social labor therefore may experience the value form as an external force that thwarts the realization of this will. c) Finally, there is the question of the social costs of commodity production and consumption. The commodity is a wall that separates consumers and producers from each other. Producers know little or nothing of the effects the use of the commodity will have on consumers, whether it enriches their lives or leads to greater risks and alienation. Consumers know little or nothing of the effects the labor process that created the commodity had on its producers, for instance, whether it enhanced their creativity or demeaned them. The information available to consumers is generally limited to the price at which the commodity is offered, while the information available to producers is systematically limited to the amount of consumer demand at a given price. Given this lack of information built into commodity exchange, by and large those who produce commodities are not free to take their effects upon consumers consciously into account in their production, and those who purchase commodities are not free to take the conditions of production consciously into account in their purchase. Rather than a free and reciprocal consideration of all relevant costs, we have here a systematic ignoring of that

77

significant set of costs that is part of commodity production without itself being measured in commodity prices.

Provisionally I conclude that the Hegelian reading of the value form in terms of notion (*Begriff*) categories fails. Marx's categorization of the value form in terms of essence categories, and the negative evaluation of that form that follows from this, can both be suported with arguments. Marx did not propose this categorization and evaluation simply in order to derive negative forms from a negative starting point.

V

The Simple Commodity Form
and the Money Form

In the previous chapter the beginning of
Capital was placed in the context of the general theory of historical
materialism. The philosophical dimension of this theory aims at the
systematic ordering of different forms of social production according to
principles immanent in social production, "sociality" and "productiveness." The form of direct and restricted sociality and low productivity must
come first in the ordering. It embodies a structure of simple unity in that
societies embodying this form have social relations that are relatively
immediate and transparent. The value form is a form of social production
with indirect and unrestricted sociality and high productiveness. Is the value
form the ultimate form of social production? This is the basic question of
Capital. Marx held that "value," "abstract labor," "commodity" (and later
"money," "capital," and so on), are principles that stand above the social
community, alien forces that impose a social bond while mystifying the
underlying social relations. In the terms of dialectical logic the value form
thus counts as a stage of difference. As such it must be ordered after a
structure of simple unity. But it cannot claim to be the ultimate form of
social production. There is at least the logical possibility of a form that
would capture unity-in-difference, a possibility Marx identified with the
socialist form.

In order to justify this set of claims the immanent determinations of the
value form must be examined in detail. The value form has itself a series of
forms in terms of which its intelligibility is grasped. In a systematic ordering

79

of these determinations the familiar dialectical principle holds. The ordering of the determinations of the value form itself commences with a form of simple unity, i.e. the simplest and most abstract structure within which the value form is manifested. Then the ordering must progress to a stage of difference, after which it culminates in a structure of unity-in-difference, each stage being more complex and concrete than what went before. In this chapter the dialectic of the simple commodity form and the money form will be presented, completing the discussion of Part I of *Capital I*. They are the first two determinations of the value form, and represent categories of simple unity and difference, respectively. A diagram of the categorial progression here can be found in section C. below. (A depiction of Marx's complete system of categories is given in the Appendix.)

A. The Simple Commodity Form

1. *The Dialectic of the Simple Commodity Form*

The value form of social production is defined by a structure within which private labor undertaken in isolation establishes itself as social labor through the exchange of commodities. The simplest manner in which this general structure can be manifested is one where commodities are directly exchanged for each other. We may term this "the simple commodity form." The simple commodity form can itself be manifested in a number of different ways, and here too the philosophical dimension of Marx's theory consists in ensuring that the ordering of these manifestations is both immanent and necessary.

Take two commodities, A and B. When x of commodity A is exchanged for y of commodity B, the two private (concrete) labors that produced A and B are both established as social (abstract) labor. They are thereby shown to possess a common feature, which Marx termed "value." When x of commodity A is exchanged for y of commodity B the value of commodity A is manifested in commodity B. This is the simplest form within which value can be manifested. Marx terms it *the elementary or accidental form* of value. It is a form of simple unity, since B is a single commodity.

This is obviously a quite inadequate manifestation of the value form. The value form is a form of social production. Production on a society-wide scale necessarily involves many different sorts of commodities. In the elementary form these other commodities are present implicitly,[1] but are not explicitly acknowledged. Hence we must move to a more concrete and complex category in which the fact that the value of commodity A can be expressed in any of an indefinite number of different commodities is explicitly stated. This is the category of *the total or expanded form* of value,

80

wherein the value of x amount of commodity A takes on phenomenal form in y of commodity B, z of C, n of D, and so on. The transition from the elementary form to the expanded form is a dialectical ordering in which a category of simple unity is systematically prior to one of difference.

We can approach this transition from another perspective. The category "elementary form," a category of simple unity, defines a structure within which the value of one commodity is manifested in some second commodity. Within this structure it is necessarily the case that there is a dominant structural tendency to manifest the value of the initial commodity in a third, fourth, fifth, etc., commodity. They manifest its value equally well, and commodity exchange can take place on a society-wide scale only with this extension. This structural tendency thus eventuates in a new structure that demands a new category, a category of difference.

The expanded form is more complex and concrete than the elementary form. As such it comes closer to being a form that corresponds to, or manifests more adequately, the value form of social production, the value created and measured by abstract labor: "For the first time this value shows itself in its true light as a congelation of undifferentiated human labor. For the labor that creates it, now stands expressly revealed as labour that ranks equally with every other sort of human labour, no matter what its form."[2] Nonetheless, in this structure the moment of difference has a predominance that ultimately makes it too an inadequate manifestation of the value form. The underlying unity of value is manifested only through an indefinite succession of different commodities. This is the structure of what Hegel termed the "bad infinite" that in principle can never attain completion.[3] And this indefinite succession must be repeated indefinitely, as each different commodity takes its turn in having its underlying value take on phenomènal form.

Just as dialectical logic motivates moving from a category fixing a structure where simple unity predominates to one where difference is emphasized, so too it motivates moving from this latter sort of category to one where unity and difference are at least provisionally in balance. More specifically, the category "expanded form" defines a structure in which commodity A manifests its value in commodities B, C, D, etc. It is necesssrily the case that there is a dominant structural tendency for the exchanging partners to reverse this and to manifest the values of commodities B, C, D, and so on, in some commodity A. This tendency is based on the manner in which this eases generalized commodity exchange. This brings us to *the general form of value*, where the value of *any* given commodity is manifested in the form of a single commodity that is simultaneously a universal commodity. This general form is a unity in which all different commodities

81

can express their value. We have at last a unity which unites all differences, an identity of identity and differences, a stable form which manifests the value form to the greatest extent possible within the simple commodity form (i.e. to the greatest extent possible under the condition that commodities alone are considered).

This categorial progression may be taken as a paradigm case for how a systematic reconstruction of categories should proceed. Marx's ordering proceeds through an incorporation of the negative (the moment of difference) until the point where there is a full development of the determinations of a categorial level. And this is the crucial feature of a dialectical ordering. The move from a category of unity, through one of difference, to one of unity-in-difference is not a mere external schema artifically imposed on a given content. Instead this provides a way of capturing the immanent unfolding of that content, its inner intelligibility.

2. Contrast with Hegel

In terms of a contrast with Hegel, it is true that Marx incorporated historical materials into his account much more than Hegel ever did. Marx connected the systematic progression of forms of simple commodity exchange with the historical stages of trade. Yet as argued above, this stress on history is not imcompatible with Hegel's approach. And Marx, no less than Hegel, did not allow a historical genesis to substitute for a systematic derivation.

There is a radical difference between Marx and Hegel here, but it does not lie in this direction. It lies instead in the distinction between a dialectic with affirmative and positive results as opposed to one with critical and negative results. But this distinction is not captured by saying that Marx derived purely negative forms from a purely negative starting point. For Hegel the end result of the dialectic is affirmative and positive. In the Marxian dialectic we have just examined, the result is in one respect positive and affirmative and in another respect critical and negative. It is this, and not any derivation of purely negative forms from a purely negative starting point, that is distinctive of the Marxian dialectic.

The positive aspect of the dialectic of simple commodity exchange is that each successive category more adequately expresses the structure of the underlying value form. Value is a principle of unity that allows many different commodities to be compared, and the general form manifests it fairly adequately in that it provides a single measure for a plurality of different exchange-values. This means that positive features of the value form are present in a more explicit and developed fashion in the general form than in the elementary or expanded forms. Marx holds that there are three main positive aspects of the form of value in contrast to other forms of

82

social production, two of which involve its sociality and one its productiveness. The value form a) leads to an expansion of the human community beyond all provincialism; b) leads to the development of human personality, *Positive* as new wants and new needs are developed in a variety of different directions; and c) leads to an expansion of society's productive capacity. Greater structural tendencies in each of these directions are clearly present within the expanded form of value in comparison to the elementary form, and these tendencies are greater yet within the general form. Structural possibilities at first latent are made more and more explicit. In this sense Marx's dialectic is, like Hegel's oriented towards positive, affirmative results.

In this same progression of categories, however, something else is going on as well. The underlying principle of unity, value, is both constituted and measured by abstract human labor. But precisely this is ever more hidden as we progress to the general form. Instead of the underlying form of social production becoming ever more intelligible, we have what Marx terms "fetishism" wherein the social relations constituting value become masked as relations among things (this refers to the indirectness of the sociality of form of social production).[4] From this perspective the dialectic arrives at a negative result.

This is unprecedented in Hegelian dialectics. Our understanding of the relationship between Hegel and Marx depends upon our evaluation of this. For later stages of *Capital* will also consist of a systematic progression of categories that is at once affirmative and critical. There are only two possibilities open here. Either Marx has hit upon a new type of dialectic, or Marx has given us a theory that appears dialectical at first glance but which is in fact not dialectical, avoiding the unequivocally affirmative results that proper dialectical logic leads to. If we can show that the further determinations emerge according to dialectical logic, then the case for the former will be strengthened. If these futher determinations are arbitrary, then the latter view gains plausibility.

B. The Dialectic of the Money Form

1. The Money Form as a Category of Difference

We are now ready to make a transition from one level of categories to another. Within any dialectical progression there will be certain nodal points that set off one group of categories from the next. Of course the transition from one determination to the next is especially crucial at these points. The most direct and plausible transition occurs when the last category of the prior level is identical with the first category of the next. The last category of the simple commodity form is the general form of value. There is an immediate transition from this to the money form:

> There is no difference between (the) forms, except that, in the latter (i.e. the money form) gold has assumed the equivalent form... The progress consists in this alone, that the character of direct and universal exchangeability—in other words, the universal, equivalent form—has now, by social custom, become finally identified with the substance, gold.[5]

To say that a commodity is the universal commodity in which all other commodities can express their value means that besides the simple commodity form commodities also have a further determination, the money form. In the last chapter the value form was described as that form of social production in which privately undertaken labor proves itself as social through the exchange of commodities. The money form is a manifestation of the value form in that money too reflects the structure within which potentially social labor is privately undergone. When a commodity takes on the money form this manifests that it is to be put up for exchange in order to prove (or disprove) the social quality of the privately undertaken labor that produced it:

> In exchange the products of individuals only manifest themselves as products of general labour by taking the form of *money*. This relativity, however, originates from the fact that they must present themselves as the form of existence of general labour, and can be reduced to it only as relative, merely quantitatively different expressions of social labour...In exchange they appear as general social labour; and the extent to which they can appear as general social labour depends on the extent to which they can present themselves as social labour, that is, on the extent of the commodities for which they can be exchanged, and therefore on the expansion of the market, of trade; on the range of commodities in which they can be expressed as exchange-value.[6]

Or, again:

> All commodities can be converted into money...because in the form of *money* their use-value and their particular natural form become extinct. They are materialized labour, therefore convertible into any form of real labour.[7]

Money is thus "an essential and necessary form of existence of the commodity which must manifest itself as exchange-value, as general social labour."[8] In this sense "value" is the intrinsic measure of the social aspect of privately produced commodities, while money is its external measure.[9]

In contrast to the simple commodity form, the money form captures a structure of difference. The commodity is a "contradictory" unity of use-value and exchange-value.[10] In the dialectic of the simple commodity form this unity is at first presented in a simple and immediate fashion. Exchange-value is captured in the use-value of another commodity, or in a series of other commodities. But in the money form the contradiction within the simple unity of the commodity gets explicitly expressed in the *difference* between commodity and money:

> The definition of a product as exchange value thus necessarily implies that exchange value obtains a separate existence, in isolation from the product. The exchange value which is separated from commodities and exists alongside them as itself a commodity, this is—*money*. In the form of *money*, all properties of the commodity as exchange value appear as an object distinct from it, as a form of social existence separated from the natural existence of the commodity.[11]
>
> The exchangeability of the commodity exists as a thing beside it, as money, as something different from the commodity, something no longer directly identical with it.[12]

Ordering the category "simple commodity form" prior to the "money form" is thus not a mere "determination of concepts." The categorial ordering captures the objective relationship between structures. One is relatively more concrete and complex than the other, explictly incorporating a moment of difference that had previously been abstracted from.

2. *Hegelian objections to the Dialectic of the Money Form*

Just as the simple commodity form (a category of simple unity) is a principle underlying a dialectical progression from a category of simple unity to one of difference to one of unity-in-difference, so too the money form (a category of difference) is a principle for a dialectical progression. Here too theoretical comprehension demands a systematic rather than haphazard reconstruction of the object. Forms or structures of money that are objectively simpler and more abstract than others must be captured in categories that are presented earlier in the categorial ordering.

The systematic ordering proposed by Marx first moves from "money as measure of value" to "money as means of circulation" (C-M-C), and then culminates with "money as end of exchange" (M-C-M). In the present section I shall present some Hegelian objections to this linear progression, objections that accuse Marx of not following a strict dialectical logic in the derivation of money as an end of exchange.[13] Then in the next section I shall discuss Marx's ordering in detail, and show how it does follow dialectical logic. In the concluding section I shall consider Hegelian objections to

Marx's general categorization of the money form.

On the level of the money form the crucial categorial transition is from money as a means for the circulation of commodities. (C-M-C) to money as the goal of economic transactions (M-C-M). A Hegelian could question whether this move fails when measured by the strict criteria for making a dialectical transition. Why couldn't M-C-M be just a partial circuit within a wider C-M-C circuit? Marx's first reply to this question pointed out that it is certainly possible that money could be made the ultimate goal of exchange. But a mere possibility is not sufficient dialectical motivation for the shift in question. Dialectical transitions, after all, are supposed to involve necessity. A second justification for the transition is the greediness of money holders. This also does not establish a necessity for the transition. And it fails for another reason. "Greediness" introduces an anthropological-psychological motivation, when according to Marx's own terms what is required is a motivation immanent to a specifically economic dialectic.

The third motivation comes closest to hitting the mark from the Hegelian view. Marx discussed how phases in what he termed the "metamorphosis" of commodities into money and back could be interrupted. Just because one has sold a commodity for money does not mean one will automatically find at once someone else with a commodity to be purchased; just because one has bought a commodity does not imply that one will find at once a third partner to whom one's commodity can be sold. At this point it is possible for elementary forms of the creditor/debtor relationship to arise (e.g. prepaid rents, the selling of a future harvest, etc.) Once this occurs, eventually the creditor will face the imperative to sell in order to pay off the debt. At this point money has become the end of the transaction, and not a mere means of circulation.

This may provide a superior motivation for the transition. But here too a mere possibility has been explicated. No strict dialectical necessity for the transition has been provided. From the standpoint of dialectical method there is also a problem in the introduction of the category of "credit" at this stage of the theory. In Marx's system credit is a complex and concrete category. It supposedly is to be explained later in the theory (in Volume III), and the explanation there is supposedly based on the category of money as end. In a dialectical (linear) ordering one cannot use what is to be explained later as a part of the explanation for the earlier principle which is to explain it. A Marxist might reply that the debtor/creditor relationship naturally arises prior to the fully developed credit system considered in Volume III. The problem then shifts to whether that which arises "naturally," contingent as it may be, can play a role in a strictly systematic ordering where transitions are supposed to have a certain necessity to them.

Given the lack of sufficient motivation, the question once again arises whether Marx was guilty of a petitio. By assuming that money must of necessity become the goal of economic transactions, Marx can get the negative results he wished to obtain. Instead of a truly dialectical progression, Marx's theory here consists of a mere extrapolation from one negative form to another. Instead of a progressive overcoming of contradictions as in a true dialectic, we have an increase of contradictions as the ordering unfolds. And, as the references to "greediness" and the "naturally" arising credit relations show, the theory also is not a systematic progression from one category to the next that strictly follows dialectical logic. The theory instead is characterized by a quid pro quo of picture-thinking and intelligible principles. Whenever the logic of a principled ordering breaks down, Marx resorts to intuitions of a contingent nature to provide the ordering with a plausibility that it lacks on strictly systematic grounds. Needless to say, from the perspective of orthodox Hegelianism this is an illicit procedure. And one may detect a petitio here too: Marx introduced these contingent intuitions in order to get to the negative results he wished to obtain.

3. The Dialectic of the Money Form

The most direct way to respond to the objections regarding linearity is to show how the transitions from money as a measure of value to money as a means of circulation, and then to money as the end of exchange, follow a strict dialectical logic. There are systematic reasons for these moves that have nothing to do with mere possibilities, mere contingencies, mere intuitions.

The simplest determination of the money form is "money as a measure of value." Instead of a simple exchange of commodities, the commodities to be exchanged have a money form, i.e. a price. Money as a measure of value is a category of simple unity. Each separate commodity has its unique value expressed in monetary terms prior to coming into contact with any other commodity. But this is an abstract unity, in which a moment of difference is implicit. Money as a measure of value at first seems to apply to each alone, but in reality applies to all taken together. In other words, money is supposed to define each commodity apart from the others. But by a dialectical twist it brings each unity into contact with myriad other commodities. We thus have a systematic reason to move from a category of unity to one of difference.

Another way of presenting this transition is the following. The category "money as measure" defines a structure in which each single commodity has a money price attached to it, expressing its value. Within this structure it is necessarily the case that there is a structural tendency for money to mediate an exchange connecting different commodities. This generates a new structure, which explicitly includes an element of difference that had previously been abstracted from. The transition to a new category, one that captures this element of difference, thus has dialectical necessity. This brings us to the next most complex determination of money, money as a means of circulation, whereby one commodity can be sold in order then to purchase a second commodity (C-M-C). (Under this heading Marx also considers specifically economic issues connected with currency and coin— the velocity of circulation, the factors that determine the precise amount of currency required, etc.—that for our purposes can be passed over.)

Money as a medium of circulation is a category of difference in two senses. First, in the circuit C-M-C, two (or more; the circuit can be continued indefinitely) different commodities are brought into play. Second, there is the possibility of the circuit being interrupted. It is possible that those who sold cannot find the commodity they wish to purchase, and it is possible that those who have purchased cannot find buyers for the commodity they need to sell. Marx went on to derive the next categorial transition from this possibility.

In the previous section we saw that for Hegelians a mere possiblity does not provide sufficient warrant for a dialectical transition from one category to the next. This is true enough. Whether in a particular case a buyer cannot find a seller, or a sellar not find a buyer, is contingent, and this possibility can play no role in a systematic ordering of categories. But it is not contingent that within the C-M-C circuit there is a structural tendency for the two parts of the circuit to be separated. It is necessarily the case that there is this tendency, and this necessity is not weakened by the possibility that not every individual event will exhibit that tendency. Because it is necessarily the case that there is a structural tendency for the circuit to be interrupted, the *difference* between the phases C-M and M-C is what should be emphasized. There is a unity here, established by money as the middle term.[14] But in a structure where there is a structural tendency for this unity to break down it is the moment of difference that predominates. This is so even if in particular instantiations of such a categorial structure the fragmentation remains only a possibility.

This is exactly parallel to many cases discussed by Hegel. With Hegel, for example, the category "unhappy consciousness" articulates a structure of difference between the human and the divine.[15] Hegel would insist that this remains the case even if in concrete instances this unhappiness is only a possibility. Many Medieval Christians and Jews perhaps did not feel estranged from the God that was so distant from them. Whether or not that possibility actually eventuated in specific instances is irrevelant from the perspective of categorial analysis. Categorial analysis is concerned with whether an immanent tendency towards fragmentation and difference is the dominant feature of the structure in question. It is a matter of what follows "proximately and for the most part," of dominant structural tendencies. And just as Hegel asserted that the dominant structural tendency built into religions of unhappy consciousness is the emergence of fragmentation, of difference, of a gulf between the divine and human poles, so Marx derived a parallel conclusion regarding the structure articulated by the category of money as a medium of circulation: "To say that these two independent and antithetical acts (i.e. C-M and M-C) have an intrinsic unity, are essentially one, is the same as to say that this intrinsic oneness expresses itself in an external antithesis. If the interval in time between the two complementary phases of the complete metamorphosis of a commodity become too great, if the split between the sale and the purchase become too pronounced, the intimate connexion between them their oneness, asserts itself by producing — a crisis."[16]

The transition to the next stage in the dialectic of money is fairly straightforward. Within the C-M-C circuit the different moments of the circuit, C-M and M-C, are only precariously connected. The structural tendency toward the separation of these moments itself necessarily generates a structural tendency to overcome this separation. This brings us to the category of money proper, where money is no longer a mere means to facilitate the exchange of commodities. Instead it becomes the end of exchange itself. When exchange is undertaken in order to accumulate a hoard, or in order to collect a reserve fund to make payments as bills become due, or in order to possess a universal money that can be used throughout the world market, the C-M-C circuit is replaced by a M-C-M circuit.

It is dialectical logic, and not any reference to contingent intuitions, or psychological states of mind ("greediness"), or mere empirical (contingent) possibilities, that motivates the move to money as an end of exchange. For the accumulation of money *qua* money provides a principle of unity that can overcome the structural tendency towards fragmentation immanent within the circuit of money as a means of circulation. If I have accumulated money beforehand by making it the end of my exchange, then even if I cannot find anyone to purchase my commodities, I myself can still purchase commodities I desire from others (money as hoard). Or if I have previously purchased without exchanging money for my purchase, then I can later undertake exchange with money as its end (money as means of purchase). This too maintains the unity of the circuit. Or, finally, if I wish to be able to engage in continuous (unified) exchange of different commodities anywhere in the global market, I must first have made the accumulation of universal money the end of my economic activity. In each case money forms a principle of unity that both incorporates the moment of difference articulated in the previous category and overcomes the structural tendency to fragmentation present at the previous stage.[17]

Of all the forms of value considered up to this point, money as end of exchange captures the structure of value the most adequately: "Value, therefore, being the active factor in such a process, and assuming at one time the form of money, at another that of commodities, but through all these changes preserving itself. . . it requires some independent form, by means of which its identity may at any time be established. And this form it possesses only in the shape of money. It is under the form of money that value begins and ends, and begins again, every act of its own spontaneous generation."[18] Thus with universal money we have reached a form of money that is the fullest expression of the money form; now "Its real mode of existence in this sphere adequately corresponds to its ideal concept."[19] We thus have reached closure on the second level of categories.

A systematic account of the linear ordering of the determinations of the money form has been provided. The deriviation of money as an end of exchange can be justified in strict dialectical terms that do not rest on any quid pro quo of intuition and dialectical reasoning. This provides a forwards justification for the ordering, i.e. one that traces the linear progression of the theory. But dialectical theory in Hegel also has a backwards justification as well. "Philosophy is its own time apprehended in thoughts." This means that dialectical thinking begins with an unapprehended totality and seeks to reconstruct its intelligibility in thought. Categorial moves in Hegel are often justified by the need to account for the given totality; the need to overcome shortcomings in the previous categories does not provide the only warrant for dialectical transitions. Could Marx, with full dialectical justification, also have legitimated the move to money as an end of exchange on the grounds that this move is necessary if we are to account for the totality being investigated, the capitalist mode of production? The C-M-C circuit cannot account for this mode of production. Since that is the object we wish to reconstruct in thought, a Marxist could say that this too justified moving to the M-C-M circuit. Orthodox Hegelians, however, feel that this sort of move is not justified in Marx's theory the way it is in Hegel's. With Hegel the aim towards which the categorial progression is heading is the affirmation of a true reality. The truth of the final category legitimates the truth of the moves up to it. However with Marx the final end point of the theory is a negative to be critiqued, an untruth. Marx's dialectic "progresses" by increasing contradictions, and not by the progressive

90

overcoming of contradictions. Therefore any given categorial transition in Marx cannot be justified by reference to its end point.[20]

This is not convincing. For one thing, the point made in section A.2 regarding the commodity form holds for the money form as well. When we move from money as measure of value through money as means of circulation to money as the end of exchange there is a greater structural tendency for the expansion of the human community, for the development of human personality as new wants and needs emerge[21], and for an expansion of society's productive capacity. In this sense the dialectic *is* deriving social forms that are progressively more developed. Of course it is true that Marx simultaneously insisted that these higher forms involve futher fetishism. But there is no good reason to restrict the backwards justification of a dialectical progression to orderings that aim at an unequivocally affirmative final category. The point of a dialectical theory of categories is the systematic reconstruction of the determinations that make a given whole intelligible. This is what allows for backwards justifications, i.e. justifying a move to a next category on the grounds that it is necessary in order to arrive at an end point that will make the object of investigation intelligible. And this is *common* to both the Hegelian dialectic aiming at a theoretical reconciliation with a given whole alleged to be true, and the Marxian dialectic aiming at a theoretical (and practical) critique of its object. Any refusal to grant Marx backwards justifications is based on an a priori desire to reject the Marxian project, and not on the intrinsic nature of a dialectical theories.

4. Money as Essence

Besides objecting to the linear progression of the money form, Hegelians have also questioned the basic categorial structure Marx employed in the categorization of money. Once money has become an end in itself it is treated by Marx as a *subject* that remains identical in its transformations. In the M-C-M circuit money is not just a functional means of exchange; it is a reflexive unity with itself, a subject.

This comes out quite clearly in the following passage: "In simple circulation, C-M-C, the value of commodities attained at the most a form independent of their use-values, i.e., the form of money; but that same value now in the circulation M-C-M . . . suddenly presents itself as an independent substance, endowed with a motion of its own, passing through a life-process of its own, in which money and commodities are mere forms which it assumes and casts off in turn. Nay, more: it enters now, so to say, into private relations with itself."[22] In Hegelian terms, Marx treats money according to a *Wesenslogik* in which money as a real subject stands over

91

against human society, having priority over human society as an essence has priority over its determinations. In other words, one pole of the structure—that of value in its money form, value as process—is given priority over the other, i.e. over the human activity of exchanging money and commodities:

> The need for exchange and for the transformation of the product into a pure exchange value progresses in step with the division of labour, i.e. with the increasingly social character of production. But as the latter grows, so grows the power of *money*, i.e. the exchange relation establishes itself as a power external to and independent of the producers. What originally appeared as a means to promote production becomes a relation alien to the producers.[23]

From the orthodox Hegelian perspective the social totality seems to be grasped here in a one-sided fashion. And here too Marx's theory might be said to be constructed in order to arrive at results that can be critiqued. Hartmann writes:

> How is the social *whole* grasped with this progression?. . . The theory lacks an intelligible motivation for this one-sidedness. Or, to speak more precisely: read forwards as an argument (i.e. without making the intent to criticize a false end point the basis of the proof) the theory lacks motivation. . . Read backwards the motivation for the one-sidedness lies in the premises of the critical project. The theory wishes to reconstruct the negative aspect of society, and it conceives this negative aspect in being given over to an alien objectivity ("commodity," "money"). . . The theory cannot show the appropriateness and necessity of handling "commodity" and "money" in terms of an essence logic that grants them a dominating role over against humans (a domination that becomes sharper with capital itself).[24]

At this point three responses can be given. First, not all structures that can be made intelligible under the general category of essence are of the same sort. In some essence structures there is no element of freedom whatsoever, no moment of difference, of individuality.[25] In other essence structures there is an element of freedom, difference, and individuality, although it is subordinate and underdeveloped. Marx's account of money as a real subject makes use of the latter sort of essence structure. Individuals are subsumed under money as a real subject, and so an essence structure is present. However the individuals engaging in money transactions have the Lockean liberty to dispose of their persons and possessions as they see fit. It is true that this liberty is not the whole story. As we shall see, it masks a structurally enforced coercion. But nonetheless it remains part of the story. Marx did stress the object side of the structure—value as money in process, as

92

essence—but his analysis of the total structure is not completely one-sided. The autonomy of the individuals within this structure may be far from complete, but it is sufficient to avoid their complete subordination within the essence structure.

Second, we ought not to forget Marx's theory of fetishism here. In the categorial interpretation of the capitalist mode of production proposed by Marx, commodities, money, and later captial, have an independence over against human subjects. But this is only because underlying social relations are masked. Money functions (as essence) not because human activity is intrinsically reduced to being a mere moment in its circuit. It functions this way because of the manner in which the human community is structured. The social form within which human activity occurs (the isolation of commodity producers from each other; the value form) creates the structural tendency for money to function in this manner (money becomes the force that unites the separate producers together). What we have here is not a rigid structure of essence that negates the very possibility of any independent human activity. Instead we have an essence structure that will give way as soon as the social relations upon which it is based are acknowledged and transformed. From this perspective Marx did *not* give a one-sided stress to money as the real subject, the essence of the social world. Even here Marx's theory points to social movements as being the ultimate real subjects of social processes.

Finally, the overall context of the development of the value form must be kept in mind. There is a comparative aspect to Marx's theory that the above cirtïcism misses. *All* forms of social production by definition involve a social dimension of labor. In *all* forms humans are mediated socially with each other. Marx admitted that this holds for the value form as well. But if he had stressed this aspect, common to all forms of social production, he would have failed to accomplish the central theoretical task of *contrasting* the value form with other social forms. That task demands that emphasis be placed on what distinguishes the manner in which the value form mediates social life. Within the value form this social mediation is accomplished through the commodity, money and, later, capital, forms. These forms stand over and against society, as if they had some objective power. Within the value form (considered at the present stage of abstraction) socio-economic decisions are uncoupled from social considerations and made in terms of independent objective factors (e.g. the need to sell in order to buy, the need to attain a reserve of money, etc.). One might applaud this on the grounds that it leads to a tremendous increase in technical rationality.[26] Or one may accept it on the grounds of its technical efficiency, while seeking to avoid its deplorable social consequences[27] Or one may take the position

93

Marx held, and assert that these deplorable consequences cannot be removed as long as the commodity form and the money form hold sway. What one *cannot* say is that there is not something unique about this manner of instituting social mediations, something that has to do with the impersonal and objective power commodities and money appear to have over the participants in generalized commodity exchange. And Marx meant precisely this when he employed a *Wesenslogik* here.

C. Closing Remarks

We can now begin to flesh out the architectonic of Marx's theory:

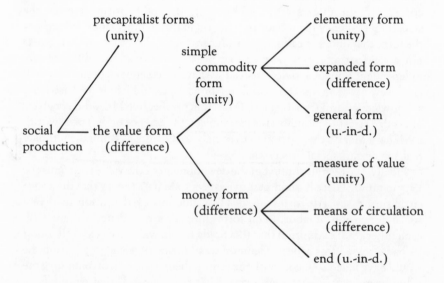

This diagram should be read both left to right and top to bottom as moving from the simple and abstract to the complex and concrete. A number of comments can be made regarding this architectonic. First, the above diagram does not present a sequence of historical stages. The simple commodity form does not model the development of some precapitalist stage of simple commodity production. Nor can the logical development of the money form be justified in terms of a logic of historical stages.

The belief that the initial stages of *Capital* capture a historical stage of simple commodity production following the law of value is widespread. But it is based upon a misunderstanding of Marx's dialectical method. Marx did not attempt to explain how capital arose in his systematic ordering of

94

categories (that is the task of the theory of original accumulation, which is a digression from that ordering; see Chapter VII below). Instead he began with the totality that is the capitalist mode of production, abstracted out its simplest determinations, and then progressed in a step-by-step fashion to more complex and concrete determinations of that mode of production. Taken as a whole, *Capital* provides a systematic reconstruction of a historical phenomenon, not a historical account of the genesis of that phenomenom. There are sections of *Capital* that describe historical developments, but they do not determine the categorial ordering of the theory. Thus the value that is a principle for grasping the simple commodity form does not characterize a precapitalist historical stage of simple commodity production. It is "entirely pecular" to capitalism:

> It has become apparent in the course of our presentation that value, which appeared as an abstraction, is possible only as such an abstraction, as soon as money is posited; this circulation of money in turn leads to capital, hence can be fully developed only on the foundation of capital, just as, generally, only on this foundation can circulation seize hold of all moments of production... *The concept of value is entirely peculiar to the most modern economy, since it is the most abstract expression of capital itself and of the production resting on it. In the concept of value, its secret (is) betrayed.*[28]

The above passage also implies that the categorial development of money aims at placing the various forms of money in their proper systematic place within a reconstruction of capitalism. This is confirmed in other places as well, for instance where Marx wrote that, "Abstract wealth, value, money, hence *abstract labour*, develop in the measure that concrete labour becomes a totality of different modes of labour embracing the world market."[29] This, of course, does not take place in any precapitalist historical stage.

It must be admitted that Marx himself did point out a parallel between the stages of the dialectic of the money form and a sequence of historical periods. To the extent that there are such parallels, Marx can hardly be faulted for pointing them out. But the logical justification of the dialectic does not rest on this parallel. It rests instead on the systematic role the determinations of money play in the reconstruction in thought of the value form. Even if capitalism turned out to have arisen in a quite different fashion from that sketched by Marx, the logical relations among "commodity," "money," and "captial" would remain untouched.

Second, besides an exclusively historical reading of *Capital* there is an opposite sort of reading to be avoided as well. *Capital* is not based on imposing an a priori scheme on the object of investigation. The talk of unity, difference, and unity-in-difference may suggest that in my reading of *Capital*

95

some rigid triadic machine churns out categories in a quasi-metaphysical fashion. This is not the case. The connections between categories of unity, of difference, and of unity-in-difference, and the fact that dialectical orderings connecting these sorts of categories can occur on various levels of abstraction and complexity, are merely general principles for the systematic construction of a linear progression of categories. They in no way determine the content of this progression. The content comes from the specific realm being investigated. Just as Hegel's project in the *Logic* was to provide a systematic ordering of the categories employed by traditional philosophy in attempting to grasp the intelligibility of the world, so Marx's project was to provide a systematic ordering of the categories employed in political economy in order to capture the intelligibility of the social world.

The chain of thought goes as follows. If one wishes to grasp the basic intelligibility of the capitalist mode of production, this can only be done through categories. If one wishes to employ these categories reflectively, this can only be done by exhibiting their immanent connections. The immanent connections among categories can be brought out by ordering them in a systematic fashion. And the progression from unity to difference to unity-in-difference is an aid in constructing an ordering that is both systematic and immanent.

It should always be remembered that in the present work I am examining only one feature of *Capital*. Marx defended many significant empirical and historical claims. But he also defended another sort of claim as well. Categories define structures, and from these structures certain structural tendencies necessarily arise. Suppose that the structure defined by a category of simple unity (e.g. "money as measure of value") necessarily involves structural tendencies that point to differences not explicitly taken into account in that category. This would justify moving to a category where that moment of difference was made explicit (e.g. "money as means of circulation"; see section B.3 above). And if a structure defined by a category of difference can be shown to necessarily involve structural tendencies that point to an explicit unifying of explicit differences, then this justifies moving to a category of unity-in-difference (e.g. "money as end of exchange"). In this manner claims of systematic necessity can be defended, i.e. claims asserting that one category must of necessity be ordered prior to another.[30]

In a systematic progression of the categories that make the capitalist mode of production intelligible, it is *necessarily* the case that the "elementary form" of commodity exchange is prior to the "expanded form," which is prior to the "general form," and that this is prior to "money as measure of value," which in turn systematically precedes "money as means of circulation," from which "money as end in itself" follows. Each earlier

96

category is simpler and more abstract than the one that follows; each transition is justified in terms of the principle that categories of unity are to be ordered prior to categories of difference, which in turn are to be ordered prior to categories of unity-in-difference. The principles for a systematic ordering of this sort were taken over from Hegel's dialectical logic. The claims of necessity in *Capital* are those that are formulated in terms of this dialectical logic.

One final point. This dimension of Marx's theory is not of theoretical significance only. Practical issues are also involved here. For instance, there is no doubt that Marx would have been hostile to policies aiming at instituting socialism in which the market perpetually retained a major role. He would insist that these polices are ultimately incoherent. "Socialism" implies the social control of the economy ("direct sociality" in the language of the previous chapter). "Market" implies a social framework in which money is an end in itself, outside social control. Further, Marx believed that this was *necessarily* the case. In order to argue for such a claim, a list of historical examples of market societies that failed to attain socialism would not suffice. That could only justify contingent empirical statements of the sort "market societies up until now have not been socialist." In order to make a stronger claim Marx began with the most general category of market societies, the "value form" that defines the general structure of commodity exchange, and argued that money necessarily develops into an objective power standing above the human community. His argument rests upon showing how the category "money as end in itself" could be immanently derived from the value form. If Marx had not had recourse to Hegelian dialectical logic he could not have formulated a claim of necessity here. This does not imply that socialists must advocate immediately abolishing all markets. But it does mean that accepting the dialectical ordering in *Capital* implies accepting that socialism involves moving more and more areas of social life outside the value form (or, more concretely, outside the commodity form and the money form).[31]

VI

The Initial Determinations of the Capital Form: Labor Power as Commodity; Exploitation

A. The Capital Form, Capital in Production, and Labor Power as Commodity

In section 1, I present Marx's account of the transitions from M-C-M to the capital form (M-C-M'), from the capital form to capital in production, and from capital in production to labor power as commodity. These transitions can all be questioned from the perspective of dialectical logic. In *The Just Economy*, a recent defense of Hegel's examination of civil society, Richard Dien Winfield attacks each of these moves. In section 2, I present his objections. In section 3, I respond to his arguments. Doing so provides a welcome opportunity to clarify further the nature of dialectical social theories. Section 4 is an excursus on a feminist account of Marx's category of labor power as commodity.

1. Marx's Systematic Ordering

The last category in the dialectic of the simple money form was money as the end of exchange, M-C-M. Once again a satisfactory dialectical transition takes us immediately from the last category of the prior level to the first category of the next level. In Chapter IV of *Captial I* Marx accomplished this in the following way. Agreeing with both Aristotle and Locke,[1] Marx argued that once money has been made the end of exchange it is necessarily the case that a structural tendency arises for the parties engaged in exchange to seek to increase their money holdings. The circuir M-C-M in itself appears

98

unintelligible. For who would exchange simply in order to end up with precisely the same amount of money as that held at the beginning? We thus must introduce a circuit that ends not with M but with a M' that includes the initial M plus some delta M, some surplus value. With this we have a direct transition from the last determination of the simple money form to the captial form of value.

"Capital" brings the value form dialectic to closure. It goes beyond the simple unity of the commodity form, and beyond the difference between commodity and money introduced with the money form. The category of "capital" defines a structure within which commodity and money are united in difference:

$$\text{Capital}$$
$$M-C-M'$$

Marx wrote:

> Value now becomes value in process, money in process, and, as such, capital. It comes out of circulation, enters into it again, preserves and multiplies itself within its circuit, comes back out of it with expanded bulk, and begins the same round ever afresh. M-M', money which begets money...[2]

As in the case of "money," "capital" is both a determination of the more universal category "value," and itself a universal with its own forms or determinations. Specifically, "capital" has three forms under it in Marx's account. The first concerns capital as a single self-expanding unit engaged in the production of surplus value. The second concerns the circulation process between different branches of industrial captial. The third concerns the unity of different industrial capitals of different sizes, and the unity of different types of capital, unities-in-difference that are established through the shared distribution of the same surplus. These different forms are logically related as unity, difference, and unity-in-difference, respectively. Hence the ordering is a systematic one, with objectivity simpler and more abstract forms being considered prior to those that are objectively more complex and concrete.

At first it might appear that capital as a principle of unity uniting the M-C-M' circuit involves the circulation process, and that therefore circulation should be considered first. But at the present stage of abstraction it is assumed that all commodities exhange at their values. We thus cannot

99

Δ_M

explain how a M' equal to the initial M invested plus some delta m emerges by reference to circulation (this is the topic of Chapter V of *Capital I*). If we assume that in the M-C part of the circuit the capitalist buys certain commodities (raw materials, tools, labor power) at their full value, then by definition delta M cannot arise through purchasing them at less than their full value. Likewise if we assume that the capitalist sells the commodity at its full value in the C-M' part of the circuit, delta M obviously cannot arise through selling it as more than its value. This leaves only the interval between which certain commodities are purchased and different sorts of commodities are produced, i.e. the production process.

What is "capital in production"? How is it to be comprehended? Once again if the aim of the theory is a systematic reconstruction in thought of the object realm, we cannot simply list features of the production process randomly. Instead determinations that are objectively simpler and more abstract must be ordered prior to those are more complex and concrete. In other words, the first determination of the capital form, capital as simple unity in production, itself is the principle for a dialectic of futher determinations. And these determinations are also ordered according to dialectical logic. On this level "labor power as commodity" is a category of simple unity. "Exploitation" and "the production process proper" will turn out to be categories of difference and of unity-in-difference, respectively.

In a sense the notion of "labor power as commodity," introduced by Marx in *Capital I* Chapter VI, has been implicit in the theory all along. The theory began with the concept of the value form, of generalized commodity production. Commodity production is only generalized when the agents of the production process find themselves in the commodity form.[3] What is new here is that the focus is now not on commodity exchange, but on the production process as it occurs within generalized commodity exchange. What is the simplest and most abstract way of conceiving this production process? As one, Marx answered, in which *all* imputs take on the commodity form. The relatively indeterminate circuit of capital now begins to get fleshed out:

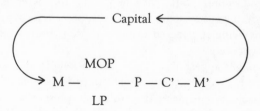

The initial investment money (M) is used to purchase two sorts of commodities, the means of produciton (MOP: raw materials, tools, factories, etc.) and labor power. The exchange value of the latter sort of commodity, like all other commodities, on this level of abstraction, is fixed by the amount of socially necessary labor time required to produce it. The value of labor power is thus fixed by the value of its consumption basket, i.e. by the amount of abstract socially necessary labor time it takes to produce the bundle of commodities that is required to produce and reproduce labor power as a commodity. Labor power then goes to work on the means of production in a production process (P), producing a new commodity (C') that is then sold (M'). This, of course, presupposes that labor power is available as a commodity that can be purchased. And this assumes that labor power is "free" in a double sense, i.e. on the one hand that the worker "as a free man can dispose of his labour-power as his own commodity, and that on the other hand he has no other commodity for sale, is short of everything necessary for the realization of his labour-power."[4] In other words, the capital form is defined initially by a basic social relation: one group purchases the labor power of another within a structure in which the former owns and controls[5] the means of production while the latter does not.

Why is the category that represents this structure logically to be characterized as one of simple unity on this level of the theory? There are two reasons for this. We are now considering what is essentially a complex process from a single perspective. At this stage the labor process is considered solely as a process of the transformation of use-values from one shape (raw materials, intermediate products, etc.). into another (finished products). Labor power is considered solely in its role as the agent of this transformation. This is an abstract and oversimplified view, as we shall see. Second, at the present stage we are also abstracting from any social antagonism that may be latent in the commodity form. At this point both the seller and the buyer of labor power are each conceptualized as free and equal, two partners whose wills are immediately united in the wage contract.[6]

We have already noted how categories in Hegel's theory are overdetermined. We should note in passing that the same may be said of determinations in Marx's theory. In so far as the categories discussed in *Capital* are determinations of the value form, and in so far as this is a category of difference, all of these determinations are categories of difference. But in so far as the dialectical progression goes through a number of different levels, the determinations of the value form may be characterized in other terms as well. "Labor power as commodity" is a category of simple unity falling under "capital in production." Nonetheless as a determination of the value form there remains an essential component of *difference* in the structure it articulates, the difference between owning/controlling and not owning/controlling the means of production.[7]

We may conclude this section with a summary diagram of Marx's system of economic categories thusfar.

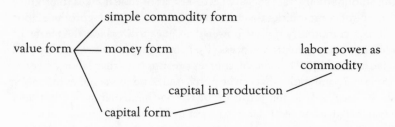

simple commodity form

value form money form   labor power as
                               commodity

                capital in production

capital form

2. Hegelian Objections to Marx's Ordering

Regarding the derivation of the capital form from commodity exchange, Winfield accepts the position implicit in Hegel's *Philosophy of Right*. For Hegel the capital circuit is subordinate to commodity exchange, not the reverse as with Marx.[8] Hegel held that the move from commodity exchange mediated by money to capital does not take us to a new categorial level. Winfield presents two arguments in favor of Hegel's position. First, the M-C-M' circuit is merely one possible form commodity exchange might take. To assert otherwise is to deny the autonomy of those participating in commodity exchange, who could freely decide to engage solely in nonprofit transactions.[9] Second, when an owner does intend to offer a commodity for sale at a gain, it still depends upon the free decisions of others whether this intention will be realized. There is no guarantee whatsoever that these decisions will be forthcoming. Therefore the capital circle is subordinate to the autonomous choices made by those engaged in commodity exchange.[10]

Turning to the move from the capital form (M-C-M') to capital in production, Hegel did not hold that comprehension of the capital form demanded beginning with capital in production. In contrast, in attempting to account for how M' can exceed the M initially invested, Marx limited the discussion to capital invested in production. He held that only an examination of production can account for the gain that constitutes capital. In his defense of the Hegelian standpoint Winfield points out that gains can be won through the exchange of objects that have not been produced, i.e. found objects. Gains can also be won by capitalist merchants who do not concern themselves with production at all. It is also possible for financial capitalists to win gains in transactions that do not involve produced commodities. Winfield writes, "the basic interaction of capital need not rest upon any intervening production process, but may simply involve speculative buying and selling."[11]

Even when the commodity has been produced by the sellar, the gain stems from the free agreement of a buyer to purchase it at a price above the seller's costs. If we wish to understand gain we must examine the free agreements of economic agents. There is no value at which commodities "must" be exchanged. Hence there is no mystery regarding how a surplus can arise when commodities are exchanged at their values. And this mystery was Marx's motivation for turning to capital in production. At best, production is but a part of the story. At worst, the move to production leads us to lose sight of how the increase from M to M' is accounted for: with some mutual expressions of free will gains are made, with other they are not; that is all one can say.

Finally, in his discussion of capitalist industrial production Marx limited his analysis to production undertaken by laborers who have hired out their labor power to the private owners of firms for a wage. But this is just one of a number of different ways capitalist production can be organized: "Just as commodity relations permit any market agent, from individual to state, to play the role of 'capitalist', so they enable commodity producing capital to take any form the market permits, be it a private business whose owner is the sole employee, a worker co-operative whose members draw dividends rather than wages, a share-holding corporation whose employees receive stocks as well as wages, or a state enterprise employing wage labor."[12] The theory of capitalist production constructed by Marx ignores these possibilities. Marx, therefore, was wrong to claim that "labor power as commodity" must necessarily follow "capital in production" in a dialectical ordering of social categories.

3. Replies

The above objections go to the heart of this stage of Marx's theory. They also raise two essential issues regarding the nature of systematic theories of categories. I shall group Winfields's objections under the two headings of civil freedom and categorial universality. Some of the points made here have been introduced in the previous chapter. However the issues with which we are concerned are so central that further consideration in the present context is warranted.

a) Civil freedom

A number of Winfield's objections can be reduced to an argument regarding Marx's alleged neglect of civil freedom. This argument involves two presuppositions. The first is a socio-economic thesis regarding market societies, the second a principle of dialectical methodology. The socio-

103

economic thesis asserts that the economic freedom of those engaging in commodity exchange makes the results of economic activity indeterminate: "What makes commodities exchangeable are the concurring decisions of their respective owners, who are independent market agents, free to decide what they need and how they will dispose over their own commodities. In entering the transactions through which exchange value is determined, they need not be swayed by any particular external consideration, nor follow any putative model of 'economic rationality'."[13] The methodological thesis is not stated explicitly by Winfield, but it is implicit throughout his critique of Marx. It states that a transition from one socio-economic category to the next can only claim systematic necessity if all possible agents would necessarily act in the manner specified by the new determination. Whenever it is logically possible for some economic agents to not act in the specified manner, then the transition is not justified.

Putting these two theses together we can formulate Winfield's general argument as follows: at crucial junctures in his theory Marx ignored the freedom of those engaged in commodity exchange; he claimed that a move from one category to another was systematically necessary, despite the fact that this freedom ensures that it is logically possible for economic agents to not act in the manner specified by the new determination; therefore Marx's systematic ordering of economic categories cannot be accepted. This argument was behind denying the necessity of the transition to the capital form; the participants in commodity exchange could choose to abstain from participating in a M-C-M' circuit. The argument was also used to question Marx's move to capital in production. If gains are made, they are explained by the free decisions of contracting partners; production may or may not be part of that story. And this argument was made as well when Winfield denied that commodity exchange is regulated by labor values.

Interestingly enough, what I have termed "Winfield's socio-economic thesis" is not controversial from a Marxist standpoint. Marx did not regard the freedom of commodity exchange as illusory. He felt that this was a crucial factor in establishing that capitalism counts as both a historical and moral advance over earlier modes of production.

In contrast the methodological thesis is extremely controversial. Socio-economic categories define fundamental socio-economic structures. As structures within which the freedom of the will is manifested, these structures allow for a multitude of individual occurrences. Nonetheless there may be structural parameters that constrain individual decisions. If so, it may be the case that certain structural tendencies are present. *These tendencies may hold through, rather than despite, the free choices of agents operating under these parameters.* Winfield himself grants this when he states

104

that the "ubiquitous element of market freedom does not preclude the working of definite laws governing the individual and global consequences of exchange transactions."[14] Why?

The question we now must pose concerns the appropriate topic for categorial analysis. Is it the myraid contingent choices that individuals might possibly make, were they to act within the structure defined by a given category? Or should our interest be directed instead to the general structural tendencies that hold on the given categorial level? I believe that the former is a matter for individual biography, while the latter is the proper concern for dialectical social theories. And I believe that this was Hegel's position as well.

Consider the category "property" in *The Philosophy of Right*. This defines a structure within which persons objectify their will in external objects. On the level of individual biography persons are free to do this in a harmonious fashion. Yet the structural parameters of the situation—on this level of abstraction persons are motivated by self-interest alone, and no legal framework is present—necessarily lead to a structural tendency for nonmalicious wrong, fraud, and crime to arise. Hegel correctly used this as a basis for arguing that the move from the category "property" to the category "crime" was systematically necessary. He proposed this transition despite the fact that it is logically possible for persons to refrain from engaging in the behavior specified by the latter determination.

The argument for moving from the circuit of commodity and money exchange to the capital circuit is exactly parallel. It is logically possible (in the sense of formal logic) that those engaged in the M-C-M circuit could freely choose to remain within that circuit, trading without regard for gain. But within this structure the self-interest of agents would be considerably furthered if they could receive a gain, and there is no institutional framework present that would check this self-interest. Given these parameters Marx maintained that there is a dominant structural tendency for some to seek to acquire a surplus. This points beyond the category "money," and so Marx quite correctly introduced the category "capital."[15]

It is also true that under conditions of legality capital can be won only when those engaged in commodity exchange make certain sorts of free decisions. Marx recognized this fact with the category of "market prices" in Volume III, and elsewhere. However this merely explains why one unit of capital rather than another survives. If there necessarily is a structural tendency for the capital form to arise, then there will necessarily be a structural tendency for those participating in commodity exchange to deal with *some* unit of capital or other. They may still make decisions freely, but they do so within the parameters set by the capital form.[16]

Finally, on the level of individual biography it is certainly the case that individuals may exchange commodities for gain without regard for labor productivity, i.e. labor values. On the present categorial level the law of value simply states that in the medium-to-long run there is a dominant structural tendency for commodity exchange to be regulated by labor productivity. In order to consider whether this law holds we must examine the structural parameters operative on the present level. The capital form on this level of abstraction involves two sorts of structural parameters. For one thing, abstraction is made from complicating factors, such as different commodities having different circulation times, imbalances in supply and demand, and so on. Also motivations of exceptional benevolence or exceptional masochism are ruled out in favor of motivations of self-interest.

At any particular time economic agents may opt for exchange at any of a wide variety of ratios, depending upon any number of contingencies. But if we rule out exceptional benevolence or exceptional masochism as significant motivations given the structural parameters of the situation, then we may assume that individuals generally will not freely choose to engage in forms of exchange that are systematically disadvantageous to themselves. In the medium-to-long run producers with greater labor productivity will not freely choose to refrain from taking advantage of this. And if consumers are offered commodities from more productive firms that are cheaper than, and comparable in quality to, those offered by other firms, then in the medium-to-long term they will not freely choose to refrain from taking advantage of this.[17] It is thus possible to hold that the law of value governs commodity exchange and the capital circuit without denying the autonomy of those engaged in exchange. Thus Marx's question regarding how a surplus might arise when commodities exchange at their values remains a legitimate query.

b) *Categorial universality*

The second issue raised by Winfield's objections is that of categorial universality. In defending Hegel's analysis of civil society over Marx's theory in *Capital*, Winfield pointed out that there are other species of the capital circuit besides that in which capital is involved in production. And there are other species of capital in production besides that in which wage labor is sold to private capitalists. The underlying thesis in both cases is that Marx's failure to grasp the capital form in its full categorial universality undermined his systematic ordering.

Let us examine the notion of categorial universality more closely. One could argue that the term is equivocal. The same category can be used in different theoretical contexts. It is possible to distinguish employing a category as a genus from employing it as a determination in a dialectical progression of categories. It could very well be the case that the appropriate notion of universality is different in these two different contexts.

The universality appropriate to a genus is characterized by inclusivity. By this I mean that it would be mistaken to consider some of its species in a manner that implied that other of its species are to be excluded from membership in the genus. Consider the category "deception" taken as a genus. Under this heading fall diverse species ranging from self-deceptions regarding one's accomplishments to deceptions regarding the terms of a contract for the exchange of external objects. Any attempt to define the category in terms of one of these species alone would be illegitimate. However when we examine the same category from the standpoint of a dialectical progression of categories things appear differently. It is possible that species that must be treated together *qua* instances of the same genus fall on different levels from a systematic standpoint. Some of these species may embody structures that are on a relatively abstract and simple level, while others may manifest structures that are more complex and concrete. In Hegel's *Philosophy of Spirit*, for example, individual self-deception falls on the level of subjective spirit. From a systematic perspective it thus must be ordered prior to deceptions regarding contractual exchange, a detemination on the level of objective spirit ("fraud").

Armed with this distinction it is possible to mount a defense of Marx against Winfield's attack. Marx can be defended by showing that there are plausible reasons for asserting that different species of capital fall on different levels from a systematic standpoint.

If we treat "capital" as a genus, then the circuit in which capital is involved in production is just one species among many, with no special theoretical privilege over the others. Marx was well aware of the existence of different species of capital. He talked of commodities that have a price without having a value, including under this heading commodities that are exchanged without having been produced. Whenever they are sold for gain they are part of a circuit of capital. It is also the case that hundreds of pages in *Capital* are devoted to the analysis of merchant capital, financial capital, rent, and other species of the M-C-M' circuit where the capital in question is not involved in production. And regarding capital that is involved in production, Marx was fully cognizant of other species besides wage labor hired by private capitalists. (All of this would come as a great surprise to readers of Winfield who were not familiar with Marx's own writings.)

Marx's theoretical objective, however, was not the enumeration of the species of capital. It was rather the dialectical reconstruction in thought of the categories that capture the intelligibility of the capitalist mode of production. From this systematic perspective different species of capital fall on different levels.

In the previous chapter we saw that the indefinite multiplication of conventional needs is an essential feature of market societies. This implies

107

that the exchange for gain of nonproduced items, commodities that have not been transformed in any manner in response to this indefinite multiplication of needs, necessarily is a peripheral matter in societies based on generalized commodity exchange. The production of the commodities in the capital circuit is therefore essential to capital in a way that gain based on the trade of found objects is not. Hence Marx had a stong reason for treating the former prior to the latter in his systematic ordering of economic categories.[18]

Regarding merchant capital, the exchange of objects for gain by those not themselves engaged in the production of those objects is not unique to any specific form of production. Merchant trade can also be found at the interstices of feudal, slave, and kinship societies, and these are all instances of the immediately social form of social production. As such it does not belong at the present stage of Marx's theory, where the most elementary and fundamental categories defining the value form are being introduced. And as for financial capital, there is a growing consensus among even non-Marxist economists that economies in which capital is predominantly invested in speculative transactions are not healthy. This suggests that Marx's insistence that this species of capital is secondary from a systematic point of view is quite plausible.

Finally, regarding labor within capitalist production, Marx held that here too it would be mistaken to see all species as falling on the same categorial level. The social relation in which nationalized capitalist firms hire laborers involves the state. Hence from a systematic standpoint it would be illicit to consider it on an abstract level of the theory where the state had not yet been introduced. Marx likewise was well aware of the possibility of self-employment. However as we shall see he felt that the capital form includes a dominant structural tendency towards the concentration and centralization of capital.[19] This in turn implies a tendency for this form of labor to be of peripheral importance. From this Marx concluded that it was legitimate to abstract initally from this species of capitalist production. And as for workers cooperatives, Marx saw them as extremely complex. On the one hand he agreed that they are species of capitalist production. However he also insisted that they include elements that point away from the capital form. Therefore he considered them at a very late stage in his categorial reconstruction of the capital form.[20]

I have established that a general rejection of Marx's theory on the grounds that Marx did not treat capital in its full categorial universality does not withstand scrutiny. The various species of capital mentioned by Winfield are all explicitly acknowledged in *Capital*. And there are good reasons for thinking that these species do not fall on the same level from a systematic perspective. Marx's derivation of the capital form, capital in production, and labor power as commodity, has been shown to be cogent. Before proceeding to subsequent derivations I would first like to consider a quite different sort of objection to the category "labor power as commodity."

4. Excursus: Labor Power and Domestic Labor

There is a major difficulty on this stage of Marx's theory. It should at least be mentioned, even if it is not central to the confrontation of Hegel and Marx. The treatment in *Capital* of labor power as a commodity is fundamentally incomplete. It ignores all investigation into the concrete material practices whereby labor power is produced as a commodity. If we take the phrase "generalized commodity production" literally, it implies that only commodities and commodified labor go into the making of commodities. And yet in the making of the commodity "labor power" this is most definitely *not* the case. There is a form of labor that does not take on the value form, yet is implicit in the capital/wage labor structure that has been outlined: The unpaid domestic labor of women. Can Marx's theory deal with *this* form of labor?

This question could be dismissed if any one of three conditions held. First, a theory of a specific form of social production can legitimately bracket out conditions for the production of commodities that are natural and common to all forms of production (e.g. the air that laborers breathe). Second, merely private matters likewise are not within the scope of the theory (e.g. personal quirks that have no socio-economic significance). Finally, the theory at this stage can overlook forms of labor that belong on a more concrete and complex level (labor within the state apparatus, for example). None of these conditions holds here. Unless one falls into a crass biologism, domestic labor cannot be seen as "natural." Nor is it an exclusively private matter.[21] It is clearly part of the *social* division of labor, even if it does not produce commodities that are socially exchanged. Nor can we say that it is similar to parts of the social division of labor that have yet to appear in the linear ordering, types that are subjected to social forms (e.g. the state form) that have not yet been introduced in the theory. The unpaid domestic labor that produces labor power as a commodity obviously belongs on the same categorial level as that labor power that is produced. Both are part of the same structure, rather than parts of distinct structures that could be considered separately. This connection has been forcefully expressed by Barbara Bradby:

> 'Labour-power' derives its value from an appropriation of unpaid female labour, primarily by men. This labour is clearly more 'socially necessary' than any other, since without it, labour-power would have neither use-value nor

109

exchange-value. The use-value of labour-power, the capacity to work, is itself the appropriation of unpaid female labour; its exchange-value is simply the market value of the commodity inputs to the labour process plus any surplus the worker can win for his own surplus consumption. The exchange-value of labour-power is worth nothing without unpaid female labour to process the commodity inputs into new labour-power. *The wage relation is therefore an exchange of use-value for exchange-value of labour-power, which takes place paradigmatically between men, on the basis of an appropriation of unpaid female labour.*[22]

Marx's neglect of this point leads Bradby to a fundamental attack on value theory:

> Why should it be so significant that *labour* underlies the valorisation process, if another, equally time-consuming and socially necessary form of work, does not get valorised at all? Marx's theory of class struggle is an excellent theory of relations between men, but it flounders when it comes to women, and reveals itself as rooted in a male ideology.[23]

This rejection of "hegemony of value" has profound practical implications that Bradby does not shirk from:

> If domestic labour is simply part of the reproduction of the capitalist wage-relation, then clearly women's interests lie with men's at an economic level, in bettering, or subverting the wage-relation. For feminists to endorse this analysis is to encourage women to join with men in their struggle to avoid being put in the position of women, or 'feminised' through their lack of authority in the labour-process and the way in which a large part of their work is 'unpaid'. But if we analyse things differently, and say that the mysterious 'use-value of labour power' (that 'unique quality' of labour-power as a commodity in Marx, that enables it to produce more than its 'costs of reproduction') is quite simply and unmysteriously the appropriation of unpaid female labour by the male worker, then the idea of women supporting men in their trade union and labour-process struggles seem quite simply, perverse, 'false consciousness' of a kind which is itself anti-women, and repressive of female work.[24]

The first point to make in response is to accept that the structure analyzed at this stage of the theory does include *both* labor power as a commodity and the unpaid domestic labor that produces labor power as a commodity. Second, given this structure there is indeed a structural tendency for antagonisms between those engaged in wage labor and those engaged in unpaid domestic labor. A gender-based conflict around social production exists that cannot be reduced to a class analysis. Marx is to be faulted for not bringing these two points out.[25]

However this does not in principle undermine value analysis. This is not simply because value analysis retains its place for wage labor, leaving us with an unresolved dualism. Thinking through the logic of unpaid domestic labor in all its specificity within the present form of social production leads us back to, and not away from, value theory. Even though such labor is not itself produced as a commodity and does not participate in the valorization process, it is still subjected to the commodity form, the money form, and the capital form. Unpaid domestic labor increasingly depends on purchased commodities (refrigerators, stoves, packaged food, etc.), and less and less on items produced within the household itself for immediate use. Successful completion of this labor thus increasingly depends upon sufficient money to purchase these commodities. And the extent of access to money for this purpose is a function of the success of labor power within the household in being sold to capital for a wage[26] (or the success of the household in accumulating capital, in which case unpaid domestic labor may be eliminated entirely as household chores are performed by hired wage labor). In the social division of labor as a whole, the commodity form, the money form, and the capital form structure domestic labor in a society of generalized commodity production quite as much as they structure wage labor, despite the fact that the latter is commodified and the former is not.

It follows that the stance that male/female solidarity in class struggle is based on false consciousness cannot be accepted. This is not simply due to the fact that this view ignores the presence of women in the labor market. The alternative between either a total identity of interests between those engaged in unpaid domestic labor and those engaged in wage labor, or a total divergence of interest between them, simply cannot be accepted. A rough parallel can be drawn from Marx's discussion in Volume III of industrial capitalists and landlords. There is an antagonism here in that the rents claimed by the latter are seen as a deduction from the profits of the former. The interests of landlords in maximizing rents thus fundamentally conflicts with the interests of capitalists in maximizing their retained profits. And yet simultaneously it is also the case that both share a common interest in maintaining a system in which rents and profits are defined as private property which they are legally entitled to hold. In the short-to-medium term their interests may diverge. But in the long term they can be expected to unite in defense of the system that benefits both. In an analogous (if inverse) fashion, and despite all the structural tendencies for conflict between those engaged in domestic labor and those who shirk this socially necessary work, both of these groups share a long term interest as a result of both being subjected to the commodity form, the money form, and the capital form.

B. Exploitation

1. Marx's Derivation of the Category

We now come to what is perhaps the central — and the most controversial — claim in *Capital*, the main topic of Part III of *Capital I* (Chapters VII-XI): the capitalist mode of production is necessarily exploitative. Or, in other words, within a systematic ordering of economic categories the category "exploitation" necessarily follows from the initial determination of the capital form, "labor power as commodity." Before presenting an argument for this transition we first must define the notions of "surplus product," "surplus labor," and "surplus value." "Surplus product" is the aggregate of goods and services that is not distributed to the producers of those goods and services. "Surplus labor" is the aggregate amount of labor required to produce that surplus product. And if the goods and services are commodities, i.e. if they have taken on the value form, then "surplus value" refers to the surplus product considered in terms specific to this form of social production.

The argument for the derivation of "exploitation" is as follows. The category "labor power as commodity" defines a structure in which disparities of wealth lead one class to own/control considerable productive resources while another does not, with the latter class selling its labor power to the former. It is a category of simple unity in that it refers to the reciprocal agreement in the wage contract that directly unites wage labor and capital. However, given the structural parameters defined by the category, a dominant structural tendency necessarily arises that points away from simple unity. The controllers of capital possess both the productive resources of the society and a considerable reserve fund. Their subsistence is thereby guaranteed. Workers, in contrast, do not possess any reserves beyond their hands and minds, which they must hire out if they and their families are to survive. Wage labor thus must bargain wage contracts with the owners/controllers of the means of production from a structurally weaker position.[27] This structural weakness will necessarily tend to be reflected in the terms of the wage contract.

112

Assume that labor power is sold at its value. If the value of any commodity is fixed by the amount of abstract and socially necessary labor time it takes to create that commodity, then the value of the commodity labor power will be fixed by the abstract and socially necessary labor time it takes to create the commodity labor power. Labor power as a commodity is produced and reproduced through food, shelter, clothing, and other natural and socially specific goods and services. Hence the value of labor power is fixed by the time required to produce the goods and services in the workers' basic commodity basket. When the worker is paid an amount sufficient to purchase this basket, labor power is paid at its value. But due to the structurally weak position in which it entered the wage bargaining, it will be forced to produce commodities with more value than the value of labor power itself.

> The past labor that is embodied in the labour power, and the living labour that it can call into action; the daily cost of maintaining it, and its daily expenditure in work, are two totally different things. The former determines the exchange-value of the labour power, the latter is its use-value. The fact that half a day's labour is necessary to keep the labourer alive during twenty-four hours, does not in any way prevent him from working a whole day. Therefore, the value of labour power, and the value which that labor power creates in the labour process, are two entirely different magnitudes; and this difference of the two values was what the capitalist had in view, when he was purchasing the labour power.[28]

The production process is now seen to be fundamentally two-fold. On the one hand, it involves a transformation of use-values. On the other hand, it is a valorization process, i.e. a process aiming at the production of surplus value. In this sense difference has been introduced where before there had been simple unity. Also it is necessarily the case that there is a dominant structural tendency for there to be a fundamental antagonism between wage labor and capital.[29] This stems from the fact that wage laborers are forced to engage in surplus labor, creating a surplus product that is then appropriated by capital in the form of surplus value. This too points beyond simple unity to difference. Hence dialectical logic demands that we introduce a category in which the moment of difference is explicit, and this category is "exploitation."

Before turning to criticisms of this derivation some terms referring to aspects of the structure defined by the category "exploitation" should be defined. From the perspective of production as a valorization process the value of the raw materials and instruments used in production goes into the value of the final product unchanged. They are therefore termed "constant capital." In contrast, labor power is a commodity with the peculiar use-value of producing exchange-value. Once the commodity labor power has been purchased by the capitalist, he or she then used it by setting it to labor. In the laboring process the worker is creating value. The capitalist will require that laboring continue until a greater value is created than the value of the labor power purchased. In this manner a surplus value is produced. The value of labor power, referring to a commodity with the unique feature of having the use-value of producing more value than its exchange-value, is hence termed "variable capital." At this point surplus value that results from a simple prolongation of the workday can be distinguished from surplus value that results from advances is productivity within a given workday (especially important are advances in the industries producing the commodity basket necessary for the production of labor power). This is the distinction between *absolute* and *relative surplus value*.

2. Hegelian Objections

a) Exploitation and the labor theory of value

From the standpoint of a dialectical theory constructed in a systematic and linear fashion a first question to be asked concerns how a given category is principled by earlier, more abstract, determinations. The labor theory of value clearly is a principle for the derivation of the category "exploitation." "Exploitation" is defined in terms of the difference between the value that labor power creates, measured by socially necessary labor time, and the value of labor power, measured by the socially necessary labor time it takes to produce the commodities necessary for the production and reproduction of the commodity labor power. If the labor theory of value is abandoned, then Marx's category of exploitation may not be able to be formulated.

A general reason for abandoning the labor theory of value according to orthodox Hegelians is that it ignores the autonomy of the participants in market exchange. In the present context the autonomy of wage laborers is denied when it is asserted that laborers "must" exchange their labor power at some predetermined value. This rules out the possibility that wage laborers could assert their market freedom by insisting that they share increases in social wealth.[30] If this possibility is excluded a priori, then it is easy enough to go on to derive the category "exploitation." But the arbitrariness of this procedure undermines any claim to have established that capitalism is inherently exploitative.

114

b) Exploitation and constant capital

The labor theory of value determines another facet of the category "exploitation" and, through it, later stages of the theory as well. Due to the labor theory of value the category "exploitation" refers to variable capital alone when accounting for surplus value. Both fixed constant capital (e.g. machinery that remains after one production period) and circulating constant capital (e.g. raw materials and machinery used up in one production period) are neglected. This neglect of constant capital crucially determines the future development of the theory in that constant capital is treated as a subsequent determination to be derived from variable capital. Variable capital is the source of surplus value, which is then invested in the expansion of constant capital, the means of production.

In terms of dialectical logic Heglians have asserted that there is a general methodological problem with this procedure. Dialectical theories attempt to reconstruct a concrete realm in thought. A reconstruction in thought of the concrete sees the concrete in terms of a superimposed set of structures, defined in a system of categories. Dialectical theorists first deconstruct these structures and then reconstruct them in a systematic fashion. In this process it is legitimate to distinguish structures that are more abstract and simple from those that are more complex and concrete. This provides the ontological basis for a logical ordering of one category prior to another. What is not legitimate, however, is to take two aspects of a single structure, two aspects on the same ontological/categorial level, and separate them, treating one as principle and the other as principled. At this stage of the theory Marx set constant capital equal to zero, and treated wage labor alone as relevant to the valorization process. He was concerned here only with the rate of surplus value (the proportion s/v) rather than with the rate of profit measured in terms of the return to the entire investment ($s/c + v$). He did this in order to construct a linear ordering of categories where "expolitation" (surplus value) was a principle for the derivation of constant capital, and where the rate of surplus value was likewise logically prior to the rate of profit.[31] But in reality any structure in which an s is produced presupposes c as well as v. Marx is guilty of "abstracting from mutually conditioning, coexisting, economic factors."[32] This goes against the canons of dialectical logic. Value theory is thereby undermined.[33]

The neglect of constant capital undermines the category "exploitation" in a number of other respects as well. First, it may very well be the case that labor receives more in industrialized capitalism with advanced constant capital than it would in non-industrialized circumstances where the means of production were owned by the workers themselves either individually or collectively. If this is the case, then what sense does it make to term a

115

situation where workers have more benefits "exploitative" relative to one in which they have fewer? Second, once the role of constant capital has been acknowledged we can see that the labor process *must* be extended beyond the point at which a value equal to the value of labor power has been reached. Under industrialized conditions it is not just the reproduction of labor power that must be covered; the production of the means of production must be provided for. Otherwise it would not be possible to produce, replace, or expand constant capital.[34]

Third, workers may very well have to labor longer and more intensively in "non-exploitative" conditions lacking advanced constant capital than they do in supposedly "exploitative" conditions with developed means of production. If this can in principle occur, then it seems that the terms *nonexploitative* and *exploitative* are being used in illegitimate ways. At least some of the social wealth produced through "exploitation" is the source of the advanced means of production that in principle may ease work conditions. If one wishes to have such advanced industrial production it is simply wrong to suggest—as Marx does with the category of "exploitation" —that workers could somehow receive back the total surplus product and still work under industrialized conditions.

Finally, Marxist economists have provided rigorous proof of the thesis that the exploitation of labor power is the necessary and sufficient condition for the existence of a positive rate of gain. The claim that there is a necessary connection between the category "capital" and the category "exploitation" seems to have been verified once and for all with this proof of what Morishima has termed "the fundamental Marxian theorem."[35] However other mathematical economists have been quick to point out that labor power is not the only productive factor that possesses the property of exploitability. In the system of simultaneous equations used by mathematical economists to model capitalism, there are more variables than there are equations. In order to arrive at a solution to the system one of the variables must be set equal to 1. If labor power is selected as this *numeraire* commodity the fundamental Marxian theorem follows. But *any* element in constant capital (economists have a special attraction to corn) could be made the numeraire commodity, as long as it is directly or indirectly an input in the production of every other commodity. Whatever element is selected, it can be shown that now *it* is the commodity that possesses the property of exploitability.[36] Once again the conclusion must be that Marx's categorial ordering is arbitrary; there is no unique connection between the category "capital" and the category "exploitation (of labor power)."

3. Replies to Objections

a) *Exploitation and the labor theory of value*

According to the first objection Marx's category "exploitation," formulated in terms of the labor theory of value, fails to take into account the autonomy of wage laborers. "Exploitation" is measured by the difference between the value of labor power and the value created by labor. By implying that labor power must be sold at its value, this approach fails to include the possibility of workers freely agreeing to wage contracts that allow them to participate in an expansion of social wealth.

This objection fails to grasp that the category "value of labor power" is not defined in terms of some minimum subsistence level fixed once and for all. It is not defined in a manner totally unconnected from the level of productive capacity attained in given circumstances, or from the extent of labor's share in productive advance. It still remains an abstract category in that fluctuations in the labor market are ignored and only the reproduction costs of the commodity labor power are taken into account. But in some historical and social contexts more is required to reproduce the commodity labor power than in other cases where social wealth is not developed, or where laborers do not share in its expansion. Marx could not be clearer on this. He referred to a "historical and moral component" that goes into the value of labor power, unlike that of other commodities.[37] This component is connected with the development of a society's productive capacity, so that in general "The more productive one country is relative to another in the world market, the higher will be its wages as compared with the other."[38] Thus, "the workers themselves... achieve a certain quantitative participation in the general growth of wealth."[39] Since we may assume that this participation is not unilaterally granted to workers by beneficient capitalists, we may conclude that it is won by the action of the workers themselves. The labor theory of value thus allows room for workers to exercise autonomy in the detemination of the value of labor power.

Did Marx undermine his category of "exploitation" when he granted (insisted upon) the above point? If in principle the value of labor power can expand along with productivity advances, how can one argue that it is impossible in principle for it to expand to the point where any notion of "exploitation" is ruled out? And if this cannot be done, how can the category "exploitation" follow that of "labor power as commodity" in a categorial ordering claiming systematic necessity?

A number of things must be distinguished: a) labor power sharing in the expansion of social wealth, b) this sharing being proportional to advances in productive capacity, c) this sharing being maintained over time, and d) this sharing of the fruits of productive advance excluding those who have not themselves contributed to the production of social wealth. The above objection implicitly assumes that all four can hold at once. But a) and b) are possibilities that may or may not occur, depending primarily on the level of growth in the economy and the organization, leadership, and combativity of

117

the working class. And c) is an impossibility, given the necessary structural tendencies in capitalism for there to be recurrent crises and for such crises to be overcome through declines in the living standards of the working class. However since the category of "crisis" has not yet been introduced into the theory, we cannot make use of this point here. This leaves d). Even under the most favorable circumstances it is not possible to prevent a considerable portion of the fruits of productive advance from being appropriated by those who in any plausible usage of the term must be considered unproductive, from the idle rich to speculators, from coupon clippers to the owners of consulting firms specializing in union-busting tactics. This is impossible for a very simple reason. Struggles regarding the social surplus do not take place in a neutral setting. They occur within the structure fixed previously in the category "labor power as commodity," i.e. within a framework where one party to the struggle owns and controls the society's productive resources and the other does not. If laborers were ever to threaten victory in all four areas this would set off a capital strike at once. In such an investment strike those who control society's productive resources (not to mention the media and the state apparatus) are, of course, better able to hold out. As long as society's productive resources are held in private hands, i.e. as long as the capital form is operative, it is necessarily the case that there is a general structural tendency for labor to be defeated. We may conclude, then, that the possibility of labor sharing in productive advances does not lessen the applicability of the category "exploitation" as long as the capital form remains in place.

In this context Marx's following remark on the Physiocrats is of interest. In it Marx insisted both that the value of labor power was not some fixed minimum and that this variability in its value does not undermine the notion of exploitation.

> Without being in any way clear as to the nature of value, they could conceive the value of labour-power, so far as it was necessary to their inquiry, as a definite magnitude. If moreover they made the mistake of conceiving this *minimum* as an unchangeable magnitude—which in their view is determined entirely by nature and not by *the stage of historical development, which is itself a magnitude subject to fluctuations*—this in no way affects the abstract correctness of their conclusions, since *the difference between the value of labour power and the value it creates does not at all depend on whether the value is assumed to be great or small*.[40]

Before turning to the next section it is interesting to note in passing that the necessary conceptual connection between "labor power as commodity" and "exploitation" can be held even if one does not accept the labor theory

118

of value. The key factor in the transition from the one category to the other is that the freedom and equality that appears to characterize the structure defined by the former category necessarily tends to give way to a structure characterized by inequality and coercion. Max Weber was one of Marx's most vehement critics. But the greatest of bourgeoise sociologists, unlike most of his epigone, was honest enough to admit that structural coercion underlies the wage contract:

> In a private economy. . . coercion is exercised to a considerable extent by the private owners of the means of production and acquisition, to whom the law guarantees their property and whose power can thus manifest itself in the competitive struggle of the market. . . In the labor market it is left to the "free" discretion of the parties to accept the conditions imposed by those who are economically stronger by virtue of the legal guaranty of their property. . . A legal order which contains ever so many "freedoms" and "empowerments" can nonetheless in its practical effects facilitate a quantitative and qualitative increase not only of coercion in general but quite specifically of authoritarian coercion.[41]

b) *Exploitation and constant capital*

The second Hegelian objection to the category "exploitation" proposed that Marx's derivation of the category depended upon an illegitimate and undialectical abstraction from the role played by constant capital. Once constant capital is acknowledged, the objection continued, one must acknowledge as well that some surplus labor must be undertaken to provide the constant capital necessary for production. Further, this may be to the benefit of wage labor; advanced constant capital may ease work conditions. Finally, mathematical economists have established that many different sorts of commodity inputs to production, those stemming from constant capital as well as from variable capital, can be said to have the property "exploitability." It was thus arbitrary for Marx to single out labor power for special consideration.

First of all, Marx is well aware that the structures defined by the categories "labor power as commodity" and "exploitation" involve constant capital. Without constant capital labor power would not be hired and no surplus could arise. In fact, Marx ridiculed as "absurd" a thought experiment of John Stuart Mill's precisely on the grounds that it overlooked the role of constant capital:

> With regard to this wonderful illustration, we note first of all that, as a result of a discovery, corn is supposed to be produced without seeds (raw materials) and without fixed capital; that is without raw materials and without tools, by

119

means of mere manual labour, out of air, water and earth. This absurd presupposition contains nothing but the assumption that a product can be produced *without constant capital*, that is, simply by means of newly applied labour.[42]

And this, Marx insisted, is "an almost impossible contingency in capitalist production."[43]

What of the fact that Marx set constant capital equal to zero in his calculations at this stage of the theory? There are two distinct things this might mean. It might be taken to imply that we can pretend that constant capital is not present on this stage of analysis. This would indeed be objectionable. But this is not Marx's reasoning. Consider the following passage in which Marx defends setting constant capital equal to zero: "This is merely an application of a mathematical rule, employed whenever we operate with constant and variable magnitudes, related to each other by the symbols of addition and subtraction only."[44] Marx's point is that the magnitude of constant capital is the same on both the input and the output side of the production equation *and thus can be cancelled.* This is entirely different from pretending that constant capital isn't present at all. Thus the objection we are considering misses the mark entirely.

For Marx constant capital is absolutely crucial in defining the category "labor power as commodity." Labor power becomes a commodity only when the means of production confront the workers as alien objects possessed by others, i.e. only when they take on the social form of constant capital. It is an essential feature of dialectical theories that earlier stages are incorporated into the later ones. Marx rigorously adhered to this. Throughout the remainder of *Capital* constant capital is thus retained as the social form of the means of production. This remains so even when, for certain purposes of calculation, constant capital is cancelled from both sides of an equation. If the means of production were not in the social form of constant capital there would be no exploitation of labor power as a commodity. Thus it can hardly be the case that Marx's theory of exploitation ignores constant capital.

It is also the case that workers may fare better in terms of work conditions under capitalism with advanced means of production than in nonexploitative situations in nonindustrialized settings.[45] In terms of the linear ordering of categories in *Capital*, once again we see that it is a mistake to see the progression simply as a dialectic in which negative forms follow negative forms. The theory in *Capital* is more complex than this. It is affirmative and critical at once. Despite all of its negative features, for Marx capitalism plays a progressive role in the development of human society. In that exploitation allows constant capital to expand, it too has a positive dimension for Marx.[46]

All of this implies that workers in principle *cannot* receive back all of what they have created. Workers cannot receive back the total product for their personal consumption and simultaneously enjoy the benefits of advanced productive capacity. Some of the total product must be set aside to produce, replace, and expand the means of production that are necessary for production. In the *Critique of the Gotha Program* Marx explicitly pointed out that in socialism too a portion of the total social product must be deducted for these (and other) purposes prior to the distribution of whatever remained to the workers.[47]

This brings us the the crucial point. Besides the quantitative dimension of the category "exploitation" a qualitive element also must be included. The production of a surplus product is a necessary condition for the applicability of Marx's concept of exploitation, but it is not a sufficient condition. To arrive at a sufficient condition we must add that the surplus product produced by wage laborers is not under their control. Since wage laborers do not possess such control under the capital form the category "exploitation" is operative, even if a portion of this surplus would have to be directed towards investment in means of production under any alternative social form.

This aspect of Marx's category has been widely overlooked.[48] This is connected to the way in which the Hegelian dimension of *Capital* has been overlooked. Later categories articulate structures of social ontology which retain the structures articulated by earlier categories. The structure articulated by the category of "exploitation" includes the lack of control over society's productive resources that is captured in the prior category "labor power as commodity." Without this qualitative dimension of the category "exploitation" one would have to draw the absurd conclusion that the model of society sketched in the *Critique of the Gotha Program* (in which distribution is based on the principle "to each according to his or her needs") also involves exploitation. After all, in this model some of the total social product would be invested in means of production rather than distributed back to those engaged in labor. However even if a *tremendously* greater percentage of the total social product were *not* distributed back to the producers than is currently the case under capitalism, this would not count as exploitation as long as the allocation were decided upon by those workers themselves within institutions of proletarian democracy.

This leaves the last question: why select the "exploitation" *of labor power* as the next category? Constant capital is equally necessary for producing a social surplus, and it is certainly a fact that those who have purchased

121

constant capital wish to "exploit" it as well.

We must keep in mind what precisely the theory in *Capital* is all about. At the most fundamental level it is a reconstruction in thought of the dialectic of a form of social production. The goal is to examine one specific form of social production in order to contrast it systematically with other forms. If our interest is to contrast one type of *social* division of labor with another, then clearly it is the position of the *social agents* of production that defines that structure.

The point can be put another way. In the capital form the defining social relation is essentially one in which one social group purchases the labor power of another social group. Means of production are not constant capital by nature. They are constant capital only within this specific social form. Therefore this social form is logically prior to constant capital. As Marx wrote:

> The utilization of the products of previous labour, of labour in general, as materials, tools, means of subsistence, is necessary if the worker wants to use his products for new production. This particular mode of consumption of his products is productive. But what on earth has this kind of utilization, this mode of consumption of his product, to do with the domination of his product over him, with its existence as capital, with the concentration in the hands of individual capitalists of the right to dispose of raw materials and means of subsistence and the exclusion of the workers from ownership of their products? What has it to do with the fact that first of all they have to hand over their product gratis to a third party in order to buy it back again with their own labour and, what is more, they have to give him more labour in exchange than is contained in the product and thus have to create more surplus product for him?[49]

The "exploitability" of the items of constant capital would be of great interest in a technical account of production. But in a theory of the social form of production only the exploitability of wage labor is of interest. We shall return to the question of constant capital at later stages of the theory.

4. Excursus on Roemer

John Roemer has constructed a number of thought experiments that seem to suggest that the Marxian category of exploitation is inadequate. Considering these cases in detail would take us too far afield. However I would like to note that every thought experiment introduced by Roemer to criticize the Marxian notion of exploitation grants all economic agents access to sufficient subsistence goods. Under this circumstance the move to the Marxian category of exploitation indeed cannot be carried out. But this is all irrelevant if we are talking about a situation in which inequalities generated by the capital form do not magically cease before some agents lose access to means of subsistence. And that, of course, was precisely what Marx was talking about.

For instance Roemer constructs a situation in which, starting from an initially egalitarian distribution of goods, an egalitarian distribution results despite the fact that some agents engage in surplus labor that creates a surplus product that is then appropriated by others.[50] Roemer concludes that according to Marx's notion of exploitation this situation would have to be termed "exploitative" despite its egalitarianism. If this were the case, then the Marxian notion would indeed generate a bizarre result. However the bizarre idea here is Roemer's belief that the situation he has constructed has anything to do with Marx's category of exploitation. Marx's systematic ordering progresses from "the capital form" to "exploitation." Roemer's example begins with a situation where the capital form is *not* operative (i.e. an initially egalitarian situation where all agents have access to means of subsistence). The fact that one need not move to the category of exploitation from *this* starting point is thus completely irrelevant to Marx's systematic claim. This is but one example of how the neglect of the dialectical (systematic) dimension of Marx's theory vitiates the attempt by analytical Marxists to go beyond Marx. I hope to establish this in detail in a subsequent work.

VII

Categories of the Production
Process Proper

Up until this point in the theory it has been fairly easy to trace the categorial ordering in *Capital*. From this point on, however, it becomes a bit more difficult to see the forest for the trees. Marx incorporated a tremendous amount of historical data in the remainder of Volume I, and he spent much less time accounting for the transitions from one determination to the next than he did at the beginning of the book. Some of the reasons for this are contingent.[1] But the fundamental reason is that Marx thought it quite important to transmit the history of struggles at the point of production. By no means do I wish to question this decision. However the aim of the present study is to bring out the *systematic* connections between the different stages of Marx's theory. The logic underlying Marx's categorial progression must be uncovered if we are to reply to the orthodox Hegelian assertion that *Capital* is a confused jumble of pseudo-systematic dialectics and empirical history.

A. Simple Cooperation and Capital as Principle of Organization

1. Hegelian Objections

The next major category after "exploitation" is the category "simple cooperation," introduced in Chapter XIII of Volume I. This category describes a structure within which laborers cooperate together in a process of production. The main structural tendency within this structure is for these laborers to generate greater output per unit input than that generated by

124

isolated individuals laboring apart. Marx then followed this with an analysis of cooperation organized along capitalist lines. Here the capitalist serves as commander (overseer, manager) of the production process, organizing a division of labor aimed at increasing relative surplus value within the firm.

Hegelians have raised a number of complaints against this part of Marx's account.[2] The first concerns the content of the category "simple cooperation." This has been taken to refer to a species-being model, an anthropological picture of humans working together in harmony. We have already mentioned the Hegelian point that the species-being model is a Utopian picture-thought that has no place in a dialectical theory.

Another complaint concerns the systematic place of this category. We may inquire whether it logically follows from the earlier categories and whether it logically leads to successive categories. On both counts "simple cooperation" seems to be lacking. Marx did not provide any systematic grounds for a transition from "exploitation" to "simple cooperation." Nor did Marx provide any systematic motive for moving from the positive picture of harmonious cooperation to the negative social form of production under capital. Lacing a satisfactory systematic account of the transition, Marx substituted a genetic story of how the capitalist manager came to replace the master of the workshop. This quid pro quo of the historical for the systematic does not measure up to the Hegelian standards of dialectical theory building that Marx himself elsewhere invoked.

When we ask why Marx might have abandoned dialectical logic at this point, Hegelians have argued that this was due to Marx's desire to construct a critical theory. Marx arbitrarily inserted a Utopian model into the theory to serve as a normative standard for the critique of cooperation organized by capital; in contrast to the pure model of cooperation, production under the control of the capitalist is "alienated." From the Hegelian perspective such an approach is inherently external to the object being investigated. And in comparison to such a Utopian picture *any* concrete social form would appear to involve negative features such as alienation.

2. Replies to Objections

Let us turn first to the question of the systematic ordering at this stage of the theory. "Simple cooperation" indeed does not follow from the category "exploitation." From the systematic point of view "exploitation" instead provides the principle for the derivation of "the capitalist production process proper." In dialectical terms "exploitation" fixes a structure of difference, where one class with an interest in furthering its appropriation of surplus value faces another whose fundamental interest is to resist that appropriation. In the production process proper these two antagonistic social forces are united in their difference at the point of production.

125

What role does "simple cooperation" play here? "Simple cooperation" does not characterize a specific stage in the reconstruction in thought of the value form. It characterizes instead the general region of social production. It expresses instead a fact that is invariant across *all* forms of social production: from the most alienating to the most nonalienating form of production, per capita output generally increases with cooperation. Why did Marx insert a discussion of "simple cooperation" in the middle of the dialectical reconstruction of the capital form? The obvious answer is that this is the aspect of social production in general that is of most relevance to the specific categories about to be introduced. Referring back to the general region of social production at this point makes us more sensitive to the unique features of the production process under the capital form.

This does not mean that the category "simple cooperation" expresses a species-being model to be used as a standard for an external critique of the capital form. "Simple cooperation" is not a picture of one special type of social production, characterized by completely harmonious labor relations. Once again, this category defines the entire region of social production, and not one supposedly pure form of it.

Turning back to the systematic progression in *Capital*, from a systematic perspective "simple cooperation" is not a principle for the derivation of "capital as principle of organization." Unlike "labor power as a commodity" and "exploitation," the category "the production process proper" has a number of different social forms ordered under it. The simplest and most abstract structure within which capital and labor are united at the point of production is one in which capital is simply a principle for the organization of the production process. Capital simply unites wage laborers at a common point of production, leaving the actual labor process untouched. This can be termed the "formal subsumption of labor under capital," or "capital as principle of organization (of the production process)." The ordering connecting the categories here can be depicted as follows:

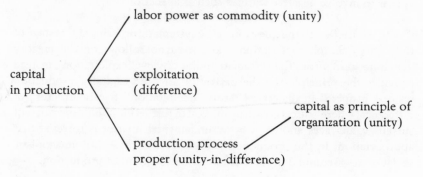

We can now move on to the next stage in the dialectic of the production process proper.

[handwritten: ⌐──> Process ; temporal]

B. Capital as Principle of Transformation

1. Manufacturing, Big Industry, and the Alienation of Wage Labor

In Chapter XIII of *Capital I* Marx described how the formal subsumption of labor was historically the first stage of capitalist production. Marx then went on to discuss two subsequent historical stages, characterized by the real subsumption of labor under capital. The first is captured with the category of "manufacturing," introduced in Chapter XIV of Volume I. Here instead of simply overseeing different producers cooperating while employing traditional techniques, the capitalist transforms the labor process by creating the detail laborer. This expands the relative surplus value produced. It also transforms social relations within the work process; increased planning on the part of the capitalist meets its dialectical opposite in the workers' increased loss of control on the shop floor. Manufacturing is then followed by "big industry," where new machinery is introduced that increases output per worker. Marx's discussion of this stage in Volume I, Chapter XV (and continuing in Parts V and VI, Chapters XVI-XXII), is filled with great historical detail. He seems to account for the transition to big industry in terms of the historical limits of manufacturing, especially its inability to produce a sufficient output to meet the demand of what is, for the first time, truly a world market. With big industry the loss of control on the shop floor is increased. The alienation workers experience increases as well, as capital's domination over wage labor advances.

2. Hegelian Objections

It should come as no surprise that Hegelians would object to how Marx's theory unfolds here. There are two Hegelian criticisms that can be made in this context. The first refers to the linear progression of the theory. The second concerns the categorization of the captial/wage labor relation.

a) The linear ordering

Marx himself recognized that the linear progression in which categories are introduced according to a strictly systematic dialectical logic is compromised when transitions are justifed historically.[3] And yet that is precisely what seems to occur in this part of his theory. To some extent Marx proposed a causal account of the rise of manufacturing and big industry, seeing them as brought about by the extension of demand in the world market, improved communications and transportation, and so on. To some extent he proposed teleological considerations to account for the change: manufacturing must give way to big industry because it is

127

capitalism's mission to "develop the productive forces." If *Capital* were to be measured by the standards of history alone, these explanations might warrant consideration.[4] But when measured by the standards of categorial theories ordered by dialectical logic, neither explanation carries any weight whatsoever. As Marx himself insisted, the historical order and the systematic order are not isomorphic. Any argument that derives a conclusion regarding the latter from the former is inherently fallacious.

b) *Wesenslogik*

Two closely related points can be made under this heading. First, when Marx discussed the capital/wage labor relationship within the context of capital's transformation of the labor process, he conceived it as an essence structure in which labor power is viewed as an "appendage" to capital. The point can be put as follows: "Capital, together with the laborers subordinate to it, is treated as a dominant historical subject...If such a dominant historical subject is granted, no falsification of the theory can ever be proposed. Everything occurring in the economic world must appear as exploitation. A non-dual, pluralistic social structure, or a balance of forces between capital and labor that hinders exploitation, is not thinkable—and not describable...The relation of capital and labor is grasped without compromise as 'essence' and 'moment'."[5] But even if we grant for the sake of the argument that coercion characterized earlier structures in the theory, when we turn to the more concrete and complex structure of the production process proper there are new determinations missing from the earlier, more abstract, levels. These new determinations might well reverse any structural tendency towards coercion that held on the more abstract levels. More specifically, within the present level wage laborers are set to work together at a common site of production. This leads to a structural tendency for associations among laborers to arise, a tendency that is introduced here for the first time in the theory. Could this factor not reverse the dominance of capital? Could it not lead to a notion (*Begriff*) structure within which labor and capital are co-principles, as opposed to an essence (*Wesen*) structure in which capital alone reigns supreme? If so, then Marx's use of categories taken from the second section of Hegel's *Logic* must be rejected.

A second reason for Marx's use of *Wesen* categories in describing the capital/wage labor relation here was his belief that there is a necessary structural tendency for wage labor to be alienated within capitalist production. A Hegelian could ask whether Marx established the systematic connection between capital in production and alienated labor. When Marx discussed alienation at this stage of *Capital* he referred to the horrors of the Industrial Revolution. He described in considerable historical detail the historical shapes alienation took among factory workers in England in the eighteenth and nineteenth centuries. But how is this of *systematic* relevance? How does this establish that in principle *any* transformation of the labor process imposed by capital to futher surplus value must be alienating? Has not Marx illicitly substituted historical stories for the systematic theoretical argument that would be required for a necessary connection to be established? After all, it may be the case that alienation is not fundamentally connected to the general capital form, or to capital in the production process. In may be that it is instead connected to the specific phemonema of manufacturing and big industry when these phenomena emerge in *any* social form of production. In this case the alienation that Marx described would follow from the process of industrialization, and not from the inner nature of capital.

Obviously this is no mere theoretical question regarding how different categories should be systematically ordered. Whether one derives "alienation" from the capital form or from industrialization determines one's position on the practical question of working towards an alternative to capitalism. With the former ordering, practical struggles in this direction have a theoretical justification they would lack if alienation is an inevitable by-product of industrial development within *any* social form. By opting for the former Marx could be accused of designing his systematic ordering in a fashion that leads to the practical conclusion he wished to obtain.[6]

3. Replies to Objection

a) The linear ordering

From a systematic perspective the move from the formal subjugation of wage labor under capital to its real subsumption in manufacturing and big industry is indeed inadequate. At best it presents an ideal type of the historical development England underwent in the centuries prior to Marx. No argument can establish any logical necessity for this pattern being repeated elsewhere.[7] It is true that Marx did trace this historical picture in great detail. However we cannot conclude from this that he introduced historical considerations in order to substitute them for a systematic progression of economic categories. An alternative reading is that Marx did provide a distinct systematic argument for a categorial derivation, with "manufacturing" and "big industry" providing historical examples of the derived category.

The previous category derived in the systematic ordering was "capital as principle of organization." This category fixes an immediate unity of capital and wage labor at the point of production. Capital unifies different labor processes under one roof in an immediate and direct fashion. Within this structure it is necessarily the case that a tension arises between i) the inherent tendency of capital to maximize surplus value, and ii) a production process that has not been transformed to maximize surplus value. If we add to this the power that comes from capital's ownership and control over the various factors of production, we may conclude that it is necessarily the case that a structural tendency emerges for capital to initiate a transformation of the production process. This points beyond unity to difference in a number of ways. For one thing, capital declares its antagonism to any from of labor process it has not transformed. The element of difference also comes to the fore in that capital will seek a transformation that increases surplus value even at the cost of increased exploitation, increased alienation, and the formation of a reserve army of the unemployed, all of which are against the interests of labor. Further, at the point of production and elsewhere, labor tends to resist capital's attempt to transform the labor process whenever this ignores labor's interests. For this reason too the category that captures this structure is one of difference.[8] Given these structural tendencies immanent within the structure defined by the category "capital as principle of organization," dialectical logic mandates a systematic transition to a category of difference, which may be termed "capital as principle of transformation."

A whole series of historical examples can be introduced to illustrate the category "capital as principle of transformation." Marx discussed "manufacturing" and "big industry," but a myriad of combined and uneven forms that have had historical reality could be selected. The key point is that these historical illustrations may claim a place in *Capital* without undermining the systematic nature of the theory. Reference to historical matters thus does not *replace* the logical argument here. It *complements* it by providing empirical examples of a categorial structure.

This approach also can provide a reply to those who find *Capital* to be an outdated reflection of nineteenth century capitalism. Many today believe that we are no longer in the stage of big industry. Instead the present historical stage of production might be better captured with a term such as *the global factory.*[9] If one accepted this view, it would follow that *Capital* is outdated in this respect. But if one wishes to grasp the intelligibility of the historical move from big industry to the global factory, it is impossible to avoid employing categories such as "the capital form" and, on a more concrete level, "capital as a principle for transformation" of the labor process. And one needs to grasp the systematic place of such categories. For example, an adequate understanding of the rise of the global factory presupposes not only the concept of the transformation of the labor process, but also the more basic concepts of "labor power as commodity" and "exploitation." In this sense *Capital* is *not* outdated. For how could a theory become outdated by the process in which new historical illustrations of its categories arise?

130

b) Wesenslogik

There are two things to consider under this heading: can wage labor be a co-principle of production alongside capital? and might the alienation in the capitalist production process be a function of industrialization rather than the capital form? If these questions are answered in the affirmative, then Marx's use of a categorial framework taken from the section of Hegel's *Logic* discussing "essence" is inappropriate.

With regards to the former issue, Marx certainly did not make labor into the passive victim of the unfolding of capital's inexorable logic. Consider the following passage: "So soon as the gradually surging revolt of the working-class compelled Pariament to shorten compulsorily the hours of labour..."[10] In this characteristic passage labor is by no means seen as a puppet of capital. Likewise capital cannot transform the labor process at will. Through its self-organziation the working class is capable of engaging in struggles at the point of production over this transformation. The eventual results reflect this struggle rather than the mere acquiesence of labor.[11] In other words, the capital/wage labor relation is one of mutuality. Each pole is mediated through the other; neither can reduce the other to a mere moment of itself.[12] And in principle each side can attain a self-consciousness of this reciprocal interdependence. Does not this suggest that capital and wage labor are co-principles in a dynamic unity-in-difference that can be categorized in *Begriff* terms?

Despite all this, Marx insisted that "essence" is nonetheless an appropriate categorial framework for grasping the intelligibility of the process he described. Why? The chief reason is because as long as the capital form is operative the weapons at the disposal of capital are necessarily far more extensive than the weapons in labor's arsenal. Labor is capable of resisting capital's demands, especially when it organizes itself. However in non-revolutionary situations this resistance is primarily defensive in nature. There is no contradiction in Marx's perspective as long as we recall that different sorts of structures fit under the general heading of "essence." In some, individuals have no independence whatsoever from the underlying essence. In others, individuals are constantly asserting an independence that is continually being negated by the underlying essence. For Marx the former is not an accurate description of the capital/labor relationship, while the latter is.

Marx has two arguments in support of this claim. Ths first refers to the manner in which investment decisions are imposed upon wage labor. As long as the capital form is in place those who control capital decide investment strategy. This simple fact undermines any attempt to view wage labor as a full co-principle in the production process. It also makes whatever fruits do result from labor's independent self-organization extremely

131

precarious. For a number of structural tendencies necessarily arise from this arrangement. If labor in a particular area has won a share of increasing productivity, capital investments over time will be made elsewhere, *ceteris paribus*. If labor has strong organizations in one particular area, capital investment over time will generally be made elsewhere. If the skills of a particular labor force are required for a particular labor process, so that investment in lower-paid and less-organized areas is not immediately feasible, then capital investment will generally be made in forms of technology that reduce or eliminate those skills. This does not imply that capital can ever successfully reduce labor to a mere appendage of itself. But it does suggest that labor's capacity for autonomous activity is severely restricted as long as the capital form is operative, and that any attempt to see labor as an equal co-principle alongside capital is to be dismissed.

This leads us back to the second issue, whether Marx mistakenly blamed capitalism for inevitable negative features of industrialization. It is certainly correct to say that industrialization has numerous negative features that would hold in any social context. For example, it always involves a risk of injury. But not everything with negative features is properly termed "alienating" in the Marxist sense of the term. Many forms of physical exercise, for instance, also involve a degree of risk, yet we generally do not say that those who engage in these forms of exercise are alienated. This suggests that the crucial component of alienation in the workplace concerns whether or not the risks (and other negative features) inherently connected with industrialization are freely taken on by those exposed to them, analogously to the way risks are freely taken on by those who exercise. The above argument that capital and wage labor are not co-principles of production implies that this is not generally the case. The category of "capital as principle of transformation" follows "labor power as commodity" and "exploitation," dialectically incorporating the structures articulated in those earlier categories. We have seen that a form of structural coercion operates in the wage agreement, stemming from a lack of material equality in the contracting partners. There is a structural tendency for the production process that follows the wage agreement to reflect this coercion. "Alienation" can be defined for now as the manifestation of this structural tendency within the production process proper. (A fuller definition will be provided in section C.4 below.)

This argument does not imply that alienation in the production process could not follow from other social forms besides the capital form. That remains an open question. At this point of the theory it also remains open whether the later determinations of the capital form might reverse the structural tendency to alienation. But Marx had good reasons to assert that

132

on the present categorial level capital is an essence that lords over the workers subjected to it in the production process. This topic will arise again in the section on accumulation, to which we now turn.

C. Accumulation

1. Accumulation and Simple Accumulation

The transition from "capital as principle of transformation" to "accumulation" is straightforward (Captial I, part VII).[13] The former defines a structure in which capital is able to increase the surplus it appropriates by transforming the labor process. It is necessarily the case that there is a structural tendency for these results to be reinvested in the next period of production. And in order to be reinvested, of course, these results must be accumulated rather than consumed. "Capital as principle of transformation" was a category of difference, which stressed the antagonism between capital and wage labor at the point of production. "Accumulation" unites the transformation of the labor process set off by capital, and the forms of resistance labor takes in response, within a single on-going process, a unity-in-difference.

Unlike "capital as principle of organization" and "capital as principle of transformation," "accumulation" is itself a universal category whose full determination requires a dialectic of forms of its own. Once we have introduced the notion of accumulation it follows at once that the simplest category on this stage will be "simple accumulation," derived by Marx in Chapter XXIII. In the structure defined by this category, each subsequent cycle begins with the same level of means of production and labor power as the previous one. Everything else appropriated is unproductively consumed by the capitalists in control of production. This is clearly the least complex form of accumulation possible, hence it should come first in the systematic ordering here.

2. Expanded Accumulation and Original Accumulation: A Hegelian Critique

The other main categories discussed in this section of Capital are "expanded accumulation" (considered in Chapters XXIV and XXV of Volume I) and "original (or primitive) accumulation" (Part VIII, Chapters XXVI-XXXIII). "Expanded accumulation" defines a structure in which part of the surplus appropriated by capitalists is devoted to increased investment in constant capital and wage labor. "Original accumulation" describes the initial process whereby the means of production were appropriated by the newly rising capitalist class, at the cost of the

133

expropriation of formerly self-sufficient peasants. Both of these determinations present difficulties from a systematic perspective.

The category "expanded accumulation" follows that of "simple accumulation." The move from "simple accumulation" to "expanded accumulation" seems to be based upon a teleological-functional account of a historical process. Capital's mission is to develop the productive forces; this is accomplished better under expanded accumulation than simple accumulation; therefore the move to expanded accumulation is made. Even if teleological-functional explanations were not as questionable as they are, they still would not be equivalent to a systematic derivation according to a dialectical logic.

Regarding the move to original accumulation, the case is even worse. In ordering "accumulation" after the category "exploitation" Marx proposed to explain the expansion of capital by surplus value extracted from labor power. The latter is systematically prior to the former; it is a principle while the former is what is principled. But the structure defined by the category "exploitation," in which surplus value was initially produced, also required the presence of constant capital. For the sake of explicating the category of surplus value Marx set constant capital $= 0$. But this was, of course, a theoretical abstraction that was not realistic even on the abstract level. Accordingly, we now face a paradox: surplus value, which is supposed to explain constant capital, itself *presupposes* the constant capital it is to explain. In order to break through this circularity Marx distinguished subsequent constant capital, derived from surplus value, from the constant capital accumulated at the initial stage. This created the problem of accounting for the initial constant capital without undermining the claim that all subsequent constant capital rests on exploitation. Marx did this by interrupting the systematic progression of categories and introducing a historical account of primitive accumulation. Marx recounted the acts of extra-economic force whereby peasants lost their independence and became wage laborers, while simultaneously initial capital was being accumulated in the hands of those who were to hire them. There is not the slightest pretence here of adhering to systematic considerations. Instead the systematic progression was abandoned as Marx abruptly shifted to a historical account.

From this three other Hegelian criticisms follow. First, in a systematic theory historical considerations can have only an illustrative function, whereas here a genetic account has exclusive emphasis and is not subordinate to any systematic explanation.[14] Second, the foundation for the theory is now a merely contingent one, as contingent as the historical story Marx related. Third, capital is treated as a continuous historical subject, whose present form bears the trace of its past guilt. This arbitrarily excludes the possibility that capital today may not have any historical continuity with the initial accumulation. It excludes a priori the possibility that capital could be accumulated in quite other processes (e.g. abstinence or credit) than the acts of violence Marx described: "Capital...is not a continuous historical subject with its origin in original accumulation, in social repression. It continually forms itself anew without such an origin, through refraining from consumption, through abstinence and the building of stocks...Capital is formed inner-economically through saving and credit, where interest is paid back through the production made possible by capital."[15] Marx can once again be accused of having committed a petitio, of structuring his theory to get to the negative results he wished to obtain.[16]

Finally, even if for the sake of the argument we assume that the theory of original accumulation could historically account for the initial constant capital without undermining the systematic theory, there is still the question whether the systematic account is cogent in itself. An orthodox Hegelian would still insist that constant capital is set equal to zero, initially, solely in order to allow the subsequent derivation of constant capital from exploited labor power. The ordering does not stem from the immanent nature of the capitalist mode of production itself; it stems instead from how the theory is constructed. And Marx constructed the theory to get to negative conclusions regarding this mode of production.

3. An Alternative Reading

a) The systematic derivation of expanded accumulation

When we examine the categoral progression initiated by "simple accumulation" we do indeed face a problem from the standpoint of dialectical logic. This problem must be resolved before we can reply to the ojbections mentioned in the previous section.

On any given categorial level the dialectical explication of the category defining that level involves a logical progression from an initial category of simple unity, to a determination where the moment of difference is stressed, to one of unity-in-difference. Only after this sequence has been completed has the theory attained closure on the given level, thus providing systematic grounds for a transition to the next level. In the present context the defining category is "accumulation." "Simple accumulation" clearly is a category of simple unity, the first step in a systematic grasp of "accumulation" on this level of abstraction. Dialectical logic demands that if a reconstruction is to proceed in a systematic, step-by-step fashion a category of difference comes next. But what is the category of difference that follows? Neither of the two candidates provided by Marx, expanded accumulation and original accumulation, fits. Leaving aside original accumulation for the moment, I believe there is a systematic imperative to insert a determination between simple

135

and expanded accumulation. This category should fix a structure that articulates some element of difference that necessarily emerges as a dominant structural tendency within simple accumulation. And it should fix a structure that itself necessarily has a dominant structural tendency pointing towards expanded accumulation.

One candidate might be a category that referred to spheres of production not yet incorporated under the capital form, such as domestic labor in the household or simple commodity production. These spheres could be considered as an element of difference relative to simple accumulation in that they are not included within the circuit of the simple accumulation of capital. Then expanded accumulation could be considered as the unity-in-difference that imposes the capital form on what had previously been "different" from it. For example, clothes were once provided through unpaid domestic labor or through purchases from simple commodity producers. With the expansion of capital accumulation clothes became commodities purchased from the textile industry.

This proposal will not work. Domestic labor has already been introduced with the category of "labor power as a commodity." And any reference to simple commodity production introduces a reference to something outside the capital form, which does not seem appropriate within a dialectic of the capital form. We require an element of difference latent in simple accumulation itself, something that when explicitly posited stands both in opposition to, and in systematic connection with, the structure of simple accumulation.

Each succeeding category incorporates structures defined by earlier categories. "Simple accumulation" incorporates the drive to appropriate surplus value defined by the categories "exploitation," "capital as principle of organization," and "capital as principle of transformation." From this it follows that it is necessarily the case that a dominant structural tendency will arise for surplus production to proceed past the point where the consumption needs of capitalists and the investment requried to maintain production at the same level are provided for. Alternatively, even if the consumption needs of capitalists were always to increase, there would be a tendency for surplus production to occur at a faster rate than the rate of this increase. Either way simple accumulation tends to proceed to the point where a reserve fund will slowly accumulate. This fund, not being incorporated within simple accumulation, constitutes a moment of "difference" standing in opposition to the structure of simple accumulation. Expanded accumulation would then incorporate this difference within a structure of unity-in-difference, as is systematically required. This occurs when some of the surplus is invested productively in expanded means of production and labor

136

power in order to lead to a higher level of production. With this the dialectic of the forms of accumulation, and of the production process proper, has reached closure.

b) *Replies to Objection*

On the above reading there is no confusion between system and history at this stage of Marx's theory. Whether simple accumulation historically led to expanded accumulation is irrelevant to the categorial ordering. (Historically, of course, the earliest capitalist firms were most definitely already engaged in *expanded* accumulation.) The systematic justification of a category rests solely upon whether it adds a further determination to the categories that have gone before, and whether it furthers the explication of the form of social production being investigated. From this point of view the present set of categories fits plausibly in the linear progression constituting the reconstruction of capitalism in thought.

Turning to the category "original accumulation," it is true that a historical account of the transition to capitalism is not part of a systematic account of capitalism. The former cannot be seamlessly incorporated within the latter; it requires a different sort of theory with a different object and a different method. But there is no reason for us to read the discussion of original accumulation as if it were intended as part of Marx's systematic theory. It neither has a place in the linear progression of categories proper, nor is it a historical example of a category on the present stage of the theory. It is instead a *digression* from Marx's systematic ordering, however important it may be for understanding the historical transition from precapitalist society to capitalism. As such the fact that it does not fit into the systematic ordering is, of course, exactly what is to be expected.

Two sorts of objections could still be posed to the category "original accumulation." First, one might hold the view that an author can never be allowed to introduce digressions. This perspective is rather odd, to say the least. Or it could be held that this particular digression is more than a mere digression in that it prejudices the course of the systematic theory. Hegelians have argued that original accumulation both introduces contingencies in the course of the theory and unfairly saddles present capitalism with historical guilt.

As for the objection that original accumulation reduces Marx's theory to contingencies, the presence of contingencies in the historical process whereby certain structures arise does not imply that no logical ordering of these structures or derivation of essential structural tendencies is possible. Marx's historical digression on the topic of original accumulation thus in no sense undermines the systematic rigor of his theory.

What of the claim that original accumulation saddles capitalism with

137

guilt it does not deserve? On this view capital can today be formed through saving and credit. Whatever social repression occurred in the initial accumulation process is therefore irrelevant. Against this we must keep in mind the following. First, primitive accumulation is not something that took place once and for all in the past. As capitalism continues its expansion throughout the globe and into new areas of social life, primitive accumulation continues as well. Second, there is no question in Marx's account of the sins of the parent being visited upon the child. It is a central thesis of the present section of *Capital* that the mechanisms of simple and expanded accumulation are *not* the same as those of original accumulation. Marx was thus well aware that any evaluation of the latter could not be carried over to the former modes of accumulation.

Finally, "credit" and "abstinence" can be taken in two senses. They could be taken in an ahistorical fashion, as referring to common features of many different types of social production. But then they do not seem to be appropriate candidates for the theoretical task at hand, the contrast of the capitalist form of social production with other forms. Or these terms can be taken in a sense that applies to capitalism specifically. But then they must be recognized as relatively concrete and complex categories that do not belong at the present level of abstraction. "Abstinence" leads to capital accumulation only in the presence of other factors, i.e. only when an initial capital fund that could be consumed nonproductively is present. Others who lack such a fund engage in many forms of abstinence that do *not* lead to capital accumulation. "Abstinence" does not explain where this fund comes from. Likewise the initial capital lent out in credit is presupposed when the capital accumulation created by credit is discussed. Explanations of capital accumulation based on abstinence and credit thus must themselves account for the initial distribution of resources. Marx's category of "original accumulation" addresses this problem head on, while the alternative explanations do not. In other words, "abstinence" and "credit" *presuppose* a functioning system of capital accumulation. Once capital accumulation is established, then the abstinence of those with capital resources can indeed be a factor in explaining why of two economic agents with comparable initial resources one expanded and one did not. Likewise once capital accumulation is established those with excess capital resources will lend them out on credit, and access to credit can indeed be a factor in explaining why of two capitalists with comparable initial resources one was able to expand and the other was not. But both of these categories serve as principles for explaining the relative positions of capitalists *within* an already functioning accumulation process. They thus do not account for that process itself. They are principles on a much more concrete level than is appropriate to consider at this stage of the systematic progression of socio-economic categories.

The question of the systematic place of constant capital remains. I have already noted that from a concrete quantitative economic standpoint there is no doubt that constant capital is a factor coexisting simultaneously with labor. From this perspective there is hence little justification for seeing concrete capital as somehow "subsequent" to labor. A Leontiff input/ output scheme treating all factors simultaneously would be more appropriate. However before concluding that Marx made an error in attempting to order constant capital subsequently to surplus value and the production process there are three points that should be considered.

The first point is the familiar one already mentioned in the above discussion of "labor power as commodity." The project of *Capital* is not simply the presentation of quantitative models of the concrete economy. The point is to make intelligible a *social* model of production, and that involves uncovering the basic social relations that define that mode of production. In Marx's view the basic social relation of capitalism is the capital/wage labor relation. Constant capital is certainly relevant to this social relation, but from the standpoint of social relations it occurs within the context of the capital/wage labor relation, and not vice-versa.[17]

Another way of stating the same point is to note that placing the introduction of constant capital later in the systematic progression is necessary if a fundamental category mistake is to be avoided. This is the category mistake of treating the nonsocial as social. It often appears that structural tendencies stemming from social relations are instead due to machinery.[18] Two examples are mentioned by Marx. One involves the familiar claim that machinery "causes" unemployment. Marx insisted this is not the case:

> It is an undoubted fact that machinery, as such, is not responsible for "setting free" the workman from the means of subsistence. It cheapens and increases production in that branch which it seizes on, and at first makes no change in the mass of the means of subsistence produced in other branches. Hence, after its introduction, the society possesses as much, if not more, of the necessaries of life than before, for the labourers thrown out of work; and that quite apart from the enormous share of the annual produce wasted by the non-workers.[19]

The best way of combatting theoretically the illusion that machinery is the source of social problems such as unemployment is to consider the social relations defining the capital form in themselves prior to turning to constant capital.

The other example involves the claim that "capital" has certain productive powers of its own, as when machinery is referred to as "capital."

139

But capital is a social relation. It is a social form that may be imposed upon machinery, but it is not immanent in the machinery itself. This is a crucial respect in which Marx's position differs from that of other political economists: "The economists continually mix up the definite, specific form in which these things constitute capital with their nature as things and as simple elements of every labour process. The mystification contained in capital—as *employer of labour*—is not explained by them, but it is constantly expressed by them unconsciously, for it is inseparable from the material aspect of capital."[20] In order to become conscious of the true state of affairs a theory is required that considers the "specific form" of capital initially, and only then moves to consider machinery *qua* determined by that specific form.

The second point is also familiar. As orthodox Hegelians continually insist, the purpose of a systematic ordering is *not* to set out the factual genesis of its object. To set constant capital equal to zero at the beginning would be nonsense if this were intended as a genetic claim; surplus value is never accumulated without constant capital being presupposed. But the point of a dialectical reconstruction is *not* to provide a genetic account. From the fact that in the real order constant capital is not subsequent to variable capital we cannot conclude that this is the case in the systematic ordering. Unless of course we hold that one ordering maps directly onto the other, and this is a thesis rejected by both Hegel and Marx.

Third, there is an argument from intentionality. In general the underlying intention and the end intended must be considered as being prior to the means employed to attain the intended end. There is certainly reciprocal impact here; the selection of ends must be guided by the available means. Still the ends have conceptual priority in theorizing means/ends relations. Now labor is an intentional process. Within this process constant capital has the position of means, with the ends (e.g. appropriation of surplus value, etc.) determined by the dynamics of the capital/wage labor relation. Therefore this social relation has conceptual priority. Further, just as constant capital has no ends of its own, so too it is not set in motion by itself. Constant capital is set in motion by wage labor, no matter how much the reverse often appears to be the case.[21] Labor may be employed as a means for the accumulation of capital; the end of the labor process may be something from which laborers are alienated. Nonetheless constant capital remains a means employed by labor to attain that end. Therefore the capital/wage labor relation may properly be treated before constant capital in a linear ordering of categories reconstructing the intelligibility of capitalism.[22]

4) Wesenslogik

a) Hegelian objections

The dominant role given to capital at earlier stages of the theory is continued the the categories of accumulation. Once again capital is seen as an essence in the Hegelian sense, a force over and above individuals. It develops from the production of surplus value to its accumulation through the unfolding of its own inner nature. And once again it may be asked whether the theory should have thematized co-principles alongside capital. If so, Marx's use of a *Wesenlogik* prejudged the analysis, for this framework rules out a priori the possibility of there being other co-principles alongside capital.

Once again we must consider whether wage labor can be conceived as a co-principle alongside capital, rather than as a subordinate moment of capital. Two points have been mentioned by orthodox Hegelians in this connection. First, when we consider whether workers are subjected to capital as an alien force, we must remember that accumulation can bring with it vast wage increases. In fact, it is in principle possible for wages to rise so high that expanded accumulation breaks down and only simple accumulation is possible.[23] How could this occur if wage labor were not a co-principle in the accumulation process? Second, a crucial component of Marx's argument for interpreting capital in essence terms is the claim that the accumulation process includes a structural tendeny for the formation of a reserve army of the unemployed (see sections 2-5 of Chapter XXV, *Capital I*). The existence of such a reserve army supposedly ensures that the asymmetry in the capital/wage labor relation remains; i.e. it ensures the continued subordination of labor. But an orthodox Hegelian wishing to question Marx's use of *Wesenlogik* might argue against deriving the concept of the reserve army from accumulation. It is logically possible that accumulation leads to an expansion of labor-intensive industries, rather than an expansion of capital-intensive ones. When the former occurs there is a structural mechanism leading to the elimination of unemployment, rather than to the formation of a reserve army of the unemployed.[24]

b) Replies

We have already noted that Marx did not define the relatively abstract category "labor power as commodity" in terms of a minimal set of subsistence goods. The structure defined by this category incorporates the possibility of an expansion of the consumption bundle whose worth defines the value of labor power. The more concrete and complex structure defined by the category "accumulation" does not introduce any new determination of labor power that would reverse this. Thus on the present level as well there is no thesis of minimal subsistence wages. Indeed, on the present, more concrete, stage of *Capital* Marx went beyond merely affirming the possibility of the value of labor power being above minimal subsistence needs. He specified the factors within the structure of accumulation that tend to bring this about: the expanded accumulation of a surplus product

141

due to productivity advances, a period of rapid capital accumulation, and the association of workers together in order to bargain with capital collectively. If these conditions are met, labor can win for itself a share in the expanded surplus product. Marx could not be more explicit about this: "It is possible with an increasing productiveness of labour, for . . . a constant growth in the mass of the labourer's means of subsistence."[25] But does the possibility of higher real wages imply that wage labor could be a co-principle of accumulation under the capital form? In the previous chapter the question was posed whether the "historical and moral" component of the value of labor power undermined the category "exploitation." I argued that it did not on the grounds that the key to this category is not the quantitative extent of the surplus product as much as it is the control of this surplus. This same argument can be made regarding accumulation. Just as "exploitation" fundamentally involved the question of the control of the surplus product, so too Marx's theory of accumulation revolves around this as well.

> Just as little as better clothing, food, and treatment, and a larger peculium, do away with the exploitation of the slave, so little do they set aside that of the wage-worker. A rise in the price of labour, as a consequence of accumulation of capital, only means, in fact, that the length and weight of the golden chain the wage-worker has already forged for himself, allow of a relaxation of the tension of it.[26]

We cannot discuss the capital/wage labor relation as if the level of real wages were the only relevant factor. That is no more than part of the story. An essence structure is not operative simply because some sort of disparity is present. For essence categories to be applicable one pole of the relation must reduce the other pole to being a subordinate moment of an on-going process under the former's direction. Under capitalism workers are personally free. However capital is the alpha and the omega of the accumulation process. Wage labor has a role in this process only in so far as it serves the interests of capital. The conditions of production that are generated in the accumulation process confront wage laborers as material facts, not under their control.[27] This is the phenomenon of alienation, which has both an objective and a subjective dimension. Alienation is objective in that it is objectively the case that accumulated investment funds, means of production, and produced inventories, confront wage laborers as "other."[28] The lived experience of this confrontation is the subjective aspect of alienation. What is of importance here is not that the apparatus of production expands as the accumulation process proceeds. This would be a feature of any non-stagnant social system, including one

142

with worker ownership and control. What is of importance instead is the specific social form this accumulation takes under capitalism, a form in which the place of wage labor is structurally subordinate:

> As long as the individual capitalist continues to operate on the same scale of production (or on an expanding one), the replacement of capital appears as an operation which does not affect the worker, since, if the means of production belonged to the worker, he would likewise have to replace them out of the gross product in order to continue reproduction on the same scale or on an expanded scale (and the latter too is necessary because of the natural increase of population). But this affects the worker in three respects. 1) The perpetuation of the means of production as property alien to him, as capital, perpetuates his condition as wage-worker and hence his fate of always having to work part of his labour-time for a third person for nothing. 2) The extension of these means of production, alias accumulation of capital, increases the extent and the size of the classes who live on the surplus labour of the worker; it worsens his position *relatively* by augmenting the relative wealth of the capitalist and his copartners, by further increasing his relative surplus labour through the division of labour, etc., and reduces that part of the gross product which is used to pay wages; finally, since the conditions of labour confront the individual worker in an ever more gigantic form and increasingly as social forces, the chance of his taking possession of them himself as is the case in small-scale industry, disappears.[29]

Even if real wages continually increase, the objective and subjective alienation built into the structure of accumulation prevents wage labor from being considered a co-principle of accumulation.[30] But it is also the case that the control over the accumulation process granted to the holders of capital keeps any rise in the value of labor power in check. What would happen if expanded accumulation were threatened by high wages? Clearly—and in the short term—either capital investment would be made in labor eliminating or deskilling technologies, were they available, or capital investment would cease in this particular firm and seek more profitable investment outlets elsewhere. Wage levels high enough to prevent expanded reproduction are thus at best highly temporary exceptions in developed capitalism:

> If the quantity of unpaid labour supplied by the working-class, and accumulated by the capitalist class, increases so rapidly that its conversion into capital requires an extraordinary addition of paid labour, then wages rise, and, all other circumstances remaining equal, the unpaid labour diminishes in proportion. But as soon as this diminution touches the point at which the surplus-labour that nourishes capital is no longer supplied in normal quantity, a reaction sets in: a smaller part of revenue is capitalised, accumulation lags,

143

and the movement of rise in wages receives a check. The rise of wages therefore is confined within limits that not only leave intact the foundations of the capitalist system, but also secure its reproduction on a progressive scale... The very nature of accumulation excludes every rise in the price of labour, which could seriously imperil the continual reproduction, on an ever-enlarging scale, of the capitalistic relation. It cannot be otherwise in a mode of production in which the labourer exists to satisfy the needs of self-expansion of existing values, instead of, on the contrary, material wealth existing to satisfy the needs of development on the part of the labourer.[31]

The second objection to Marx's use of a *Wesenslogik* in which wage labor is but a moment in the "self-expansion of existent value" had to do with how accumulation creates a reserve army of the unemployed. Against this the possibility was suggested that an expansion of labor-intensive industries could eliminate the reserve army. If wages are sufficiently low, then further investment may well be made in labor-intensive industries. As long as there is a sufficient pool of available cheap labor this may continue until the reserve army disappears. In the objection considered above, the story concludes here. However it is interesting to consider what will tend to occur next. At some point labor shortages will tend to arise. These shortages in turn will tend to raise wages. Everything else being equal, higher wages will sooner or later begin to cut into profits. At this point capitalists will seek to lower their costs in order to reestablish an acceptable profit level. It appears that they could do this equally well by lowering their constant capital costs as by lowering their labor costs. If they take the former option, a reserve army of the unemployed does not arise, and a pillar of support for Marx's categorization of the capital/wage labor relation is removed.

This reasoning is cogent as long as we abstract from social relations and examine only the quantitative, technical aspects of the situation. But of course social relations cannot be abstracted from.

From the structure of social relations we can conclude that it is necessarily the case that those who control capital will have a fairly fixed order of preference in the search for lower costs. These preferences stem from certain considerations. "Full employment" of machines does not set in motion demands by machines for better work conditions, whereas tight labor markets do set such demands in motion. "Full employment" of machines does not make it more likely that machines could win these demands, whereas tight labor markets do make this more likely for wage laborers. Ignoring the nonexistent demands of machines does not set off the possibility of a machine strike, while ignoring workers' demands in a full employment situation makes worker resistance both all but inevitable and relatively effective. Given these sorts of considerations we may rank order

144

four possible procedures for cutting costs. All else being equal, capitalists will most prefer the introduction of technologies that save constant capital while eliminating laborers from the work process.[32] Next to this they will prefer labor-saving technologies that keep the costs of constant capital level. A distant third in this preference hierarchy comes constant capital-saving technologies that require the same level of employment as before. And dead last comes constant capital-saving technologies that demand an expansion of the labor force.

Of course in considering technical innovation the preferences of capitalists form only part of the story. The other part consists of the potential technical advances that are at hand and their relative cost. If the only available technology that lowers costs is third or fourth on their preference list, or if this technology saves significantly more than an available technology from the first or second group, then in this concrete case it will be selected. But we cannot treat the availability of technical advances or their cost as exogeneous variables. The very same ordering that determines what sorts of technical innovations capitalists prefer to introduce determines the sorts of innovations they would prefer to have developed. Their ownership/control of capital allows them to influence the process of technological development along these lines. And as more is invested in pursuing a particular technology the costs associated with that technology typically come down. Therefore we may conclude that it is necessarily the case that from the capital form we can derive a general structural tendency for technological innovation in the workplace to reproduce the reserve army of the unemployed. This is not the same as asserting that this always and everywhere takes place. But the preferences of capital, and the economic power to act on those preferences, ensures that the structural tendency remains. Needless to say all this makes it quite implausible to suggest that wage labor could be a co-principle of accumulation as long as the capital from is operative.

D. Excursus: Capital and Independent Producers

In footnote 20 of the previous chapter I noted John Roemer's argument that the capital form need not involve the capital/wage labor relation in production. It might seem that if this were admitted it would force us to overturn the subsequent progression of categories in Marx's theory. This is not the case. Let us take a form of capitalist production that does not involve the capital/wage labor relation. Here independent producers (family farmers come to mind) must borrow on the capital market to acquire their production inputs, and must sell their output to repay these borrowings. Within this structure it is necessarily the case that a structural tendency

145

emerges for capital to act as a principle of organization and of transformation of the production process. When independent producers depend upon capital markets to acquire the funds necessary to purchase their inputs, they are in a certain sense formally subsumed under capital. And when capital markets provide necessary capital only to those independent producers who employ the most productive technologies, this formal subsumption gives way to something quite close to real subsumption. Despite the fact that capital does not relate to these producers as wage laborers, the capital form nonetheless grants capital the power to impose an organization of production and a transformation of the production process to which these independent producers must conform.[33] Likewise the asymmetrical social roles connecting the owners/controllers of capital and independent producers dependent on the capital market also ensures a structural tendency for the former group to maintain and expand its position through an accumulation process. Hence even if we grant that the capital form does not always involve wage labor, the subsequent stages in the systematic progression of categories do not need to be revised.

E. Conclusion

If the ordering of categories in a theory is to be justified in terms of dialectical logic, then it must progress from a determination of simply unity, through one of difference, to a final stage of unity-in-difference. Otherwise the ordering would be arbitrary, rather than a systematic progression from the simple and abstract to the concrete and complex. Such a progression is clearly found at the end of the first volume of *Capital*. The linear ordering here can be summarized as depicted here:

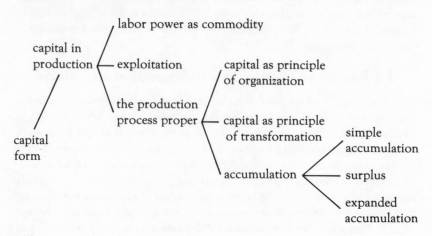

I believe that I have show that the progression of these determinations of the capital form follows dialectical logic as strictly as anything to be found in Hegel's systematic writings.

VIII

The Categories of Circulation

A. The Transition to Capital in Difference

We have examined Volume I of *Capital* in terms of a dialectical theory of categories that progresses from categories of unity to categories of difference and then to deteminations of unity-in-difference. However in a sense all of the categories of Volume I have been categories of unity. For they have gone into a categorial reconstruction of the capital form in its immediate determination as a *single* circuit of capital.

$$\text{Capital} \longleftarrow$$
$$\overset{\text{MOP}}{\underset{\text{LP}}{\rightarrow M - \qquad - P - C' - M'}}$$

When we turn to Volume II, Parts I and II stay within this same general structure. Marx discussed such topics as the distinction between fixed and circulating capital (i.e. capital invested in the machinery, factories, office buildings, etc. that endure for more than one production period, as opposed to capital invested in raw materials and labor power consumed within a given period); the velocity of money in the circuit of capital accumulation; and the velocity of commodities in this circuit. In this discussion Marx examined the influence of circulation back upon production, an influence that was not taken into account in Volume I. But the discussion of these topics does not bring us to a new categorial level. Here, just as throughout Volume I, capital is treated as if the capitalist mode of production consisted of a single entity, a single capital, that goes through the process of accumulation alone. This, of course, is an abstraction. It is only in the later sections of Volume II (Part III, Chapters XVIII-XXI) that the theory moves to a more concrete level.

From a systematic perspective the expectation is that a stage of simple unity must now give way to a stage of difference. Of course this expectation does not substitute for an argument justifying this transition. As was the case with transitions considered previously, here too the theory needs to provide immanent grounds for a move to a new level of categories. In the structure presented by the category "accumulation" we must discover an element that points forward.

A number of elements of the accumulation process have already been introduced in the course of our discussion of Volume I and the beginning chapters of Volume II: the initial investment, the process of production, the generation of surplus value within production, the accumulation of surplus value in the expanded accumulation that replaces simple accumulation, the velocity at which money and commodities travel through the circuit of accumulation, and so on. None of these factors provide the means for a transition to a higher categorial level. This leaves one critical step in the circuit unexamined: the process whereby C' goes to M'. This step refers to the buyers of the commodities offered for sale, whose purchase brings about the "realization" of the surplus value contained in the commodity.

Of course these buyers have always been present. We have stressed the role of demand in determining the socially necessary labor time; if a product is produced that goes beyond what market demand can absorb, the labor time spent producing it is socially wasted and creates no value. Yet the simplest and most abstract way to examine the capital form is to assume at first that sufficient demand is present. Then the circuit of capital can be explored in itself, in its own simple unity. But after the various moments of this circuit have been fully explored in the theory of capital accumulation, we must ask where these buyers come from.

Could not the capitalists and wage laborers of a single-circuit purchase the products of that circuit? To some extent. But given the structural parameters of the situation (commodity exchange on a society-wide scale, division of labor, the multiplication of social needs, etc.) it is all but impossible that a single circuit could ever provide for all those operating within that circuit. There is thus a dominant structural tendency for the realization of the surplus value produced in one circuit to involve demand from capitalists and wage laborers outside that circuit. A category (capital as

149

simple unity) which appears at first to unify the entire relevant manifold (the different moments of accumulation) is shown to *not* unify a relevant aspect of that manifold (the demand "outside" the circuit of capital). This is a dialectical contradiction. We thus have motivation for a move to a new level of economic determinations. We now move from a stage of simple unity to one of difference. This gives us the following structure:

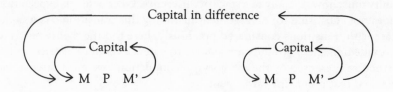

In other words, instead of unifying a single circuit, capital is now conceived as internally differentiated into two separate divisions or branches standing in internal relation to each other. Each provides necessary demand for the other. Just as Volume I consisted in an examination of capital in what from the present perspective was its simple unity, Volume II consists of an examination of capital in its internal difference.

B. The Dialectic of Capital in Difference

1. Simple Reproduction

Thus far we have discussed "capital in difference" in general terms. "Capital" is now a principle of unity that reproduces itself through circulation between two different circuits of capital. We now must specify these two distinct circuits. Each involves the investment of money, the purchase of means of production and labor power, a production process, and produced commodities that are then (hopefully for the capitalist) sold at a gain. There are numerous ways we could distinguish capital units. Different circuits could be distinguished by the amount of money invested and/or gained, the sorts of means of production used, the skills of the labor power employed in the process of production, the manner in which the produced commodities are sold, and so on. Such distinctions depend upon contingent historical circumstances. But there is one manner of distinguishing circuits that is not contingent. It has to do with the products produced in the circuit. Whatever else occurs, it always and everywhere is the case that means of production must be produced if capital accumulation is to occur. And whatever else occurs, it always and everywhere is the case that means of consumption must be produced to satisfy the wants and needs of both wage laborers and capitalists. *This* manner of distinguishing circuits of capital accumulation is immanent within the nature of capital. Accordingly, this is selected by Marx as the criterion for distinguishing the two moments of capital in difference. Marx aggregated all firms producing means of production into a single circuit of capital termed Division I, while Division II consists of the firms producing means of consumption. In setting up this abstract model of capital in difference (capital in circulation between the two divisions) Marx introduced a number of assumptions. From our perspective the most significant is that there is no mobility of capital investment between the divisions. Any surplus that is reinvested must be reinvested in the division in which it was produced. In this sense each division is categorized as self-enclosed, and yet as necessarily related to its "other," different from it. This confirms the interpretation of the present categorial level as one of difference, explicitly constructed by Marx as a stage of the reconstruction of capitalis.[1]

Our next systematic anticipation is that just as the capital form itself has a number of determinations, with "capital in circulation" as the form that captures the moment of difference in the development of the capital form, so "capital in circulation" in turn will be dialectically reconstructed in terms of a linear progression of *its* determinations. We anticipate as well that this reconstruction will proceed on this more concrete level from a category of simple unity, through one of difference, to one of unity-in-difference.

A category of immediate unity on the present theoretical level would define a structure in which the circulation between Division I and Division II leads to the reproduction of capital in a simple and abstract fashion. This occurs if the circulation process simply reproduces the same level of capital accumulation. Marx termed this "simple reproduction" (Chapter XX, Volume II). To understand this circulation process we must note that demand for means of production is generated by capital invested in both divisions (means of production are required to produce both the means of producing consumption goods and the means of producing other means of production). Likewise demand for means of consumption is generated by capital invested in both divisions (both require investment in labor power, the wages for which are then spent for means of consumption; and investment in both branches results in a surplus at least part of which is devoted towards capitalist consumption). With this in mind we can diagram a simple model of the categorial framework on this level of analysis, the circulation between the two branches of production:

151

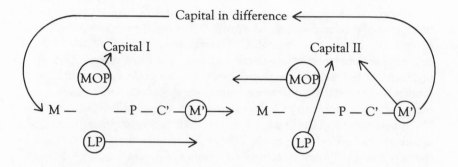

In many places the categorial structures of *Capital* can be made intelligible without reference to the quantitative dimension of value theory. However the circulation between the different divisions of capital can be most easily illustrated with the aid of some elementary quantitative relationships. We can begin by presenting the structure of capital in difference in value terms (with 'c' defined as constant capital, 'v' as variable capital, and 's' as surplus):

Capital

Division I   Division II

For simple reproduction to occur the value of the output of each division (the value of the output of Division I is $Ic + Iv + Is$; of Division II, $IIc + IIv + IIs$) must equal the demand for that output. Since the demand for the output of Division I consists of the means of production employed in Division I (Ic) and that employed in Division II (IIc), we have the following equation: $Ic + Iv + Ic = Ic + IIc$. Likewise the demand for the output of Division II consists of the means of consumption consumed by the agents in Division I ($Iv + Is$), plus the means of consumption consumed by those operating in Division II ($IIv + IIs$). This gives us a second equation: $IIc + IIv + IIs = Iv + Is + IIv + IIs$. By simple arithmetic both equations reduce to $IIc = Iv + Is$.

Given Marx's assumptions, if the circulation of capital between the two departments fits the proper proportions, simple reproduction can continue indefinitely. With this we are obviously on a more concrete and complex level than the categories of accumulation with which Volume I concluded. For the above equation goes beyond the simple category of accumulation to a specification of conditions that must be met if accumulation is to succeed within the context of the reproduction of capital on an economy-wide scale.

2. Surplus and Expanded Reproduction

The next category Marx introduced was "expanded reproduction" (Chapter XXI, *Capital II*). A systematic intention is obviously at work here. "Simple reproduction" and "expanded reproduction" are clearly ordered from the logically more abstract and simple to the more concrete and complex. They are not ordered in terms of historical stages (historically capitalists were from the first engaged in expanded reproduction). Perhaps we should settle for this, and not fetishize the search for triadic progressions. On the other hand, it is also clear that "simple reproduction" is a category of unity, and that "expanded reproduction" is a category that articulates a structure of unity-in-difference. While it is always possible to jump from one to the next within a theory, logically a moment of difference between the two is implied. If the theory is truly to progress in a step by step fashion, all such implications should be made explicit. And so just as in the previous chapter a category of difference not discussed by Marx was inserted between simple and expanded accumulation, so too one may be introduced here to mediate simple and expanded reproduction. The parallel can be taken a step further. Just as accumulation surpassing the consumption needs of capitalists within a single circuit of accumulation served as the transition to expanded accumulation, so too a surplus surpassing the consumption needs of capitalists as a whole can serve as a transition to expanded reproduction.

The key to a transition from simple reproduction lies with the generated surplus. As long as the surplus value appropriated by capital is devoted entirely to capitalist consumption (i.e. to purchasing the products of Division II) there is no contradictory element in the structure. But the earlier category of "exploitation" posits that capital has an immanent tendency to increase the surplus value it appropriates. If we add to this a premise that the consumption requirements of capitalists in general are limited (or, better, that they do not increase as fast as the appropriation of surplus), then it is necessarily the case that there is a structural tendency for a surplus to arise that is beyond those consumption needs. Marx pointed to this in this passage: "We see, then, aside from Ic which we reserve for a later analysis, that even simple reproduction, excluding accumulation proper, namely reproduction on an extended scale, necessarily includes the storing up, or hoarding, of money."[2]

This surplus introduces a contradictory element into the structure of simple reproduction. A unifying principle that does not unify aspects of a given structure is a dialectical contradiction. The category of "simple reproduction" is supposed to unify the reproduction process, yet the excess

153

surplus is a relevant part of the process that is "outside" that unity. Dialectical logic demands that the contradiction be overcome, that a higher category of unity capable of incorporating this moment of difference be introduced. This brings us to the notion of expanded reproduction.

With expanded accumulation a part of the surplus in each branch is now invested productively in the production of means of production and means of consumption, instead of being spent in unproductive capitalist consumption. Once again some elementary quantitative relationships best capture Marx's argument. Here too expanded reproduction can proceed smoothly only if there is a fixed proportion in investment in Division I and Division II. The equations are just a bit more complicated. Now the surplus 'S' is divided into three components: that which is invested in expanded constant capital (Sc); that which is invested in expanded variable capital (Sv); and that which is consumed by the capitalists (So). Since it is still the case that the total value provided by Division I must equal the demand for means of production from both divisions, and that the total value produced in Division II must equal the demand for means of consumption in both divisions, the equations are as follows:

$$C1 + V1 + Sc1 + Sv1 + So1 = C1 + Sc1 + C2 + Sc2 \text{ and}$$

$$C2 + V2 + Sc2 + Sv2 + So2 = V1 + Sv1 + So1 + V2 + Sv2 + So2$$

both of which reduce to $C2 + Sc2 = V1 + Sv1 + So1$.

Given Marx's assumptions, if the proper proportions are maintained in the circulation between the two divisions, expanded reproduction can continue indefinitely.

The categorial progression on this stage of the theory, thus, is:

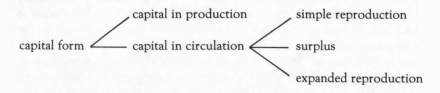

C. Hegelian Objections and Replies to the Objections

1. *A Debate Regarding Difference Within The Capital Form*
a) *An objection to Marx's position*
For Marx, the element of difference within the capital form reinforces the

categorization of capital as an alien essence standing above and beyond the individuals in society. It merely takes the interpretation of capital as essence to a higher level. In Marx's account, capital is an essence which differentiates itself into two branches. Demand is a function of capital invested in these branches. In this manner consumer demand seems to be reduced to an inessential appearance: "Thus capital *has* consumers. The consumer doesn't appear as an authentic counter to capital, but as a marionette of the two divisions of capital."[3]

The orthodox Hegelian perspective is opposed to Marx's position. Here consumer demand is viewed as an independent co-principle of capital. Accumulation occurs when the product or service offered by capital is freely accepted by consumers. When this occurs a universal will is created that is different from, yet united with, the wills of capitalists and consumers taken separately. For orthodox Hegelians this harmonious reconciliation of wills ensures that categories taken from the level of *Begriff* in Hegel's *Logic* are applicable here (although, to repeat a point made numerous times already, Hegelians grant that *Wesen* categories are also applicable here to a certain degree).

We can take the controversy a step further. Why did Marx wait until the present stage of the theory to introduce realization issues, i.e. issues connected with the completion of commodity sales? Marx held that the inner nature of capital leads capitalists to seek to produce at full capacity.[4] In reality, however, accumulation only occurs if there is sufficient demand for the goods or service produced, a point Marx did not appear to take into account in Volume I. But if consumer demand is treated as a co-principle for accumulation alongside capital, Hegelians (and others) argue, then the phenomenon of accumulation cannot be grasped within a theoretical framework that makes "capital" alone the essence of accumulation. Consumer demand thus should have been introduced as a co-principle of accumulation back in Volume I.

b) A Marxian reply

On the level of accumulation we were still operating within a single circuit of capital. On this level demand was provided either by the owners and controllers of capital or by wage laborers. Consumption or investment by capitalists obviously does not provide a distinct second co-principle alongside capital. And consumption by laborers cannot form a distinct co-principle for the simple reason that it reproduces the very capital form within which laborers are subjected:

> By converting part of his capital into labour-power, the capitalist augments the value of his entire capital. He kills two birds with one stone. He profits, not

155

only by what he receives from but by what he gives to, the labourer. The capital given in exchange for labour-power is converted into necessaries, by the consumption of which the muscles, nerves, bones, and brains of existing labourers are reproduced, and new labourers are begotten. Within the limits of what is strictly necessary, the individual consumption of the working-class is, therefore, the reconversion of the means of subsistence given by capital in exchange for labour-power, into fresh labour-power at the disposal of capital for exploitation. It is the production and reproduction of that means of production so indispensible to the capitalist: the labourer himself... The fact that the labourer consumes his means of subsistence for his own purposes, and not to please the capitalist, has no bearing on the matter. The consumption of food by a beast of burden is none the less a necessary factor in the process of production, because the beast enjoys what it eats. The maintenance and reproduction of the working-class is, and must ever be, a necessary condition to the reproduction of capital. But the capitalist may safely leave its fulfillment to the labourer's instincts of self-preservation and of propagation.[5]

Consumer demand may be a "co-principle" here in the sense of being a necessary condition for continued accumulation. But not every necessary condition is equally essential. Some necessary conditions involve the underlying structure constituting a particular process, while others involve functions that are carried out once that structure is in place. With regards to accumulation, "capital" is of the former sort and "consumer demand" is of the latter.

Turning to Volume II the argument remains much the same. Although the structure has now developed to include different circuits of capital, it remains the case that demand stems from wages paid to labor power, capitalist consumption, or capitalist investment in means of production. On this level of abstraction there is no demand outside the circulation between the two divisions of capital.[6] And it remains the case that the laborer's consumption activity is in fact clearly not independent of the capital invested: "As for the labourer, it has already been said that he is but the secondary, while the capitalist is the primary, starting point of the money thrown by the labourer into circulation. The money first advanced as variable capital is going through its second circulation when the labourer spends it to pay for means of subsistence. The capitalist class remains consequently the sole point of departure of the circulation of money."[7] Again, "labour-power already supplied, in the form of commodities, the equivalent which is to be paid to the labourer, before it is paid by the capitalist to the labourer in money-form. Hence the labourer himself creates the fund out of which the capitalist pays him. But this is not all. The money which the labourer receives is spent by him in order to preserve for the capitalist the instrument by means of which alone he can remain a capitalist.''[8] The subordinate place of wage labor within this structure confirms Marx's use of *Wesen* categories.

2. The Place of the Reproduction Schemes in Marx's Architectonic

What exactly did Marx attempt to accomplish with the categories of reproduction? It seems as if he presented the conditions of the possibility of stable capital reproduction, either with or without growth. But then how does this fit within a negative, or critical, theory? If the aim of the theory is to critique the capital form through a systematic reconstruction of its determinations, then it would seem that providing the conditions of the possibility of a stable reproduction of capital fails to further Marx's theoretical project. Of course the equilibrium equations for stability also point to the possibility of reproduction difficulties due to a disproportionality in the circulation of capital between the two departments. But in so far as this disproportionality is a mere possibility, the question remains: how does a thesis regarding a positive accomplishment of capitalism (stable reproduction) systematically fit within a categorial ordering moving towards an ever more concrete presentation of a negative social form?

> The question arises to what extent the conditions of equilibrium in the theory can serve as an antecedent for the negative, for a negative conceptualization of the realization problem. In this case the abstract level does not show how a negative proceeds from it. . . From a systematic perspective the reproduction scheme is not theoretically relevant, in so far as it deals with a mere possibility, an affirmative possibility at that, and thus does not correspond to a critical theory which takes up given negatives. In this sense the significance of the section of volume II of *Capital* would be merely to introduce the bare possibility of disturbances due to disproportionalities.[9]

If this is the case we must ask if the schemes can truly be seen as a stage in Marx's theory. For in this theory it supposedly is the case that "an abstraction can be taken as a stage only when it is disposed to the negative."[10] And pointing out a bare possibility of disturbance within schemes that are in principle stable hardly serves the purpose of critique.

This objection misses two crucial components of Marx's theory. The first has to do with crises, the second with methodology. Regarding the former we must recognize that probabilities come in differing degrees. To take an extreme case, if an event which has a 1 percent chance of occurring and one which has a 99 percent chance are both considered "merely possible," then a quite significant difference has been ignored. The equation stating the condition for simple reproduction ($Ic = IIc + IIs$) also implies that simple reproduction will break down when the proper proportional relationships between Divison I and Division II break down. Since investments in IIc and Iv are made in isolation from each other within different circuits of capital, there is no guarantee whatsoever that they will be made in the correct proportions to ensure simple reproduction. Nor is there any guarantee that Is will be generated in the right amount to correct any imbalance. In fact the odds are overwhelming that disproportionalities will arise. This suggests that within the structure defined by the category "simple reproduction" there necessarily is a structural tendency for crises in reproduction to arise due to disproportionality.[11]

The same reasoning holds even more regarding expanded reproduction. Since more variables are involved, the structural tendency for disproportions to arise is even greater. One possible root of this tendency seems to be singled out by Marx as significant enough to warrant independent consideration. The drive to accumulate surplus value leads to a structural tendency to keep investment in variable capital, a key input costs, as low as possible. But if wages fall too low, some means of consumption will go unpurchased.[12] Not being able to sell means of consumption will lead firms in Division II to reduce their purchases of the means of production necessary to produce those consumption goods and services. In this manner the downturn in Division II spreads to Division I. Here chronic dise-quilibrium and a structural problem regarding realization is based on *underconsumption*:

> Contradiction in the capitalist mode of production: the labourers as buyers of commodities are important for the market. But as sellers of their own commodity—labour-power—capitalist society tends to keep them down to the minimum price. Further contradiction: the periods in which capitalist production exerts all its forces regularly turn out to be periods of over-production, because production potentials can never be utilized to such an extent that more value may not only be produced but also be realized; but the sale of commodities, the realization of commodity-capital and thus of surplus-value, is limited, not by the consumer requirements of society in general, but by the consumer requirements of a society in which the vast majority are always poor and must always remain poor.[13]

Marx thus seems to have two distinct theories of realization problems, two ways in which circulation sets limits to production. One is based on capital in difference, considered for itself (disproportionality crises proper), and one is based on capital in its relation to effective demand (undercon-sumption crises). We shall return to this topic below. For now it is enough to note that the structural tendency to realization crises is so great that there is little difficulty in placing this stage of Marx's theory within the architechtonic of Marx's critique of capitalism as a whole.

The other difficulty with the objection is methodological in nature. Perhaps it is true that the possibility of stable capital reproduction would be somewhat difficult to fit within a purely negative theory, even if the tendency to crises is acknowledged. But if this reasoning is applied to *Capital* its circularity should be evident. It presupposes that Marx's theory is a purely negative theory whose purpose is solely critical, and then dismisses the reproduction equations on the grounds that they are not relevent to a purely negative theory. If we interpret *Capital* as a theory that dialectically reconstructs positive as well as negative aspects of the capitalist mode of production, this objection loses its force. Capitalism in certain circumstances could allow for stable reproduction at a given level and, in others, for stable extended growth. These are among its positive features. In establishing the possibility of both equilibrium and crisis, Marx points to both positive and negative features of the system. The problem here is with an interpretation that cannot account for Marx's incorporation of positive aspects of capitalism, and not with Marx's theory. To take just one example, Marx mentioned the following positive feature of expanded reproduction:

> With the development of the productivity of labour and therefore also with the development of the capitalist mode of production—which develops the social productive power of labour more than all previous modes of production—there is a steady increase in the mass of means of production (buildings, machinery, etc.) which are embodied once and for all in the process in the form of instruments of labour, and perform with steady repetition their function in it for a longer or shorter time. It was also observed that this increase is at the same time the premise and consequence of the development of the social productive power of labour. The growth, not only absolute but also relative, of wealth in this form is characteristic above all of the capitalist mode of production.[14]

3. An Illicit Abstraction?

The previous objection argued that the categories of reproduction do not fit within Marx's critical theory. The present objection points to a problem that arises even if it is granted that they do fit. In the dialectical ordering that makes up Marx's theory later categories articulate structures that incorporate those considered on the present level. We have just seen that Marx established the necessity of a tendency to crises on the present level. Marx hoped to derive from this the possibiliity of crises within more concrete structures. If the systematic ordering of categories captures the inner nature of capital, then this sort of claim could in principle be maintained. But some

159

Hegelians have questioned whether this is the case. On their view any consideration of capitalist reproduction on the present level ought not to abstract from the phenomenon of credit. For credit can in principle set right any temporary disturbances in reproduction:

> Regarding the probability of disturbances credit cannot be ignored...transcendentally credit hasn't yet been derived in the categorial progression. But in the the concrete the credit system is so narrowly bound up with commodity circulation that cyclical displacements or disproportions between Division I and Division II need not appear."[15]

Instead of tracing the inner nature of the object of investigation, Marx seems to have started out with equilibrium conditions and credit. These phenomena are inseparately connected. He then (a) went on to illicitly abstract from credit; after which he (b) pointed to crisis tendencies in the model constructed by means of that illicit abstraction; and finally (c) he later used those abstract crisis tendencies to derive structural tendencies to crises on the concrete level. This approach leads to results that cannot be justified in terms of a strict dialectical procedure:

> The disturbances on the abstract level are supposed to explain something about the concrete level. But the latter need not suffer disturbances at all, and it especially need not be disturbed by factors made operative in the abstraction.[16]

In response, first of all it is true that "credit" has not yet been explicitly introduced into the theory, if we mean by the term a distinct circuit of capital. However it is interesting to note that there is room for a certain form of credit on the present level of categories. The reproduction schemes aggregate all industries producing means of production, separating them from the aggregate of all industries producing means of consumption. Since we are on the level of capital in difference, any investment across divisions is ruled out. However *within* each division nothing necessitates that all investment funds in a particular firm must come from that firm itself. Within the structure defined on the present level, firms could provide credit for other firms within the same division as themselves.

The crux of the matter is not that Marx abstracted from credit in Volume II. Even if he had explicitly introduced credit, would that have changed his analysis? Those who offer credit are in the same position as all other controllers of capital. They allocate their investments individually, in order to maximize the return they privately appropriate. Their decisions are not motivated by the desire to maintain the equations defining simple or expanded reproduction. And even if that were their motivation, structural constraints on their decisions prevent them from having sufficient information regarding which allocations of credit maintain the relevant equation and which do not. Thus credit cannot eliminate the structural tendency to crises of disproportionality. At best it may be able to alleviate some of the symptoms of that tendency. At worst credit allocation itself includes the possibility of setting off disproportionality crisis.

A last point here returns to methodological issues. From the standpoint of dialectical logic we are not yet in a position to claim that Marx did or did not arrange matters on the present level of the theory so as to derive conclusions regarding more concrete levels. From the fact that Marx has shown that on the present level there is a structural tendency to disproportionality crises, it does not follow that we can assume that this will hold true for more concrete stages of the capital form. These more concrete structures incorporate earlier ones. Yet they also include determinations not yet introduced into the theory. The added determinations may reverse tendencies that operate on the more abstract levels (as, for example, the tendency for commodities to exchange at their values is reversed on the more concrete stages of the theory). Given the orthodox Hegelians' commitment to dialectical logic, their objection here is premature on their own terms.

4. The Underconsumption Argument

Just as the present level of categories provides principles for the further stages of the theory, it itself is derived from earlier stages. And just as we can ask whether the present level distorts the further development of the theory, so too we can ask whether the present categorial level is itself distorted by the earlier stages.

We have seen that on the present stage Marx held that chronic disequilibrium between the two divisions can arise due to insufficient purchasing power directed towards the means of consumption industries, which then reacts back on industries producing means of production. We have also seen that for Marx this is not a mere logical possibility. There is a structural tendency for this to occur. Why? The premises of the argument for this underconsumption thesis rest on the more abstract category of surplus value. The drive to maximize surplus value defines the inner nature of capital. That drive leads to a drive to minimize the share of the total product going to wages. It also leads to the drive to expand production regardless of available effective demand. ("With the development of capitalist production, the scale of production is determined less and less by the direct demand for the product and more and more by the amount of capital available in the hands of the individual capitalist, by the urge of

161

ιn inherent in his capital and by the need of continuity and
. ۔ the process of production."[17]) But reproduction occurs only if
sufficient effective demand is present. Therefore, Marx concluded, realization difficulties (underconsumption crises) are inherently connected to the inner nature of capital.

In principle this sort of derivation is a legitimate procedure within a dialectical theory, showing the relevance of an abstract determination (surplus value) to a more concrete stage (capital in circulation). But is it not the case that the tendency to underconsumption arises here only if one has already defined capital in terms of an insatiable thirst for surplus value? Once again the theory appears to rest on a petitio. If the discussion is not already prejudiced by the surplus value conception, then expanded reproduction could lead to stable growth rather than underconsumption crises: "There is no reason why the relation between wages and the value to be realized cannot be formed such that realization is stable. . . it is not at all obvious that capital must be seen as a conflict between surplus value generation and realization. But even if a conflict is granted, without the transcendental assumptions of Marx (regarding surplus value) it is a purely quantitative neoclassical optimization problem. . . The grounds (of crisis) could be of a peripheral nature, disturbances within a basic stability due to distorting proportionality (of investment), or to wages that are too low as a matter of fact, not principle."[18]

If on the abstract level of the theory Marx did not allow for any increases in real wages, and if he then derived a tendency to realization crises on a more concrete stage from this, then the objection would have considerable force. But as we have seen Marx *does* allow for increases in real wages. Further, the objection implies that raising wages that are *de facto* too low may resolve realization difficulties. But wages are typically at a *high* level immediately prior to the outbreak of crises:

> It is shere tautology to say that crises are caused by the scarcity of effective consumption, or of effective consumers. The capitalist system does not know any other modes of consumption than effective ones, except that of *sub forma pauperis* or of the swindler. That commodities are unsaleable means only that no effective purchasers have been found for them, i.e., consumners (since commodities are bought in the final analysis for productive or individual consumption). But if one were to attempt to give this tautology the semblance of a profounder justification by saying that the working-class receives too small a potion of its own product and the evil would be remedied as soom as it receives a larger share of it and its wages increase in consequence, one could only remark that crises are always prepared by precisely a period in which wages rise generally and the working-class actually gets a larger share of that

part of the annual product which is intended for consumption. From the point of view of these advocates of sound and "simple" (!) common sense, such a period should rather remove the crisis.[19]

Does this not still leave us with a mere optimization problem? Even if crises often occur after wages have increased, isn't it the case that realization difficulties could still be avoided if wages were raised yet further? From a mathematical standpoint, of course, one can eliminate the possibility of realization difficulties simply by increasing one or more of the variables determining demand. But this formal mathematics often misses the social dynamics of the situation. If the variable to be increeded is wages, in the short term this may indeed expand the domestic market and avoid realization difficulties. But the medium- to long-term results must be considered too. Higher wages tilt the balance of class forces in favor of the working class, giving it the confidence to press for further demands. There is no a priori limit to these demands; they can spontaneously move towards the point where they threaten capital's economic, political, and ideological hegemony. At some point capital must attempt to cut off this dynamic. If this reestablishes the possiblity of realization difficulties, this will seem a small price for capital to pay in order to maintain its hegemony (especially since it is always possible to attempt to compensate for a decreased internal market with increased exports). The approach of neoclassical optimization theory ignores this social dynamism. But Marx's reproduction schemes do not. For they incorporate the earlier determinations of the capital form, especially that of labor power as a commodity sold by wage laborers to the capitalist class. Here, as elsewhere, this proves to be the central principle of the capital form.

IX

The Categories of Concretion

Capital is a complex work in which numerous empirical investigations are conducted within the context of a systematic theory of economic categories. In Volume III the balance of these two components of Marx's theory falls heavily on the side of empirical studies. Perhaps this is a function of the fact that Volume III, like Volume II, was edited by Engels after Marx's death. At any rate, for the most part we shall leave the discussion of Marx's empirical arguments to social scientists. Our task here is to trace the categorial progression that continues to provide the architectonic of Marx's theory. The goal of the present chapter is to make explicit the logic behind this progression. My thesis is that here too this logic is a dialectical logic taken over from Hegel.

In Volume III we move from the abstract level of "capital in general" discussed in the first two volumes to the concrete level of many capitals. Capital in general was discussed in terms of the production (simple unity) and circulation (difference) of capital. The level of many capitals is defined by a distribution of surplus value connecting many capitals (unity-in-difference). This category of capital in distribution in turn needs to be concretely comprehended, and doing this in a systematic fashion demands tracing the dialectic of its determinations. A distribution among units of capital that are all of the same type forms a category of simple unity. These units are qualitatively the same in that they are all units of industrial capital. A concept of distribution that stems from a source that is "outside" those units of capital forms the second level here, one of difference. Finally, a concept of distribution that unites many qualitatively different sorts of capital is a more complex category of unity-in-difference that brings Capital to a close.

164

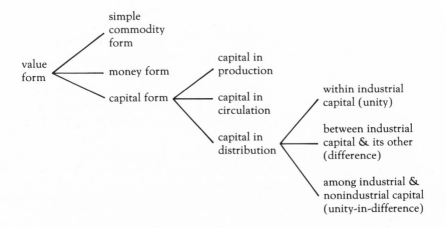

A. The Dialectic of Industrial Capital

1. The stages

A category of simple unity on the level of many capitals unites units of capital that are distinct but qualitatively the same. In Volume II Marx aggregated firms producing means of production and firms producing means of consumption into two different divisions. At the beginning of Volume III these firms are disaggregated so that we have many different units of capital competing against each other. All these different units, however, are qualitatively the same in that they are all units of industrial capital.

Often in *Capital* a particular category with a specific categorial structure is itself a principle for a systematic ordering of different determinations under it. This is the case for capital as a simple unity of many units of industrial capital, the topic of Chapters I-IX of *Capital III*. In this ordering "cost price" comes first. It provides the most simple and immediate manner of categorizing the many units of industrial capital. As the first category in Volume III, it is an immediate continuation of Volume II. In Volume II prices were assumed to be directly proportional to values. Also in Volume II Marx insisted that constant capital must be taken into account in the reproduction process of capital, against the tendency of Adam Smith and others to neglect it. The category of "cost price" develops these points. "Cost price" is a measure for determining price that takes into account constant capital as well as variable capital and surplus value, as opposed to Adam Smith's attempt to derive cost price from revenues (wages plus

165

surplus, i.e. profits and rents) alone. Different units of industrial capital can be distinguished according to the cost prices of the commodities they produce, with cost price equalling c + v + s, all calculated in value terms.

A new conceptual determination falls on this level, that of "profit." Previously Marx employed the category "surplus value," which is a function of variable capital alone. Now that constant capital has been explicitly posited as part of the cost price, we must introduce "profit" as a function of total costs, of both constant and variable capital costs.[1] If we assume that the rate of surplus value is more or less comparable across industries and firms, this implies that there is a structural tendency for the rate of profit to diverge wildly across industries and firms within the present structure. For the ratio of constant to variable capital can diverge wildly. If two industries have the same organic composition of capital (i.e. the identical ratio c/v), the same rate of exploitation, and same level of wages, there is no special problem. But suppose technological change leads certain industries to have much higher organic compositions of capital than others. Assuming a rate of surplus value of 100% we now may have

	c	+	v	+	s	=	cost price	rate of profit
industry A	90	+	10	+	10	=	110	10%
industry B	50	+	50	+	50	=	150	50%

One of the most important respects in which "cost price" is a category of simple unity on this level has to do with the fact that with this category we consider each of the many units of capital in isolation, individually. But each of the many units of capital is what it is due to its difference from other units. Its pursuit of its own profit interests necessarily brings it into contact with other units of capital, pursuing *their* profit interests. This moment of difference must be systematically incorporated if the theoretical reconstruction is to be adequate to the object reconstructed. And so Marx next introduced the category of "competition" among the many units of industrial capital. This category makes explicit the latent antagonism among the different units of industrial capital, each seeking profit on the basis of its own cost price.

An analysis of the structure defined by the category "competition" reveals that it too is not a stable determination. When individual units are forced to compete for investment with other units of capital, a structural tendency is set up that prevents products from being sold at cost prices. For in the medium term capital will not be invested in firms or sectors with lower-than-average rates of profit. When this moment of difference ("competition") is incorporated, the simple unity of cost price gives way to the complex unity-in-difference of production prices. In Marx's formulation production prices are defined as $(c + v)((1 + r)$; ("r" = rate of profit). This formula captures the structural tendency for each unit of capital to receive a profit measured as a function of total investment $(c + v)$, and not by the amount of surplus value it has itself produced (a fuction of v alone).[2] As a result the rate of profit is categorized on this stage as equal across the different units of productive capital. Returning to our earlier example, if industries A and B both sold their products for $130, they would both have a rate of profit of 30%. At these "prices of production" a stable structure is attained which unites the different units of industrial capital.[3] This brings the first level of categories in Volume III to a close:

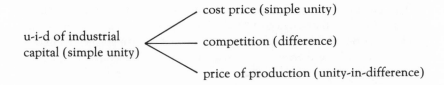

cost price (simple unity)

u-i-d of industrial   competition (difference)
capital (simple unity)

price of production (unity-in-difference)

2. Dialectical Objections

With "price of production" we have reached a new level of concreteness. Unlike Volume I and Volume II, prices are no longer directly proportional to values. When Volume III was first published, many of Marx's critics claimed to see a logical contradiction between Volume I, where commodities supposedly exchange according to prices proportional to values, and Volume III, where commodity exchange takes place by means of prices that are not proportional to values. This objection could only have been formulated in circles where even a minimal understanding of Hegel and of systematic dialectical theories was lacking.[4] It is of the essence of dialectical theories that simple and abstract determinations (prices proportional to value) lead to more complex and concrete ones (prices that are not so proportional) that cannot be simply reduced to the former. A theory can hardly be said to have refuted itself when it does what it sets out to do! More interesting, therefore, are the objections made by those who understand the sort of theory Marx attempted to construct. Two of these objections can be considered here.

Marx felt that the sum total of prices proportional to values equals the sum total of prices of production, the latter being a mere redistribution[5] of the former (in our example the sum total of values = the sum total of production prices = $260). Marx also felt that the sum total of surplus value equals the sum total of profits, with once again the latter being a mere redistribution of the former (in our example, both = $60). The first objection has to do with the cogency of these claims. From an economic standpoint, a problem stems from the fact that Marx's formula for deriving the production price of a particular output—$(1 + r)(c + v)$—treats the prices of the inputs "c" and "v" as directly proportional to their values. However c and v, the inputs of the process, are the outputs of other processes. They too should have been "transformed," i.e. purchased at prices of production. But when inputs as well as outputs are calculated in terms of prices of production in a system of simultaneous equations, the two equivalences Marx proposed can no longer both hold (except in quite exceptional cases). More than a few economists have concluded from this that the entire theoretical project of *Capital* collapses.[6]

This issue can also be posed in terms of dialectical methodology. Marx seems to have conflated categorially distinct levels. The present level is one of capital in plurality, of many capitals. As such it is distinguished from the earlier levels of the theory which treated capital in general. By equating prices proportional to values and prices of production, as well as surplus value and profits, Marx wanted to have his cake and eat it too. In effect he insisted that many capitals can be treated in precisely the same manner as capital in general, at the very moment that he also granted that capital in concretion is different from capital in general. Both positions cannot be held at once. Either a new categorial level has been reached, in which case quantitative considerations from earlier levels no longer hold; or we do not have a new categorial level, in which case the theory only appears to be a dialectical progression of categories and is in fact undialectical. From a Hegelian standpoint Marx seems to have made a fundamental error: "The mistake made by Marx was the mistake of viewing a transcendentally early (category) as identical to a transcendentally late one."[7] This goes against one of the basic canons of systematic theories of categories.

A second problem also involves both economic and logical points. Consider again the above example. Here, and in other examples Marx constructed, the rate of exploitation and the level of real wages are both kept constant across different industries, despite the fact that industry A has a much higher organic composition of capital. However increases in the organic composition of capital regularly bring increases in productivity, as Marx himself elsewhere stressed. If this is the case then we cannot have both a constant rate of exploitation and constant real wages. If we keep real wages constant, then increasing productivity leads to an increase in the rate of exploitation. With this the idea that profits stem exclusively from the surplus value produced by variable capital breaks down. For by suppostition v has not changed; what has changed is that c has increased relative to v. If this can bring about a higher rate of surplus value, then c must be treated as an independent factor of production, contributing to the level of profit in its own right. This point also appears to undermine Marx's abstract discussion of surplus value and exploitation on the earlier level of capital in general. Different c's can produce different amounts of relative surplus value, with the amount of labor remaining constant. This shows that labor alone cannot be the entire story even on the abstract level.

Marx set the rate of exploitation equal in all industries in order to avoid this conclusion. This causes the rate of profit to depend exclusively upon surplus value,[8] but it does so at the cost of transgressing a canon of dialectical logic. When dialectical logic is followed we must always remain open to the possibility that introducing new determinations on a concrete and complex stage of the theory reverses tendencies that held within structures defined on more abstract and simple levels. On the level of many capitals, different rates of c/v are essential for distinguishing different units of capital. This should have led Marx to reverse the supposition of an equal rate of surplus value, for it is plausible to assume an equal rate only when we abstract from different c/v ratios.

In the next section I shall formulate a reply to the first objection. Consideration of the second objection will be postponed until the discussion of the tendency of the rate of profit to fall.

3. Replies to Hegelian Criticisms:
The Transformation Problem

The first point to note is that the general approach used to refute Marx's thesis regarding the relationships between prices proportional to values/ prices of production and surplus values/profits is suspect. Simultaneous equations have been used to show that when input costs are measured in prices of production Marx's transformation does not work. In response to this Ernest Mandel and others have pointed out that the economic value of the inputs to production generally cannot be determined simultaneously with the outputs of the production process.[9] Their value is instead a function of the preceding production period, which typically would have employed a different technology with a level of productivity different from that in the present period. Therefore to insist that they be priced in the same manner as outputs of the present period does not make economic sense. This is an important point. But it still leaves the transformation problem standing. There still remains the question of the quantitative relationship between $c + v + s$, with all terms measured in values/surplus values, and ($c + v$) ($1 + r$), with all three terms measured in prices of production/profits.

There are still cogent reasons to deny the two sets of equivalences Marx defended.

There is also still the alleged conflation of the level of "capital in general" and "many capitals" that was said to undermine Marx's claim to employ dialectical logic here. In this context we may introduce Anwar Shaikh's contribution to the debate.[10] He grants that if the sum total of values is held equal to the sum total of prices, then the sum total of surplus values cannot equal the sum total of profits. But surplus values and profits move in the same direction. And they diverge within a quite narrow range. Further, this divergence can easily be explained in terms of the surplus value capitalists remove from the circuit of capital in their personal consumption of luxury goods. (An exceptional circumstance where profits and surplus values are equal occurs when luxury goods are not produced, i.e. with the maximally expanded reproduction termed by economists the "von Newman ray.") Therefore the level of values may still be seen as determining prices of production despite the divergence of surplus values and profits.

Shaikh's argument goes beyond merely clarifying the quantitative economic relations here. It also illuminates the relationship between capital in general and many capitals. The divergence of profits from surplus values ensures that the level of many capitals is categorially distinct from the level of capital in general. This allows a dialectical progression from one categorial level to another. Thus Marx's theory is able to show how capital in general is a principle for the determination of many capitals, without conflating the two levels.

At the very least we may conclude that Mandel, Shaikh, and others have established that quantitative objections to the so-called transformation problem are not conclusive. Before turning to the next section, however, I would like to argue against the view that the transformation problem has a crucial importance in relation to Marx's theory. I have argued that *Capital* is best read as an attempt to reconstruct systematically the categories that make the capitalist mode of production intelligible. In a linear dialectical theory of this sort the question of a quantitative equality holding between the magnitudes of different categorial levels is quite secondary. Instead the aim of such a theory is to comprehend concrete determinations through tracing their systematic derivation from abstract determinations. This is accomplished through a categorial analysis that traces how categories of simple unity define structures with inherent contradictions. They necessarily involve structural tendencies that point away from structures of simple unity and towards structures in which the element of difference is paramount. In this manner categories of difference are derived, which in turn articulate structures that necessarily involve tendencies that point toward structures of unity-in-difference. These in turn lead to structures of simple unity on a new, more concrete, level. Throughout this progression transitions are justified through uncovering dialectical contradictions, a procedure that does not in any way presuppose that relevant magnitudes on any two levels of the theory are identical. While the question of the transformation of prices proportional to values to production prices is extremely helpful in thinking about the theoretical relationship between values and prices, most Marxist and non-Marxist accounts have concentrated exclusively on the problems involved in establishing the quantitative identity of values and prices, surplus value and profits.

It is true enough that Marx himself directed considerable attention to these two equations. But there is much in his theory that points away from granting them a place of absolute centrality. Consider, for example, the relationship between "expanded accumulation" and "simple reproduction." No Marxist has ever claimed to prove that the sum total of values accumulated in expanded accumulation equals the sum total reproduced in simple reproduction. No non-Marxist has ever claimed to refute Marx based on a proof of the nonequivalence of these magnitudes. Indeed the question of the mathematical relationship between the two magnitudes hardly makes sense. The two categorial structures "expanded accumulation" and "simple reproduction" are related in a logical ordering. They are not simultaneously coexisting in the concretion. Being on distinct logical planes, the quantities appropriate to each are not truly commensurate. What is important for the theory is instead the systematic motivation for moving from one category to the next. Likewise there is no good reason to hold that the systematic relation of prices directly proportional to values and production prices crucially depends upon the quantitative identity of the magnitudes operative on each level. Here too what counts is the systematic connection between the two determinations. If "value" is prior to "price," it is so, first and foremost, because an adequate attempt to capture the intelligibility of the latter, to reconstruct it in basic categories and in this manner to comprehend it, begins with the former notion. In this sense "value" is a principle for the derivation of "price." This is a matter of tracing the dialectic of value forms. Even in cases where the question of the quantitative relationships among the various forms makes some sense, therefore, the quantitative issue is still relatively secondary, at least from the perspective of dialectical logic.

B. The Dialectic of Supply and Demand

1. The Progression of Categories

We have just traced a dialectic from cost prices through competition to prices of production, a progression from a category of simple unity, to one

171

of difference, to one of unity-in-difference. But if we take the dialectic of industrial capital as a whole, we must see it as a category of simple unity. In section A we considered the many units of industrial capital in themselves. This was an abstraction. Concretely they are essentially connected to something "other." The next stage must be to introduce this element of difference explicitly into the theory, which Marx did in Chapter X of Volume III.

The "other" confronting the many units of industrial capital is consumer demand. Comprehending this in thought requires a series of determinations. Here as elsewhere these determinations follow a systematic order.

The first category on this stage adds to the last category of the previous stage the simple determination that commodities with their prices of production are offered to particular consumers in particular markets at particular times. This is a category of simple unity in this context. This category presupposes a moment of difference that it cannot subsume under itself. This moment of difference, standing in opposition to prices of production, is consumer response. This is based on a myriad of contingent factors operating on this level of concreteness (changing fashions, temporary bottlenecks in supply, etc.) The next category, a synthesis of production prices offered and consumer response, a concrete unity that includes the moment of difference within it, is the category "market price."

It is interesting to note how little controversy has broken out regarding the "transformation" of prices of production into market prices. It has not been claimed by Marxists that there is a quantitative identity between the two levels. Nor has the lack of such identity often been proposed by non-Marxists as an argument against Marxist theory (however see section 2 below). It would indeed be difficult to maintain an identity of magnitude here. For example, a sudden increase in consumer demand may lift market prices above production prices and keep them there for an extended period. Of course this brings surplus profits to the units of capital that supply at those prices, (i.e. profits that are higher than the average rate of profit as given in the calculation of the prices of production). Over time this encourages investment in this sector, which over time leads to increased supply relative to demand, and over time this will make market prices once again approach prices of production. Yet during this interval demand could very well have shifted again. As a result, any quantitative identity between the sum total of production prices and the sum total of market prices is likely to be extremely contingent and temporary. Yet this does not in the least undermine the systematic ordering whereby "market prices" are derived from "prices of production." If the analogous relationship between "prices of production" and "prices proportional to values" had been seen in the same way, perhaps fewer polemics regarding the transformation problem would have arisen. More attention might have been paid instead to the logical structure of Marx's theory.

Another interesting point to note concerns the role played by consumer demand in the unfolding of *Capital*. *Capital* traces a systematic progression of different levels of abstraction, and consumer demand plays a different role on these different levels. "Demand" is built into the notion of "socially necessary labor time" introduced at the start of the theory in Volume I. Labor time that produces products no one purchases is socially wasted. The moment of consumption is operative here, but in a quite abstract fashion. No attempt is made to account for this demand. In Volume II this begins to get fleshed out. Demand takes various forms, from the demand of firms in both Division I and Division II for means of production produced by the firms in Division I, to the demand for items of consumption produced in Division II from wage laborers and capitalists in both departments. While more concrete than the discussion of demand in Volume I, this is still on a fairly high level of abstraction. Capital in general is considered only in its difference, i.e. the circulation between means of production-producing industries and means of consumption-producing industries. On this level, demand is treated within this fairly abstract structure. On the level of capital in general, demand is generated as a moment of capitalist reproduction. That is why "consumer demand" could not be considered as an independent co-principle alongside capital.

In Volume III we move from captial in general to many capitals, and the corresponding notion of demand becomes more concrete as well. Demand is now addressed to one or another of a group of competing capitals. The role it plays thus goes beyond the mere transition from prices of production to market prices. It also helps determine which among a group of competing capitals will survive and which will not. While "demand" is not an independent co-principle to capital in general, with respect to any given unit on the level of many capitals demand *is* as separate co-principle regarding the fate of that unit.

All this is sufficient response to those who object that *Capital* ignores the role of demand. Marx is well aware that without considering demand, socially necessary labor time cannot be determined, the capitalist system cannot be reproduced, and we cannot account for either market prices or why some among a group of competing capitals survive and others do not.[11] The question still remains, of course, whether Marx adequately grasped consumer demand in its "otherness" to capital, or whether he subjected it too much to the capital form. We shall turn to this next.

2. *Hegelian Objections and Replies*

A first Hegelian objection can be dismissed at once. Richard Winfield claims that the divergence of market prices from prices of production

173

undermines the entire Marxist project, for this shows that market prices rest on the free agreement of the two exchanging partners. In Hegelian terms, market prices are fixed by the externalization of the free will. Asserting that market prices are governed by prices of production is analogous to imposing administered prices. Both undermine this structure of freedom. The divergence of market prices shows that prices of production are not imposed. Therefore the market system is one of reciprocal freedom, contrary to Marx's view.

This issue once again concerns Marx's use of a *Wesenslogik* in understanding capitalism, i.e. the question whether an impersonal force asserts itself above the will of individuals. We can first simply note that Winfield himself implies that prices of production are the logically necessary starting point for a consideration of market prices. After having written that "the only constraint (commodity exhangers) face is the necessity of reaching agreement with other commodity owners"[12] so that "commodity exchange involves an exercise of freedom completely the reverse of what Marx laments"[13] Winfield adds that "factors of production determine the minimum price which must be met if the product is to be sold without a loss in relation to the costs of its manufacture."[14] This, of course, provides a bottom baseline for market prices; if they fall below prices of production for an extended period capitalist reproduction breaks down, whatever the willing of contracting agents might be. There are also mechanisms set off if market prices rise significantly above prices of production for an extended period, which Winfield failed to consider. This situation attracts investment into the particular sector of the market. This increases supply and lowers market prices, which thus once more approach prices of production. We see that the freedom exchanging partners have in commodity exchange is fixed within fairly narrow bounds. And this is precisely what Marx meant in asserting that prices of production are logically prior to market prices.

A more substantial Hegelian objection also involves the question of *Wesenslogik*, as well as the relation between capital in general and many capitals. On the abstract level of capital in general Marx categorized capital as an essence in the Hegelian sense. It was viewed as a force for the maximum accumulation of surplus value, a force that subjected all agents, capitalists as well as wage laborers and consumers, to its dictates. Marx clearly thought that this categorization held on the concrete level of many capitals as well. Does Marx's view capture the full concreteness of the level of many capitals? A Hegelian would object that characteristic features of the level of many capitals are abstracted from in order to make this level appear more like the level of capital in general than is warranted. Specifically, the competition among the many capitals in response to effective demand is overlooked, a competition over prices. If this concretion were fully incorporated into the categorial ordering, then the present level of many capitals could not be characterized in terms of the maximum accumulation of surplus value as capital in general was. The level of many capitals would be defined instead in terms of a balance between accumulation and realization.[15] Instead of seeing laborers and consumers as mere appendages to capital, as Marx supposedly held on the level of capital in general, on the level of many capitals a unity-in-difference, a harmonious reconciliation, would be called for. Successful accumulation requires that commodities be realized, i.e. purchased by consumers, and this in turn demands that the purchasing power of labor be sufficiently high for economic optimization. The refusal to adjust to capital in concretion as many capitals is based on Marx's wish to critique capitalism. But the inherent, essential, connection between capital and exploitation that Marx supposed part of the inner nature of capital becomes an open question, once capital in concretion is seen to depend on sufficient demand, which involves in turn the purchasing power of labor.

The first point to make in reply is that Marx certainly does incorporate competition among the many capitals over prices. That is precisely the mechanism that ensures that market prices do gravitate around prices of production within relatively fixed limits. If competition for effective demand pushes market prices below prices of production, then many firms will go out of business, allowing those that remain to push prices higher. If market prices rise significantly above prices of production, this will attract new investment in the particular market, thereby increasing supply and lowering the prices there. In the medium term, therefore, prices of production tend to regulate market prices, as Marx asserts, due pricisely to price competition among the many capitals. The key issue is whether acknowledging this competition, i.e. incorporating effective demand within the theory on the level of many capitals, reverses Marx's previous estimation of the nature of capital in general. Two distinct issues fit under this heading, both of which concern the interpretation of capital in general in terms of Wesenslogik.

We have already stated that consumer demand is a co-principle on the level of market prices in that it plays a determining role in deciding which of the many units of capital survive and which do not. Does this mean that consumer demand forms a co-principle standing alongside capital in the sense that the attempt to treat capital in essence terms breaks down? Second, does the introduction of realization considerations undermine the claim that there is an essential connection between capital accumulation and exploitation?

Turning to the capital/consumer relationship first, it is certainly true that

175

capitalist producers cannot offer products profitably if there is no one who wishes to purchase them, just as consumers cannot demand what is not profitable for capitalists to produce. In Hegelian language this means that each side is mediated by the other. There is thus reciprocal interdependence. Given this, the orthodox Hegelian will conclude that a *Begriffslogik* is applicable here to some degree, with capital and consumers as co-principles. Categorizing these relations exclusively in terms of *Wesenslogik* with capital lording over society, orthodox Hegelians argue, would be done only by those who have begged the argument and decided beforehand that this social relation is to be critiqued.

Marx too grants this element of reciprocity. And yet on the concrete level of many capitals Marx continued to insist that categories from the level of *Wesen*, not *Begriff*, best characterize this social relationship. Even when consumers play the role of helping to determine which among a group of competing capitals will survive, they are still subjected to the capital form. Why did he refuse to see consumers as co-principles alongside capital?

A general point must be kept in mind. We would be mistaken to assume that a social form characterized through *Wesen* categories by Marx necessarily must be a two-poled relation where one pole, the essence, totally dominates the other pole and reduces it to a mere appearance. For Marx a structure may still be categorized in essence terms even if the nonessential pole cannot be reduced in this fashion. The crucial thing is whether one pole sufficiently dominates the other so as to prevent it from attaining meaningful autonomy. In Marx's view the capital/consumer relation, while *not* categorizable in terms of essence on the one hand and mere illusory appearance on the other, can be grasped in terms of this second sort of essence structure.

There are two sorts of arguments that can be constructed in defense of this view. The first goes as follows: 1) If production is held constant, consumption options rest on pregiven patterns of distribution. The pattern of demand will fundamentally shift if the pattern of distribution shifts (for example an egalitarian redistribution of wealth would shift demand from luxury condominiums to affordable mass housing). 2) Distributional patterns primarily rest on who owns capital and who provides services useful to those who own capital; they rest secondarily on the level of the social wage, which generally fluctuates with the rhythms of capital accumulation (being generally greater during upswings and lower in downswings). 3) The pattern of distribution can fundamentally shift only with a shift in the underlying social relations constitutive of the capital form. 4) Therefore consumption is *not* categorially equiprimordial with capital.

Consumption decisions may structure capital, but they themselves res
pattern of distribution ultimately based on capitalist production relati ی.
Despite the reciprocity of capital and consumption it is thus captial that is
the alpha and omega of the process.

The second argument against viewing consumer demand as a co-principle
alongside capital begins by holding distributional patterns constant. In this
case consumption patterns generally shift with productivity increases, for
productivity increases generally lead to lower prices, and lower prices
generally stimulate increased demand.[16] Since within capitalism increases in
productivity generally are based upon increased capital investment, from
this perspective too capital has priority over consumer demand.

The orthodox Hegelian has three options in response. The Hegelian
could simply insist that the consumer's ability to determine which firms
survive and which do not is by definition sufficient to warrant viewing
consumer demand as a co-principle alongside capital. Given the above
arguments for the priority of capital this move does not seem convincing.
Or the Hegelian could assert that the state can intervene to address whatever
lack of reciprocity exists on this level. We must postpone discussing this
option until the following chapter, noting only how much this weakens the
initial Hegelian claim that a *Begriffslogik* operates to some degree in civil
society even when we abstract from the state.

The third response brings us to the other issue here, the question whether
exploitation can continue to be seen as part of the inner nature of capital
once the concrete stage of the theory has been reached. An orthodox
Hegelian could respond to the above by saying that the arguments thusfar
continue to ignore capital's own interest in there being a co-principle
alongside it. The interest of capital in continued capital accumulation is an
interest in overcoming realization difficulties. If produced goods and
services are not sold, no capital is accumulated. Capital's inherent interest in
solving realization problems is an interest in ensuring high demand. Unions
and the higher wages they can win help ensure high demand. Therefore the
basic interests of labor in organization and higher wages are consonant with
the fundamental interests of capital. The same structural mechanism that
sets up consumer demand as a co-principle to capital thereby also
undermines the claim that the capital/wage labor relation is inherently
exploitative.

This position is less than compelling for at least five reasons. First, while
high wages can ease demand problems they also raise costs, leading to a
general tendency by capital to raise prices to ensure (or to expand) its profit
margins, leading to the need for yet higher wages, etc. In short, a price-wage

spiral heading towards inflationary crises may eventually be set off. This can be avoided by increases in productivity that allow for both high wages and high profit margins. So the thesis rests on the very implausible premise that such increases in productivity can always and everywhere be automatically guaranteed. Second, as Marx pointed out all capitalists may want those who work for others to be paid well so that they can purchase goods. However this doesn't at all imply that they want this for their *own* employees. This is a prisoner's dilemma situation, where decisions that are rational from an individual point of view prevent what is collectively rational from being attained. Third, in periods of upswing in capital accumulation there may be enough surplus present to afford pay hikes that ease realization difficulties. In periods of downswing, however, this is not likely to be the case. Fourth, wages high enough to ease realization problems are generally high enough to create problems regarding the imposition of capitalist discipline in the workplace. The existence of highly paid jobs generally grants the working class the confidence to call into question so-called managerial perogatives regarding such things as how the workplace is to be structured. Fifth, there are alternative methods of pumping up demand to avoid realization problems that do not involve problems such as lowering profit margins and increasing labor combativity. Investment in unproductive military spending financed by state deficits, i.e. military Keynesianism, has proven to be far more compatible with capital's interests than a Keynesianism centered upon higher wages to labor.[17]

The orthodox Hegelian criticism of Marx presented by Hartmann ignores the fourth and fifth points, says that the third is irrelevant because high wages dealing with realization difficulties make it possible in principle to avoid extended economic downturns, and claims that coordinated action among capitals in principle can avoid both price-wage inflationary spirals and a shortsighted capitalist rationality that, by keeping wages low, goes against what is collectively rational for capital as a whole. Of course the fourth and fifth points, regarding how capitalists wish to retain their perogatives and military Keynesianism, are absolutely crucial. And the regularity with which periods of downturn have alternated with periods of upswing in the history of capitalism makes any supposition that significant downturns can in principle be avoided once and for all highly questionable, to put it mildly. As for the idea that capitalists may in principle coordinate their activity to attain collective rationality, it is extremely doubtful that individual capitals will forgo what is individually rational for them to do unless some external force compels this. This could only be the state, a topic reserved for the next chapter. We may conclude that on the present categorial level, at least, the orthodox Hegelian case against Marx is a weak one.

C. The Falling Rate of Profit

At this stage of the theory Marx interrupted the categorial progression to discuss a structural tendency that he felt held on the present categorial level (Chapters CII-XV, *Capital III*). He termed this "the law of the tendency for the rate of profit to fall." Marx began with an equation defining the rate of profit in terms of cost prices: $r = s/c + v$. Dividing the nominator and the denomiator on the right side by v gives us $r = (s/v)/((c/v) + 1)$. Clearly if c/v increases, while s/v either decreases, remains the same, or increases at a slower rate than c/v increases, then r declines. Marx argued that there is a tendency for decline to occur. Given the focus of the present study, only those aspects of his arguments that are connected to the question of the dialectical ordering of economic categories will be examined here. This discussion can be divided into the following issues: 1) Does the introduction of different rates of profit imply that the conceptual priority previously given to labor should be reversed? 2) Are there conclusive arguments establishing a tendency for c/v to rise? 3) Is it plausible to hold that s/v either falls, holds constant, or increases less than c/v? I argue that there are serious problems with Marx's position. This leads to a final issue: 4) If from the standpoint of dialectical logic there are problems with Marx's law of the tendency for the rate of profit to fall, is there a Marxian theory of economic crisis that can avoid these difficulties?

1. *Value Theory and Constant Capital*

On the present categorial level do principles that held on an earlier level continue in force? From the standpoint of a dialectical ordering of different categorial levels it is possible that abstract principles are reversed when new determinations are introduced in the theory. On the abstract level of capital in general, where value categories alone were employed, perhaps the productive contribution of constant capital could be neglected in order to examine the surplus value generated by surplus labor. But on the present concrete level the category "profit" has replaced that of "surplus value." Unlike surplus value profit is not a function of labor alone, but of constant capital as well. Consider a situation in which 100 units of capital are used, providing 100 units of product and a profit of 50, with a level of wages of 50. In this case the rate of profit is 33 percent. With wages held constant the effect on profit of a rise in c depends entirely on the productivity of that c, as we can see when we compare three cases, in which the same amount of capital leads to different productivity advances.[18]

	cap.	net product	profit	wages	rate of profit
initial situation	100	100	50	50	1/3
case 1	110	108	58	50	rises
case 2	110	103	53	50	constant
case 3	110	101	51	50	falls

On the most abstract level of capital in general, where c is set equal to zero, surplus value and the surplus labor might be the only relevant factors for consideration. But when we go on to the concrete level of capital in plurality, where c does not equal zero, c plays a role beyond that of a mere cost of production. It also is itself a source of the surplus generated. However on the level of many capitals Marx continued to exclude any conceptual space for capital as a value-creative force. In the terms of dialectical logic, Marx attempted to formulate a structural tendency on a concrete and complex categorial level through examining a structure that only allows abstract and simple determinations. From the standpoint of dialectical logic, whether there is a lack of factual evidence for a declining rate of profit is not the only question of interest. We must also ask whether Marx's theory rests on this categorial confusion between abstract and concrete levels.

Two points can be granted at once. First, different levels of productivity of c do affect profit rates, as the above example shows. Second, this c certainly appears to be distinct (and opposed to) the labor power that uses it. But it does not come out of thin air, nor does it come from capital investment. It ultimately comes from the creative acts of specific sorts of labor, scientific-technical labor as well as the other sorts of labor employed in the industries producing means of production.[19] Constant capital is the embodiment of these forms of labor; it is dead labor used by living labor rather than a distinct creative contribution to the labor process.

It is true that c appears as a distinct factor of production rather than as a mere combination of past labor with living labor. Why? Is it because it is inherently a distinct creative force? Hartmann answers as follows: "It is capital that allows the additional creation of value precisely when it is given out for the introduction of labor-saving machines."[20] But the fact that c is purchased by capitalists—and thus appears as distinct from (alien to) the workers employed to use it—is entirely a function of the specific social form of production that is capitalism. It is no argument that capital is inherently productive in and of itself. Imagine a system of workers' councils, with workers and their democratically elected representatives deciding upon how to employ the results of past labor in the means of production-producing industries. Under such conditions the differences in the productivity of different machines (hardly unknown to Marx!) would remain. But this would not be seen as the contribution of some second creative force. Instead it would be seen as the results of previous decisions, made by the workers themselves, to invest their labor and scientific-technical research in the production of one type of machinery rather than another. In the above example the superiority of case 1 over cases 2 and 3 would be seen as entirely due to the correctness of the decision to allocate research and labor to the industry producing the particular type of machinery used in case 1. Acknowledgement of the superiority of this machinery would not be equivalent to acknowledging a second creative contribution to production distinct from labor, for which "capital" deserves a special reward.[21] It would instead be equivalent to a decision to reallocate labor from industries producing the machines used in cases 2 and 3 to that producing machines used in case 1.

From this perspective it is the Hegelian critic of Marx who has failed to understand what is implied in a categorial ordering. When the concrete level of many capitals is attained, this does not reverse the entire previous set of determinations. Only those determinations are reversed that are incompatible with the structures defined on the more concrete level. The view that means of production represent dead labor, and that they only appear to be alien to living labor due to the capital/wage labor relation, is not at all incompatible with the move from the inner nature of capital to many capitals. It is not even incompatible with a recognition of the different degrees of productivity of machinery and the other components of c. Therefore there is no warrant for reversing those determinations now, even though we are on a more concrete level.

The next objection to be considered involves the question of constant capital as well.

2. Dialectical Logic and the Bias in Technical Change

The argument for the law of the tendency of the rate of profit to fall presupposes that the rate of profit is a negative function of the organic compostition of capital, c/v. Everything else being equal, increases in c relative to v lead to a lower rate of profit. In the mechanism where this occurs, competition forces capital units to seek the highest possible rate of

181

profit. This in turn leads to a striving for greater productivity. Greater productivity lowers costs per unit, so a firm can offer its products at a market price lower than its competitors. In this manner the firm can increase its market share. This greater productivity is won through increased investment in constant captial. When competition forces other units of capital to catch up, the result is a generalized increase in c/v, and thus a fall in the general rate of profit.

This counts, for Marx, as perhaps the basic contradiction in capitalism. As we saw in Chapter IV, the abstract form of social production (the value form) was ordered subsequently to immediately social forms of production precisely because it furthered productive capacity, expanded social cooperation, and developed human personality. With the falling rate of profit all those aspects stop well before what is technically possible has been attained.[22]

The vast literature on the tendency of the rate of profit to fall agrees on at least one point: Marx's argument does not work unless we presuppose the hidden premise that the search for productivity gains has a systematic bias in the direction of labor-saving technologies. However from the standpoint of the systems of simultaneous equations employed in mathematical economics, this bias has no foundation. Marx' argument is often rejected by mathematical economists on this ground.

This point can also be formulated in terms of dialectical logic. The question whether Marx was justified in asserting a labor-saving bias in technical change already arose in Chapter VII. There I argued that this claim was warranted; the social relations defining capital lead capital to prefer labor-saving technologies. However that was on a relatively abstract level of the theory, where the capital/wage labor relation was the topic and where competition among many capitals was abstracted from. Marx appears to assume here in Volume III that earlier categorial levels fix structural tendencies that continue to hold on later categorial levels. And so the earlier determinations of the wage labor/capital relation lead to the supposition that the bias toward labor-saving technologies continues to hold on more concrete levels of the theory. But according to dialectical logic, later categorial levels fix concrete structural tendencies. Previously considered tendencies may be put out of play altogether or operate only in a transformed sense. (For example, in Hegel's theory the structural tendencies of civil society are either put out of play or operate in a transformed manner once the more concrete level of the state has been reached.) On the concrete level of cost prices, prices of production, and market prices, c is treated as an equal factor in investment alongside v. And the force of competition demands that total cost be minimized relative to output, irrespective of how those costs are distinguished. Therefore, on the present level of concretion it would seem that technologies that lead to a reduction in the costs of constant capital would be just as welcome to the competing units of capital as labor-saving technologies. But without a systematic bias towards the latter, Marx's argument for the law of the tendency of the rate of profit to fall fails. It would seem that Marx could derive that law only by violating the canon of dialectical logic that mandates respecting the difference between abstract and concrete categorial levels.

It is true that in dialectical progressions the concrete adds new determinations to the abstract. But it is also true that the abstract is not eliminated but retained on the concrete level. In Hegel's *Philosophy of Right* it is true that civil society is transformed in its functioning once the level of the state has been reached. For instance the state has a right to interfere with property rights during wartime. But it is also true that civil society, supposedly characterized by principles of "freedom" as expressed in commodity exchange, sets structural parameters limiting the state (the state must in general respect property rights).

Marx's position in *Capital* is exactly parallel to this perspective. On the one hand, on the level of cost prices, prices of production, and market prices, the costs of constant capital are explicitly accounted for. Therefore Marx grants that capitalists will seek capital-saving technologies and employ them whenever possible. But on the other hand the capital/wage labor relationship, intrinsic to capital in general and considered on the abstract level of the theory, continues to set structural parameters to the workings on the concrete level. On the abstract level of the theory we discovered that the capital/wage labor relation, as the basic social relation of the capitalist mode of production, is an antagonistic one. It is with wage labor, not the residue of dead labor termed "constant capital," that capitalists must struggle to maintain their perogatives in the production process and over the surplus generated in it. And so Marx continued to insist on the concrete level not only that labor-saving technologies will be sought alongside capital-saving ones, but that *all else being equal* labor-saving technologies will in general be preferred. If only capital-saving technologies are available, or if they appear likely to lead to significantly greater profits, they will be employed; if both are available and appear comparably profitable, labor-saving technologies will be preferred.

Even if this argument is accepted it does not establish Marx's premise. It does establish a tendency for the technical composition of capital to increase, i.e. for an increase in the ratio of the physical mass of raw machinery, raw materials, and so on, to the mass of labor power. However this is not identical to the organic composition of capital, which is the ratio

183

between the respective values of these factors as they change over time. It is logically possible (in the sense of formal logic) for the technical composition of capital to increase without an increase in c/v. Since dialectical logic is concerned with structural tendencies and not individual occurences, this is not in itself a difficulty for Marx's position. What is a difficulty is that there does not seem to be any argument establishing a necessary structural tendency connecting increases in the technical composition of capital with increases in the organic composition. When the mass of constant capital increases, its value may fall, while the value of variable capital may rise, remain constant, or fall at a slower rate. The precise result depends upon a plurality of contingent historical circumstances, such as the nature of the technical advance, the organized strength of the working class in struggles to determine the value of labor power, etc. If this is the case then from a systematic perspective the law of the tendency of the rate of profit to fall breaks down.

Marx did grant that a fall in the value of constant capital was a countertendency to the law. But from a systematic perspective the law and countertendency are on the same level. They are equally possibilities latent in the structure defined on the present categorial stage. Marx's attempt to distinguish the level of the law from that of the countertendency infringes the canons of dialectical logic.

3. The Rate of Surplus Value

Even if c/v does rise, the rate of profit will fall only if the rate of exploitation either falls, remains constant, or rises less than the organic composition of capital. In this sense the theory of surplus value is a principle for the law of the tendency of the rate of profit to fall. In his numerical examples Marx kept the rate of surplus value constant. This supposition allowed the law to be derived. But if c/v rises, the greater productivity this implies necessarily leads either to an increase in real wages or an increase in the rate of surplus value. Since the reserve army of the unemployed and other factors hamper a rise in real wages proportional to productivity increases, there is a tendency for the rate of surplus value to rise. Of course Marx did state that a rise in the rate of surplus value is possible, and a countertendency to the law. But "the countervailing factors that Marx concedes (such as the rising rate of surplus value) are treated by Marx as secondary to the transcendentally prior thesis of the falling rate of profit."[23]

From a dialectical standpoint this objection also must be sustained. An increase in c/v would only be made if it enhanced productivity, i.e. if it was inseparable from an increase in s/v. Therefore increases in these two ratios fall on the same categorial level. In a systematic ordering there is no warrant for treating one as prior to the other. Nor is there any systematic reason for holding that c/v must increase at a faster rate than s/v. That is a thoroughly contingent matter. In some cases an increase in c relative to v may lead to a small gain in productivity (i.e. a small rise in s/v), in other cases the same increase might lead to a much larger gain. These considerations undermine Marx's derivation of the law of the tendency for the rate of profit to fall. This has potentially serious consequences for Marx's theory as a whole.

Marx placed considerable weight upon the law of the tendency of the rate of profit to fall. The law results in a "fettering" or "slumbering" of the productive forces. This was Marx's description for a state in which social needs which potentially could be met with the given level of productive capacity are not met, due to the social form within which production and distribution take place. Crises are not natural catastrophes. Crises are periods in which social needs go unmet despite the presence of ample raw materials, ready at hand factories and offices, and a willing labor force. They are thus irrational occurences. If it can be shown that a social system regularly leads to crises, this establishes the irrationality of that social system. This also sets the historical task for humanity of creating a set of institutions which combine the rational features of the present system without including its irrational features.[24] If the law of the tendency for the rate of profit to fall could be systematically derived within Marx's theory, then the critical intention of that theory would be fulfilled. Marx's derivation, however, does not work.[25] Does this mean that his critical intention is *not* fulfilled?

4. Crisis Theory

Let us examine the logic of Marx's argument more closely. Competition over sales among the many units of capital is both the motivation for introducing the productivity advances that allow one firm to undercut the maket prices of its competitors, and the force that leads these competitors to attempt to match those advances. The law of the tendency of the rate of profit to fall is thus formulated on the categorial level of market prices. Within the concrete and complex structure defined by the category market price, both capital and its "other," effective demand, are explicitly posited. However the law itself is derived in abstraction from part of the concrete structure fixed on this level. The law is derived solely from a consideration of the side of capital (c/v; s/v) with consideration of effective demand bracketed out. More specifically, Marx assumed that it is of the essence of capital to be producing at full capacity, to seek maximum accumulation and the highest rate of profit possible, and that in the concrete it cannot do otherwise than manifest this, its inner nature. When it does so, it increases c/v without regard for the long-term impact on the rate of profit. Marx's theory of the tendency of the rate of profit to fall stems from this. On this view, crises are pictured as an immanent limit to capital, in abstraction from effective demand. Given that Marx's argument doesn't hold up, two questions arise: a) did Marx formulate another sort of argument for crisis tendencies, an argument that incorporates effective demand; and b) if so, is this argument both consistent with his interpretation of capital in terms of the Hegelian category of essence and compelling in its own right?

a) Marx did propose an argument for crisis tendencies that takes into account the full categorial structure on the level of market prices, i.e. both capital and effective demand. In any given market a number of different units of capital compete. Each attempts to expand its market share. It does so through making productivity advances, which lower unit costs and therefore allow market prices to be lowered, undercutting the prices of competitors. This creates two problems for capital. First, the drive to lower unit costs leads to technical renewal. This renewal may come into conflict with the valorization of previous investment in fixed capital. In other words, technical advance may make machinery obsolete before the capital investment in that machinery has been paid off.[26] This may set off a money crisis.[27] A second problem is that this increase in productive capacity resulting from the technical renewal may exceed the ability of markets to absorb that capacity. (In this sense underconsumption is the secondary phenomenon and overproduction prior). Together these two tendencies ensure that it is necessarily the case that crises will regularly occur.[28]

Of course the lower prices brought about by the productivity advances may lead the initial market to expand. But this expansion sooner or later reaches its limits. The basic logic of the situation leads units of capital to increase productive capacity past these limits. The (temporary) expansion of the market will also have encouraged other units of capital to enter the market, giving yet further impetus to the expansion of productive capacity. The inevitable result is a tendency to overproduction; taken all together the many units of capital tend to produce far more than the market can possibly absorb. When this occurs some of this excess productive capacity must now be destroyed. Some firms in this market must go bankrupt and/or be absorbed by others. Marx held that given the interdependency of different markets, the linkages that connect suppliers, distributors, etc., it is necessarily the case that problems resulting from overproduction regularly tend to become generalized. At this point overproduction crises break out. This crisis, however, includes the seeds of its own reversal.[29] In a crisis much previous investment in constant capital cannot be regained. This leads to a devalorization of that capital.[30] It either loses all its worth, or it can be valorized only at a significantly lesser cost. This is bad news for the initial investors, but good news for other units of capital that are now able to

186

absorb what remains of worth in this constant capital at a drastically lower cost. In this manner further investment is again stimulated.[31] Thus we see in crisis a general tendency to the concentration of capitals emerging. This process also helps solve the overproduction/underconsumption difficulty. Part of the devalued investment in productive capacity is put out of play altogether, thereby addressing part of the cause for the overproduction crisis. Finally, the crisis puts workers out of work, forcing them to accept cutbacks. This is equivalent to a rise in the rate of surplus value.[32]

b) As it stands, this argument for overproduction crisis remains consistent with Marx's characterization of capital in essence terms. Capital remains an impersonal and objective force that subjects all those under it to its sway, including individual capitalists. But is this argument compelling? Let us examine a critique of the argument for overproduction crises made from a systematic viewpoint. On the abstract level of Marx's theory, the inner nature of capital—considered apart from effective demand—was asserted to consist in the drive to accumulate surplus value. On that level capital was treated as an essence in the Hegelian sense, subsuming wage laborers, consumers, and even capitalists to the imperatives of capital accumulation. On the concrete level of many units of capital in competition with each other over market prices, however, effective demand must be explicitly taken into account. On the concrete level it is not the drive to accumulate that alone defines capital; the concern for realization issues is also present. This leads each of the many units of capital to take into account each other's productive capacity. In this manner the many units of capital in principle can attain a harmonious adjustment of production to demand. When this occurs the structure is one of mutuality, rather than one in which all are subjected to an alien social form. From this perspective a *Begriffslogik* capturing the element of reciprocity would be more appropriate than the *Wesenslogik* to which Marx clung.[33]

Marx is quite willing to grant the possibility of a dynamic equilibrium between productive capacity and demand. This, after all, was a central topic of Volume II. The question is whether once such an equilibrium has been attained it will reproduce itself indefinitely. Volume III points out some factors that suggest that equilibrium can only be temporary. There are two main points to emphasize. The first is epistemological in nature. With productive forces in private hands it is impossible for a unit of capital to know the investment plans of its competitors, and therefore it is impossible for it to know what total productive capacity will be in the future. Likewise with demand a function of privately articulated decisions, it is impossible to establish demand in the future with any precision. Even if these epistemological problems could be resolved, there is a free-rider problem to be faced.

187

Each unit of capital wants to have the greatest share of the market possible. If other firms in the market lower their output while it alone doesn't, then it can expand its market share while benefitting from a situation where production and demand are pretty much in sync. But of course if all the units think along the same lines, then no one will cut their production, and overproduction crises cannot be avoided. This is not to say that cartels cannot be effective. They can be maintained over extended periods of time. But they will always be inherently fragile, and thus unlikely to provide stability. We must conclude that the sort of reciprocal harmony among units of capital referred to above is not possible, given the general inability of capitals to coordinate their planning. This inability results from the inner nature of capitalism:

> So long as things go well, competition effects an operating fraternity of the capitalist class . . . But as soon as it no longer is a question of sharing profits, but of sharing losses, everyone tries to reduce his own share to a minimum and to shove it off upon another. The class, as such, must inevitably lose. How much the individual capitalist must bear of the loss, i.e., to what extent he must share in it at all, is decided by strength and cunning, and competition then becomes a fight among hostile brothers. The antagonism between each individual capitalists' interests and those of the capitalist class as a whole, then comes to the surface, just as previously the identity of these interests operated in practice through competition.[34]

At this point the orthodox Hegelian once again would introduce the state as a *deus ex machina*, arguing that in principle the state may intervene whenever the reflection among the many units of capital, and between capital and demand, proves insufficient: for Marx's theory to be satisfactory, "a taking into account of simultaneously working extra-economic factors would have had to follow (as for instance the influence of the state through anticoncentration, antimonopoly, and anticartel legislation, fiscal measures, investment activity, interest and currency policy, etc.). It does not require any further consideration to conclude that the argumentation for crises in the Marxist form is not acceptable."[35] This topic, however, will be postponed to the next chapter.

D. The Dialectic of Nonindustrial Capital

We come at last to the conclusion of Volume III, where Marx considered those economic phenomena which are the furthest away from value considerations: merchant capital, bank capital, interest, precious metals, ground rent, etc. (Chapters XVI-XLVII). The economic details of these

188

discussions cannot be gone into here. Our main concern must be instead for the systematic place of these categories, which can be sketched as follows:

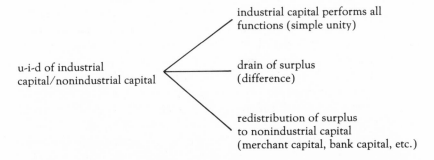

industrial capital performs all
functions (simple unity)

u-i-d of industrial
capital/nonindustrial capital

drain of surplus
(difference)

redistribution of surplus
to nonindustrial capital
(merchant capital, bank capital, etc.)

The last categorial structure considered above was that of many units of industrial capital competing over market prices. We can make the transition to the next stage in the theory by noting that certain conditions must be fulfilled if this structure is to be reproduced. Reserve funds must be available in case payments to a firm are delayed for one reason or another. Reserve funds must also be available in case the given firm itself faces a due payment. Likewise there are certain costs involved with the storage of goods at final and intermediate points of sale and with the selling process itself.[36] Reserve funds must be available to cover these costs. The simplest and most immediate manner of dealing with these and similar issues is to have the units of industrial capital directly fulfill these functions themselves. This fixes a structure of simple unity on the present level.

This structure is contradictory. On the one hand the drive of these units of capital is to maximize the surplus value they retain. On the other hand the costs involved in sales, in the hoarding of reserve funds, and so on, are all a drain on this surplus. This forms the moment of difference, of negativity, in the present dialectic. What is now called for is a way of incorporating this moment of difference within a higher level unity. This sort of unity-in-difference structure can be found when qualitatively different types of capital arise to take on these costs, and these different types of capital are united with industrial capital through a redistribution of the surplus. The different types of nonindustrial capital specialize in one of the surplus-draining functions, and perform that function more efficiently than industrial capital itself could. The sale of goods is taken over by merchant capital, reserve funds are centralized under bank capital,[37] and so on. The units of industrial capital have to redistribute the surplus[38] so that these other forms of capital also tend to get a rate of profit more or less equal to that of industrial capital. But industrial capital still is able to retain more of

189

the surplus than it otherwise would, given the greater efficiency of these other types of capital in fulfilling the functions of selling, loaning, etc.

There is one type of nonindustrial capital that warrants special mention: rent. The unity of industrial capital and rent capital is one of unity-in-difference as well. But the moment of difference here is not a surplus draining function that must be fulfilled if reproduction is to occur. The moment of difference arises instead when industrial capital confronts a necessary precondition for its reproduction that it cannot incorporate within itself in an immediate and simple fashion (i.e. *qua* a structure of simple unity). Industrial capital requires a physical context in order to produce commodities (that is expecially true regarding the land needed for production of farm commodities, of course, but the point is general). If that physical context is privately owned by a distinct stratum, then this ownership confronts industrial capital as "other."[39] The payment of rent is the incorporation of that otherness within a structure of unity-in-difference. In rent, part of the surplus generated by industrial capital is transferred to landholders within a structure that is more complex and concrete than that of industrial capital alone:

> If capital meets an alien force which it can but partially, or not at all, overcome, and which limits its investment in certain spheres, admitting it only under conditions which wholly or partly exclude that general equalisation of surplus-value to an average profit, then it is evident that the excess of the value of commodities in such spheres of production over their price of production would give rise to a surplus-profit, which could be converted into rent and as such made independent with respect to profit. Such an alien force and barrier are presented by landed property, when confronting capital in its endeavour to invest in land; such a force is the landlord vis-a-vis the capitalist.[40]

From the standpoint of Hegelian dialectical logic there is no new objection to raise against this part of Marx's theory. The fundamental objection has been made beforehand: Marx fixed the inner nature of capital in the early stages by abstracting from elements that are essentially part of that inner nature. His critical evaluation of the inner nature of capital stems from this arbitrary procedure, rather than from the nature of capital itself. Thus by the time we get to the later stages of the theory the damage has been done: "Marx's analyses of the later themes does not imply that the determination of capital is modified by them. The decisive theses of *Capital* remain undisturbed . . . In Marx's perspective capital has already been interpreted at the beginning."[41]

We have already mentioned Hartmann's view that credit should have been introduced at an earlier stage of the theory. If this had been done, the earlier prejorative interpretation of capital would have had to be modified. The arbitrary ordering of his theory, and not the inner nature of capital, led Marx to see the genesis of capital in a primitive expropriation of peasant producers rather than in saving and credit.[42] Similarly the failure to consider credit prior to the present late stage of the theory undermines the theory of crisis constructed on earlier, more abstract, stages of the theory: "Looked at closer, economically the fact that interest is not taken into account in the theory of capital makes the treatment of the crisis mechanism and its (partial) self-correcting impossible."[43] From this perspective it could be that crises really stem from concrete phenomena that are only contingently related to the inner nature of capital, phenomena such as the stock market.[44]

I have already discussed these issues at the appropriate earlier levels of the theory. Only a few comments need to be added here. First, an examination of interest and credit that wishes to comprehend the social relations involved cannot just point out that interest is attached to many capitals and that credit is a reward for waiting. If we want to grasp the social relations here we have to ask how it is that some accumulate enough money capital to be able to live off the interest. Why are they able to lend money capital, rather than spend it on consumption? The standard answer is that lenders have different time preferences. But "time preferences" are more than a natural fact regarding different psychological propensities. They are social facts that depend on a social form. Because some parties own the society's productive resources and some do not, some are able to accumulate considerable reserve funds while others are not. As a result some are able to develop the "time preference" required to lend funds out for interest while others are not. In other words from the standpoint of social relations "interest" and "credit" logically presuppose the capital form. Hence it is entirely proper for Marx to consider the latter first in his systematic ordering of categories.

The point can be put another way. According to the objection, abstracting from interest and credit prevents an adequate comprehension of capital. This would hold only if considering interest and credit earlier in the theory would force us to revise the fundamental structures articulated in Marx's category of "capital." Does the existence of credit and interest undermine the capital/wage labor relation? Not at all. It *reinforces* that relation. Credit lent to capital to further capital accumulation is qualitatively distinct from consumer credit; it occupies entirely distinct branches of banks, is made on entirely distinct criteria, and so on.[45] This elementary fact cannot be grasped unless we *presuppose* an understanding of the capital/wage labor relation. Hence it is legitimate to consider this relation first in the categorial progression.

191

On the subject of crises it is entirely true that crises cannot be concretely understood unless credit, bank capital, stock markets, etc., are taken into account. But it is also true that basic mechanisms setting off crises *can* be understood without a consideration of these phenomena. The fact that stock markets both exacerbate other crisis tendencies and create new ones of their own in no way suggests that the systematic ordering proposed by Marx must be abandoned. The mechanisms leading to overproduction crises discussed above would remain even if all stock markets were abolished. And credit can no more remove the immanent tendency to overproduction crises than it can remove the tendency to disproportionality crises.[46]

E. Evaluation of the Final Stages of the Capital Form

Before the final discussion of the last stage of *Capital*, we should take a quick look back at the beginning of the work. *Capital* is part of the general theory of historical materialism. The philosophical dimension of this theory consists in the attempt to order various forms of social production in a systematic fashion. From this perspective the dialectic in *Capital* has a two-fold objective: to establish a) that the value form (the money form, the capital form) of social production is an advance over immediately social forms of social production, and b) that there are immanent shortcomings in the value form that ultimately prevent it from being an adequate form of social production, with "adequate" meaning "capable of attaining a dialectical reconciliation of individual/universal (community)."

Throughout this study I have argued that the complexity of Marx's objective is manifested in the complexity of his dialectical progression of economic categories. Unlike Hegel's systematic theories, the progression is not a simple teleology. It does not simply move to (normatively) higher and higher stages, to forms that are to be affirmed more than those that have gone before, to categorial levels that are progressively "truer." But neither is Marx's theory simply a derivation of negative forms from negative forms, with each succeeding form more worthy of critique than the preceding one. It is not simply a dysteleology. Instead, as the determinations of the value form progress, those aspects that make the value form an advance over the immediately social forms of social production develop as well. Simultaneously, those aspects that ultimately prevent the value form from being an adequate form of social production also develop.

On the last stages of his linear ordering these contradictory features reach their most aggravated shape. Credit, for instance, is a complex and concrete manifestation of those aspects of the value form that mark it as an advance over immediately social forms of social production. Credit is a form to be affirmed for two reasons: 1) it allows the productive capacity of the society to be developed to the greatest extent possible within the capital form ("The credit system accelerates the material development of the productive forces and the establishment of the world-market. It is the historical mission of the capitalist system of production to raise these material foundations...to a certain degree of perfection."[47] and 2) it also constitutes a social advance. The value form is a form of *social* production; although it is privately undertaken, the labor within it is social labor. When decisions regarding investments are made privately by the owners of capital this is covered over. But in the credit form these decisions—while still undertaken privately— explicitly take on a social character they lacked before:

> We have seen that the average profit of the individual capitalist, or of every individual capital, is determined not by the surplus-labour appropriated at first hand by each capital, but by the quantity of total surplus-labour appropriated by the total capital, from which each individual capital receives its dividend only proportional to its aliquot part of the total capital. This social character of capital is first promoted and wholly realized through the full development of the credit and banking system. On the other hand this goes farther. It places all the available and even potential capital of society that is not already actively employed at the disposal of the industrial and commercial capitalists so that neither the lenders nor users of this capital are its real owners or producers. It thus does away with the private character of capital and thus contains in itself, but only in itself, the abolition of capital itself. By means of the banking system the distribution of capital as a special business, a social function, is taken out of the hands of the private capitalists and usurers.[48]

From this perspective the systematic ordering in *Capital* is teleological in the same sense as in Hegelian theory. Earlier stages in the linear order are more "untrue," and the dialectic moves towards forms that are more and more to be affirmed: "It is one of the civilising aspects of capital that it enforces this surplus-labour in a manner and under conditions which are more advantageous to the development of the productive forces, social relations, and the creation of the elements for a new and higher form than under the preceding forms of slavery, serfdom, etc."[49]

This, however, is only half the story. Marx combines the teleological nature of the categorial ordering with a critical, dystelological dimension lacking in Hegel. The very same later stages that are to be affirmed more are also simultaneously to be criticized more. The categorial structures discussed at the end of Volume III are negative forms in four respects. First,

193

the fetishism that has characterised the value form throughout reaches its highest manifestation here. In earlier stages one example of this fetishism was the tendency to see "capital" as a thing with mystical creative powers operating alongside labor. With interest capital, however, capital is granted these mystical powers in itself, apart from any connection with labor.[50] Second, the structures articulated by these later forms are inherently unstable and they push the instability of the capital form to its highest point.[51] Third, the later developments of the capital form do not reverse the fundamental social antagonism that has characterized the capital form throughout. The capital/wage labor antagonism may be more hidden in the greater fetishism of the concrete structures introduced at the conclusion of Marx's theory. But it is also in principle aggravated. These later categories such as interest and credit heighten the structural tendency for capital to be concentrated. As the concentration of capital increases, its force as an alien power standing over against labor increases as well.[52] Finally, these later categories also include structural tendencies for further sorts of social antagonisms to arise that could not be conceptualised on earlier stages of the theory. There is a latent antagonism between bank capital and industrial capital, for example, that comes violently to the fore in periods of crises.[53] Any pretense that the capital form allows for a rational ordering of social life breaks down in the face of this.[54]

This all suggests that the value form of social wealth, culminating in the most concrete forms of the capital form, cannot be the final stage in a systematic ordering of the forms of social production. A new social form of production must be introduced, one which combines the affirmative aspects of the value form while overcoming those features of it that must be criticized. This is the socialist form.

X

Conclusion

The tasks set in Chapter III have now been completed. We have traced the systematic ordering that leads from one category to the next in *Capital*, an ordering that follows a dialectical logic. We have also seen that Marx's use of dialectical logic can be defended against objections from the orthodox Hegelian standpoint. I now would like to point forward to further areas of investigation suggested by this dialectical reading of *Capital*. Three such areas will be presented here: the investigation of alternative principles to "value," the dialectic of the state form, and the proper categorization of the socialist form. Each of these topics deserves a separate study. Here a brief sketch of a future research agenda must suffice.

A. Value Theory and Its Alternatives

From the systematic perspective the category "value" must fulfill two distinct roles in Marx's theory.[1] First, it must allow us to separate the object realm to be investigated from other object realms. Second, it must provide the first (i.e. the simplest and most abstract) principle for the derivation of the progressively more complex and concrete categories that reconstruct the intelligibility of that object realm. In Chapter IV, I argued that "value" can be used in fulfilling the first task. In Chapters IV-IX, I established that "value" can fulfill the second role. Beginning from "value" we can systematically proceed to a step-by-step categorial reconstruction of generalized commodity production.

195

Even if all this is granted, however, a question still remains: Might not there be some other category that could help us accomplish these two tasks just as well, if not better, than the category value? If this were the case, then one could construct a theory of the sort Marx set out to construct in *Capital* without employing the category of value.

There is not space to be exhaustive here. Instead I shall briefly and provisionally examine three of the most significant theoretical alternatives to Marxian value theory: neoclassical economics, Weberian social theory, and Neo-Ricardian (Sraffian) economics. Each view presupposes an alternative to replace "value" as the foundational category in the analysis of the capitalist mode of production: "Utility," "formal rationality," and "prices of production," respectively. In order to make this discussion more manageable I shall simply assume that a system of socio-economic determinations could in principle be derived from each of these different starting points.

1. Utility

Neoclassical economics has usually been seen by Marxists as a primary example of a nondialectical theory. It has been seen as empiricist, as "vulgar economics." On this view neoclassical economics is solely concerned with operations on the most concrete level of the economy, and not at all with underlying structures captured in more abstract principles.

This is a somewhat unfair charge against neoclassical economics. In principle the neoclassical position could be presented as a dialectical theory. Not all of the fundamental determinations used in neoclassical theory fall on the same categorial level. The notion of "utility" is clearly its most basic thought determination, an abstract and simple principle for grasping the intelligibility of capitalism.

Let us imagine a neoclassical economist who has somehow been deeply influenced by Hegel and attempts to derive a categorial theory using "utility" as a starting point. Let us even further suppose for the sake of the argument that beginning with this notion the theorist is able to move in a step-by-step fashion through various other determinations, arriving at the end with capitalism in its concreteness. Such a neoclassical Hegelian would have a number of reasons for considering this as superior to a reconstruction based on value theory. Advantages in both simplicity and comprehension could be claimed. This approach is simpler than Marx's in that beginning with utility rather than value avoids the difficulties of any transformation of values into prices, difficulties that linger after decades of discussion. And it is a more comprehensive approach in that it can account for the intelligibility of trade in found objects, rare paintings, and so on. Labor considerations seem to be fairly irrelevant here, whereas the question of the utility of these objects clearly is not.

Marxists should not underestimate these advantages. Nonetheless, utility theory must be rejected on the elementary grounds that the concept of "utility" fails to fulfill the central function assigned to the initial category in a reconstruction of the capitalist mode of production. It fails to delimit that form of social production from others. The purchaser of slaves, the guild master bringing craft works to market, the bureaucrat working out a centralized plan for the allocation of goods, the participants in workers councils where such plans would be worked out democratically, all essentially employ utility calculations in their economic decision making.

At this point our neoclassical Hegelian might attempt to specify various ways utility considerations operate in the different modes of production. There clearly is something that distinguishes a slave owner, socially defined as a "person," choosing how to maximize his utility in the purchase of a slave, socially defined as a "thing," from utility calculations where all that matters is effective demand in the market, or from utility calculations in which production is to be matched with democratically articulated social needs. But with this move to institutional boundary conditions the utility theorist has admitted defeat. For he or she has now admitted that to distinguish one mode of production from another one must have reference to the notion of social form, and that this is logically prior to considerations of utility if our theoretical project is to delimit one specific mode of production.

2. Technical Rationality

Weberian social theory offers an alternative to value theory that avoids the difficulty of the neoclassical position. The beginning of Weber's *Economy and Society* can be read as a reconstruction of the fundamental categories of social theory, ordered from the most simple and abstract determination ("Social Action") to more complex and concrete categories (e.g. "Political and Hierocratic Organizations"). This theory of categories attempts to reconstruct the principles of intelligibility for the social realm as a whole rather than for any historically specific case. Nonetheless in the course of this theory Weber does propose certain basic categories from which the key features of the capitalist mode of production can be derived. The central category here is that of technical (formal) rationality. Unlike the notion of utility the concept of technical rationality can fulfill the first function required of the initial determination in a reconstruction of generalized commodity production. In can clearly delimit this form of social production from others. Capitalism can indeed be grasped as a system in which formal rationality holds sway in the economic sphere, in contrast to other modes of production where traditional considerations or a material rationality are more essential.

Let us suppose that a Weberian has somehow been influenced by Hegel and attempts to work out a categorial reconstruction of capitalism. Let us further suppose that beginning with the notion of technical rationality the theorist was able to move in a step-by-step fashion through various other determinations, arriving at the end with capitalism in its concreteness. Let us even suppose for the sake of argument that our Hegelian Weberian can claim with some plausibility that this approach has both a simplicity and comprehensiveness that more than matches Marx's theory. Would we not then have to concede that this position is superior to value theory?

No. Even if our imagined Weberian categorial reconstruction could make good all these claims, one fundamental problem remains. For Weber technical rationality in capitalism involves capital accounting. Weber himself admitted that technical or formal rationality can become fully institutionalized only *after* labor has been make a formally calculable factor of production: "Persons must be present who are not only legally in the position, but are also economically compelled, to sell their labor on the market without restriction. It is in contradiction to the essence of capitalism, and development of capitalism is impossible, if such a property-less stratum is absent, a class compelled to sell its labor services to live; and it is likewise impossible if only unfree labor is at hand. *Rational capitalist calculation is possible only on the basis of free labor*; only where in consequence of the existence of workers who in the formal sense voluntarily, but actually under the compulsion of the whip of hunger, offer themselves, the costs of products may be unambiguously determined by agreement in advance."[2] In other words, we must presuppose that labor itself has taken on the commodity form. This in turn means that we must presuppose that what Marx termed "the form of value" is *already* operative and applied to labor power.

Technical rationality may successfully delimit the capitalist mode of production. But since it itself presupposes other determinations, it is not the most simple and abstract category to do so. Hence there is a more simple and abstract category that should stand at the beginning of the categorial reconstruction, and this turns out to be precisely Marx's category of value.

3. Prices of Production

Among progressive social theorists Sraffa's economics has probably provided the most influential foundation for a rejection of the labor theory of value. Unlike Ricardo's own theory, the Neo-Ricardian position of Sraffa and his followers seems to be based on an empiricist ideology. By this I mean that it appears to assume a single-tiered social ontology that does not point to any deeper level of underlying structures. Its equations relate physically specified conditions of production and real wages to prices of production and the rate of profit. All the terms of these equations are viewed as simultaneously coexisting on the same level of concreteness. In these equations "no reference to any derivative value magnitudes (is) of the slightest significance to that determination."[3]

Let us assume, just for the sake of argument, that Sraffians such as Steedman have successfully refuted the quantitative relations connecting values/surplus values to prices/profits that Marx supposed.[4] Would this be equivalent to a refutation of the labor theory of value? Not at all. Value theory has three components: the form of value, the substance of value, and the magnitude of value. Even under the most favorable view, the calculations of Steedman and others at the very most prove solely that one aspect of the magnitude of value (that concerned with its relation to prices of production) does not hold. No more, no less.

This leaves Marx's notions of the form of value and the substance of value (as well as the remaining aspects of the magnitude of value, which I shall not consider further). What place do these notions have for Neo-Ricardians? For the most part they are simply presupposed in Neo-Ricardian theory under the heading "underlying assumptions." Steedman writes, for instance, that in his book "the only economies considered are commodity economies, in which all products are produced for exchange and in which production and the allocation of labour power between industries are co-ordinated solely through the market."[5] In other words, all labor is privately undertaken, and must prove whether it counts as social labor in market exchange. But this is precisely what Marx meant by the form of value. Likewise we also find the "underlying assumption" that "unless otherwise stated, all labour is taken to be unskilled, 'simple' labour, all labour being of equal ability and equal 'intensity'... All summations of labour-time are summations of quantities of abstract labour."[6] This, of course, captures part of what Marx meant by the substance of value.[7] Far from being refuted, large chunks of value theory have been smuggled into this position under the term *underlying assumptions*.

From the standpoint of a dialectical reconstruction of fundamental categories two major shortcomings follow. First, Neo-Ricardian theory fails to explore adequately the initially presupposed determinations in and of themselves. Second, it fails to move in a step-by-step fashion from these initial determinations ("underlying assumptions") to the relatively more concrete level of physically specified inputs, labor time, and outputs.

From a systematic perspective there is a third problem as well. Sraffian

199

analysis assumes that the prices of outputs determine the prices of inputs into production. This can be the case only it we abstract from technical change. It also holds that the rate of profit is equal across the economy. And this is never the case concretely; it holds only for certain levels of abstraction. In other words, the level of prices and profits investigated by Neo-Ricardian theory is *not* that of the concrete phenomena of capitalism. Just as there is a categorial level prior to that of prices of production—implicitly acknowledged in the talk of "underlying assumptions"—so too there is a level that is subsequent to that level where technical change occurs continually and rates of profit diverge. This, however, is not acknowledged.

We may conclude that Neo-Ricardian theory is not an alternative to value theory. It is a more limited theory with a theoretical task that fits *within* value theory: the construction of a theory of prices of production as distinct district from the more abstract level of prices proportional to values and from the more concrete level of market prices. The point is not that Steedman and others ignore social relations. The point is that they consider only one level of social relations in capitalism, ignoring both the other levels and the inner logic that connects them together. If one simply wished to have a quantitative formula regarding abstract profits and prices of production, then value theory will indeed appear a waste of time. But such a formula can hardly claim to be a full reconstruction of the intelligibility of capitalism in its totality.

B. The State Form

The three volumes of *Capital* form only a fragment of what was to be Marx's complete system. Three further volumes were projected, on the state, foreign trade, and the world market.[8] It is easy to see how these further developments would follow the same sort of dialectical logic as that in *Capital*. The state, limited to a single territory, forms a category of simple unity on this advanced level. Foreign trade introduces a moment of difference, in which the state comes into contact with what is "other" than it. Finally world trade forms a dialectical unity of unity (the world market itself) and difference (the different nationally based capitals).

A problem remains. Even if this further development of the theory would be consistent with the dialectical ordering Marx did complete, it might still lead to a reversal of determinations found in *Capital*. Let us once again return to the Marx/Hegel debate from this perspective.

The orthodox Hegelian stresses that civil society belongs on the level of *Sittlichkeit*, ethical life, as opposed to that of abstract right or morality. As such it is a universal, a unity-in-difference that is categorizable in terms of a

Begriffslogik. The contrast between this perspective and that defended by Marx has been one of the central issues of the present study. However the orthodox Hegelian position goes beyond this point. For Hegelians civil society is only a relative universal. Hegelians agree with Marxists to the extent that, for Hegelians too, the moment of difference, of antagonisms among particular interests, retains a central importance within the unity-in-difference that is civil society. In other words, within the level of *Sittlichkeit* civil society is on the level of essence, *Wesen*. For the orthodox Hegelian there is a higher categorial level than that of civil society, a more affirmative social form, a higher universality. This is the state. The state transforms the manner in which civil society functions, lifting it to a reconciliation of universal and individual beyond what it could attain on its own.

Let us grant for the sake of the argument that it has been shown in the present work that Hegel failed to establish a justification for a *Begriffslogik* interpretation of civil society taken in itself. Since for Hegel civil society is a subordinate sphere whose functioning is transformed by the state, it could still be the case that civil society can indeed be viewed in *Begriff* terms in so far as it has been transformed by the state.[9] In contrast, Marxists define the state as ultimately the representative of capitalist interests. This means that while the state may follow the capital form in Marx's systematic ordering, it does not introduce new determinations that would lead the social order as a whole to be categorizable in terms of Hegel's *Begriffslogik*. Hegelians argue in reply that the Marxist position cannot account for the many forms of state legislation that go against the short- and long-term interests of capital. Whatever imbalances may exist in principle on the socio-economic level between capital and labor, capital and consumers, and among individual capitalists, in principle can be corrected through worker's-rights legislation, consumer-rights legislation, and the coordination of investment on the level of the state. The state is a distinct type of institution that can reconcile whatever antagonism remains within the level of civil society. If this were the case, then obviously Marx's conclusions would have to be drastically revised.

The move to the universality of the state is not as foreign to Marx as might at first appear. Marx thought that universal suffrage would lead to a transformed society in which the interests of the working classes were taken into account. He even speculated that universal suffrage might provide a mechanism for a peaceful transition to socialism.[10] It seems only a small step from this position to the view that universal suffrage would transform the social system sufficiently to incorporate the interests of the working classes, while still retaining a capitalist market society. Arguing for the universality of such a reformed capitalist state does not even require that this reformed

201

state fulfill the universal interest as well as a socialist system could. Every transaction involves opportunity costs, including the transition to socialism. As long as the cost of reforming capitalism were sufficiently low relative to those involved in the transition to socialism, then the former could still claim to better embody the Hegelian moment of universality—even if in the abstract the latter might be preferred.[11]

The debate on Marx's theory of the state shows no signs of abating.[12] Here I can do no more than sketch some of the familiar reasons for rejecting the Hegelian approach to the state. We can summarize the case in four propositions. If any one of these propositions were true, let alone a conjunction of them, this would be sufficient to undermine the state's claim to universality.

Concentrated economic power seeps into the political sphere, leading to a tendency to concentrated political power. The argument for this proposition is straightforward. Economic power grants those who possess it the ability to influence the political process disproportionately. Rational agents who have this ability will tend to take advantage of it. Those in capitalist society who own and control capital generally possess economic power and generally are rational. Therefore we may conclude that they generally will disproportionately influence the political process.

This may take a wide variety of forms. The owners and controllers of capital may themselves hold political office. Or others who run for office may be dependent on them for financing and therefore adjust their political program accordingly. Those with economic power have the resources to lobby extensively for their porposals. They also have the resources to set up various research groups, institutes, councils, etc. to shape public policies.[13] They have the resources as well to shape the media through which information is transmitted, whether through direct ownership or indirectly through the dependency of those media on advertising revenues.[14] In this manner public opinion can be shaped. Such features make it most unlikely that the capitalist state can attain a level of universality sufficient to make Hegel's *Begriffslogik* applicable to the social order as a whole.

The Hegelian would argue that this argument merely shows that the state must intervene in the marketplace in order to ensure equality of political opportunity. This is argued for at length by Winfield in his defense of Hegel's call for public regulation of the market. However Winfield also acknowledges that there is tendency towards the concentration and centralization of capital.[15] And concentrated economic power inevitably undermines the equality of political opportunity. At this point there are only two options. Either the demand for equality of political opportunity is given up, thereby abandoning the state's claim to universality; or new socio-economic institutions are introduced that do not involve concentrated economic power, thereby abandoning civil society as described in *The Philosophy of Right*. Either way the Hegelian project breaks down in incoherence.

The remaining three propositions consider structural factors in the capitalist state that would hold even if the points mentioned under the first did not prevent the election of a progressive political administration. In this context "progressive" connotes a serious commitment to the Hegelian objective of instituting a state that transforms civil society so as to allow for a reconciliation of universal and individual.

The state's need for revenues forces it to further capital accumulation. In order to carry out an agenda reconciling universal and individual the state would need considerable resources at its disposal. However, by definition, in a capitalist market society the main sources of wealth are privately owned and controlled. The state therefore must tax the private owners of wealth in order to acquire the necessary revenues. This means that even state officials committed to progressive policies are dependent upon the economic well-being of the taxed. The tax base is the sum total of profits, interest payments received, salaries, wages, etc. And these are all generally a function of the rate of accumulation. In order to ensure sufficient revenues, therefore, the administration must commit itself to furthering the condition of capital accumulation.[16] But we are supposing that capital accumulation involves precisely that failure to reconcile universal and individual that it was the state's task to overcome. Therefore the state cannot fulfill that task. As long as a capitalist market society exists, it is most unlikely that the state can attain a level of universality sufficient to make Hegel's *Begriffslogik* applicable to the social order as a whole.

The state's dependency on the market for government bonds forces it to serve the interests of capital. If we combine the disproportionate political influence of those who own/control capital with the state's need for revenues, we can derive a structural tendency for the state to not tax the owners and controllers of capital sufficiently to cover its revenue needs. If this is the case the resulting deficit must be covered through the sale of government bonds to private investors. This arrrangement in effect grants these private investors a veto power over state policy. If a political administration came to power that was sincerely committed to reconciling the universal and the individual, this would regularly lead it to overturn the perceived self-interest of the owners and controllers of capital. But in the eyes of the purchasers of government bonds this would not be "sound economic policy." They therefore would refuse to purchase the bonds unless interest rates were raised considerably.

This would cause the cost of credit to soar. And this would provoke a general rise in the cost of credit throughout the economy, perhaps setting off an economic downturn. Whether or not that was the case, it would lead to more and more of the state's revenues being diverted to meeting interest payments, leaving fewer and fewer resources for carrying out its initial program. If the state responded by simply printing more money, the situation would not be changed. The investors in the government bonds would simply demand higher and higher rates to offset the inevitable inflation. If the state persisted in carrying out its program despite all this, the situation would eventually deteriorate to the point where private investors decided that government bonds were too great an investment risk to continue purchasing. The state would then be forced to revamp its agenda so as to appear "prudent" and "responsible" to these investors. In this manner state policy eventually comes to reflect the perceived interests of a relatively small group of investors. The interests of the remainder of society would be incorporated only to the extent that they are compatible with the perceived interests of these investors.[17]

If there are structural factors in a capitalist market society that generally bring about this result, then it is most unlikely that the state can attain a level of universality sufficient to make Hegel's *Begriffslogik* applicable to the social order as a whole.

Capital strike is the ultimate mechanism ensuring that the state remains a capitalist state. This final proposition generalizes the case of an investment strike undertaken by the purchasers of government bonds. Let us once again imagine that a regime has come to office on a platform based on Hegel's *Philosophy of Right.* State officials sincerely wish to attain a level of concrete universality in the polity. And so they pass strict legislation regarding the provision of public goods, transfer payments to the poor, consumer rights, worker rights, the coordination of investments, etc. To some extent such legislation may be compatible with the perceived interests of capital. But there will be many cases where it is not. (Hegelians must grant this if they are to provide a systematic motivation for introducing the state as a higher-level universal than civil society.) In these cases a state that sought to obtain the universal interest would have to pass and enforce legislation that significantly went against the perceived interests of capital. How would those who own and control capital respond to this? Given the ultimately private control of investment decisions that defines capitalism, the all but inevitable result would be a capital strike. Investment funds would be hoarded, or devoted to speculation, or diverted to overseas investment, or dissipated in an orgy of luxury consumption. Such an investment strike would bring the economy to a screeching halt. Unemployment would rise drastically.

Numerous firms would go bankrupt. The limited fiscal resources of the state would be undermined. And so on.

At this point state officials would face an alternative. They could take away from the small group that owns and controls capital the ability to veto public policy through a capital strike. This would involve removing investment decisions from private hands and subjecting them to some form of public control. With this we have moved away from capitalism. Therefore at this point the Hegelian claim that a *capitalist* state can attain a level of concrete universality is put out of play. Or the state officials, fearing the social unrest set off by the capital strike, could quickly rescind the legislation that was offensive to those who own and control capital. This would be done under the guise that it was necessary to provide a favorable investment climate "to get the economy moving." This may make the economy move, but with this option the attempt to establish a universal interest has been abandoned.

The above thought experiment establishes that the private ownership of the means of production in effect grants the owners and controllers of capital an indirect veto power over state legislation. This in principle prevents the capitalist state from attaining a concrete universality. Categorizing the social order as a whole in terms of a *Begriffslogik* is thus not warranted.[18]

C. The Socialist Form of Social Production

In conclusion one final issue can be mentioned that arises in a dialectical reading of Marx's systematic works. How ought the socialist form be categorized? Three candidates can be considered. I shall argue that they can be ordered according to Hegel's dialectical progression from *being* through *essence* to *notion.*

First, Marx often uses the phrase "the association of free individuals" when discussing socialism. If the category "association" is taken without any further qualification, it defines a structure in which separate entities are externally aggregated. Marx, of course, did not accept the possessive individualism of the liberal tradition. Ironically, however, the phrase "the free association of individuals" suggests the same categorial structure we find in the liberal individualism of Hobbes and Locke. In Hegelian terms the category "association" falls on the level of Being *(Sein).* From a logical standpoint this is the simplest and most abstract level. From a sociopolitical standpoint no concretely functioning institutional framework could ever be categorized in such indeterminate terms. It needs hardly be added that a structure of this sort is incapable of institutionalizing a full development of either universality or individuality, let alone a full reconciliation of the two.

A second possibility can be found in Marx's theory of the party. Consider the following claims:

> In what relation do the Communists stand to the proletarians as a whole?. . . They have no interests separate and apart from those of the proletariat as a whole. . . They point out and bring to the front the common interests of the entire proletariat. . . In the various stages of development which the struggle of the working class against the bourgeoise has to pass through, they always and everywhere represent the interests of the movement as a whole. The Communists, therefore, are on the one hand, practically, the most advanced and resolute section of the working-class parties of every country, that section which pushes forward all others; on the other hand, theoretically, they have over the great mass of the proletariat the advantage of clearly understanding the line of march, the conditions, and the ultimate general results of the proletarian movement.[19]

This is an argument for giving the Communist Party leadership in the historical struggle to bring about the socialist form. But the argument can easily be extended and used to construct a model of socialism. If there is one group that embodies the "common interests of the entire proletariat," then why shouldn't its leadership extend into the post-revolutionary period as well? We thus have a two-tiered institutional structure. On the bottom tier there is "the great mass of the proletariat" consisting of those who are perpetually confused regarding their interests. On the top tier there is the small group of leaders who "always and everywhere" possess a correct grasp of things. In Hegelian terms this is a structure in which one pole is "essential" and the other is "inessential." An institutional framework constructed in these terms would thus be categorizable in terms of a *Wesenslogik*.

This also is more than a little ironic. For as we have seen throughout this study a major part of the Marxist critique of capitalism is that the capital form institutionalizes a *Wesenslogik*. This is not to say that a social order in which "capital" serves as an essence preventing the full development of autonomous individuality can be conflated with societies centrally controlled by a ruling bureaucratic stratum. Nonetheless when a relatively small elite claims that it embodies special qualities that grant it an exclusive right to rule, this too is an institutionalization of an essence structure, in Hegel's sense of the term. And this too prevents the full development of autonomous individuality.[20]

206

Neither the model of the free association of individuals nor that of single-party rule is an adequate model of the socialist form, if that form is to be an advance over both directly social forms of social production and the value form (see Chapter IV). However Marx sketched a third model that does meet this requirement. He believed that certain features of the Paris Commune can serve as an anticipation of future socialist societies.[21] Specifically, Marx mentioned with approval the Commune's policy that anyone holding an office in which public power (whether "political" or "economic") is exercised was to be directly elected, subject to recall, and only paid average workers' wages.

Marx's arguments for features such as these can easily be formulated in Hegelian terms. First, setting up public offices ensures that the universal interests of the community can be institutionalized. In other words, this is compatible with a complex and concrete system of institutions, as opposed to the abstract and indeterminate picture suggested by the phrase "free association of individuals." Second, individuals within the community are reconciled with the universal through the direct election of those exercising public power in those offices. Third, institutional mechanisms allow this reconciliation of individual and universal to be maintained over time. This is encouraged both through the ability of these individuals to recall public officials who are no longer serving the universal interest, and through the fact that there is no material basis for those public officials to see themselves as a class apart from other categories of workers. In all these respects Marx's model has no room whatsoever for a bureaucratic stratum that claims to embody universality while refusing to submit to open debate and decision making.

From here we could go on to derive other features of this model of council democracy, a model in the tradition of Rosa Luxemburg, Gramsci, Trotsky, and Ernest Mandel. These would include free speech, freedom of assembly, rights to form public factions, and the ability to form a plurality of parties, all of which fit under the heading of "socialist pluralism."[22] But it is time to conclude. The point to stress is that in council democracy the universal uniting individuals is not imposed upon them by an outside force such as the imperative of capital accumulation. Instead an individuality flourishes that no longer is isolated or alienated from the political community. For Marx, only this counts as true autonomy for the individual:

Only within the community has each individual the means of cultivating his gifts in all directions; hence personal freedom becomes possible only within the community.[23]

207

In capitalism, then, Marx sees an essence ("capital") that subjects the individuals under it to its imperatives. In socialist democracy he sees a universal that is reconciled with the autonomy of individuals. From the perspective of philosophical principles, therefore, Marx's move from capitalism to socialism is exactly parallel to Hegel's move from essence to the notion *(Begriff)*. The anticipation of socialism, no less than the critique of capitalism, can be grasped in terms of dialectical logic.

APPENDIX: A TABLE OF THE CATEGORIES IN CAPITAL

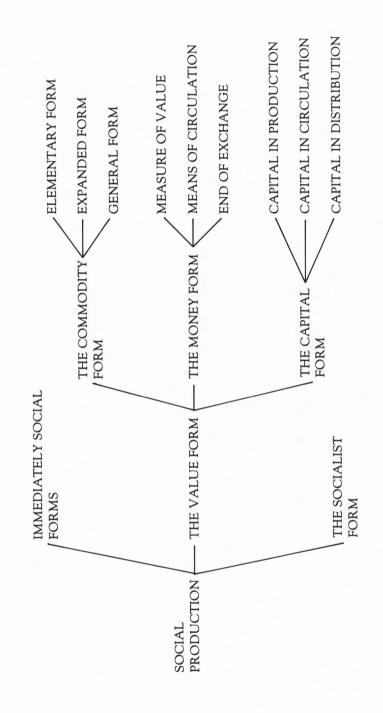

APPENDIX: (cont.)

CAPITAL IN PRODUCTION
- LABOR POWER AS COMMODITY
- EXPLOITATION
- PRODUCTION PROCESS PROPER
  - CAPITAL AS PRINCIPLE OF ORGANIZATION
  - CAPITAL AS PRINCIPLE OF TRANSFORMATION
  - ACCUMULATION
    - SIMPLE ACCUMULATION
    - SURPLUS
    - EXPANDED ACCUMULATION

CAPITAL IN CIRCULATION
- SIMPLE REPRODUCTION
- SURPLUS
- EXPANDED REPRODUCTION

CAPITAL IN DISTRIBUTION
- DISTRIBUTION WITHIN INDUSTRIAL CAPITAL
  - COST PRICES
  - COMPETITION OVER PRICE
  - PRICES OF PRODUCTION
- INDUSTRIAL CAPITAL & ITS "OTHER"
  - OFFER TO CONSUMERS
  - CONSUMER RESPONSE
  - MARKET PRICES
- DISTRIBUTION BETWEEN INDUSTRIAL & NONINDUSTRIAL CAPITAL
  - INDUSTRIAL CAPITAL PERFORMS ALL FUNCTIONS
  - DRAIN OF SURPLUS
  - REDISTRIBUTION OF SURPLUS TO NONINDUSTRIAL CAPITAL

Notes

Introduction

1. See Kojève's *Introduction to the Reading of Hegel*.

2. Chris Arthur's *The Dialectics of Labour* is an excellent investigation of Hegel's influence on the early Marx.

3. This topic is comprehensively discussed in Dick Howard's *From Marx to Kant*.

4. See Joe McCarney's provocative *The Real World of Ideology*.

5. See the collection edited by Oskar Negt, *Aktualität und Folgen der Philosophie Hegels*. Some of these criticisms are also found in *Hegel*, by Raymond Plant.

6. R.D. Winfield defends Hegel against Marxian criticisms in his paper "Hegel's Challenge to the Modern Economy."

7. Most of the major positions in this debate are covered by Richard Norman and Sean Sayers in their *Hegel, Marx and Dialectic*. A concise account of the main issues can be found in William McBride's *The Philosophy of Marx*.

8. See Derek Sayer's *Marx's Method: Ideology, Science and Criticism in 'Capital'* and Patrick Murray's *Marx's Theory of Scientific Knowledge*.

9. The classic studies on this topic are Bertell Ollman's *Alienation* and Istvan Mészàvos's *Marx's Theory of alienation*.

10. This gap has been noted often. For example, C. Prokopczyk writes that "the lack of philosophical examination and exposition of the dialectics in Marxism (or in Hegelianism, for that matter) stands in blatant conflict with the frequent and crucial references to the dialectics made by scholars dealing with Marxism and Hegelianism." *Truth and Reality in Marx and Hegel*, p. 101.

11. Engels himself (followed by Bubner) discussed the transition from "commodity" to "capital" in terms of Hegel's move from "being" to "essence" in the

Logic. (See Engel's letter to Schmidt, Nov. 1, 1891, in *Letters on Capital,* p. 259, and Bubner's study on the logic of *Capital* in his collection of essays *Dialektik und Wissenschaft.*) Arthur contrasts Marx's categories of "value" and "abstract labor" with Hegel's logical universals (see his article "Dialectics and Labour"), Pilling traces the dialectic of the forms of commodity exchange and of money in his *Marx's 'Capital': Philosophy and Political Economy,* Krahl and others have interpreted the relation between "value" and "price" in terms of the Hegelian categories of "essence" and "appearance" (this is presented in Krahl's "Bemerkungen zum Verhältnis von Kapital und Hegelscher Wesenslogik"). Zelený and others have compared the methodology in Hegel's *Logic* with that found in *Capital* (see Zelený's *The Logic of Marx),* and so on. But none of these commentators has examined *Capital* as a whole. Even Roman Rosdolsky, a Marxist scholar who pointed out the Hegelian elements in Marx's systematic writings with great force, complained that he "would only be able to touch upon the most important and theoretically interesting problem — that of the relation of Marx's work to Hegel, in particular to the *Logic* — and would not be able to deal with it in any greater depth." *(The Making of Marx's Capital,* p.xi) Mike Roth and Michael Eldred should also be mentioned. They have explored the dialectical dimension of *Capital* in more depth than other commentators. (See their *Guide to Marx's Capital.)*

12. Consider three of the most influential contemporary writers on Marx: Jon Elster, Jürgen Habermas, and Lucio Colletti. Elster's use of analytic game theory has little in common with Habermas' synthesis of speech act theory, Weber, and the Frankfurt School. And their perspectives both differ considerably from Colletti's version of Kantianism. Nonetheless all three theorists share the view that whatever remains of worth in *Capital* is there *despite* the work's Hegelian components. (See Elster's *Making Sense of Marx,* Habermas' second volume of *Theorie des kommunikativen Handelns,* and Colletti's *Marxism and Hegel, passim.)* I reply at length to Colletti's critique in "Hegelianism and Marx," while Elster's objections to the Hegelian elements in Marx's Theory are answered in my "Analytical Marxism and Marx's Systematic Dialectical Theory."

13. Empirical research alone cannot justify such strong claims. I shall show below that a dialectical derivation of the category "exploitation" from that of "capital," or of "price" from the category "value," can justify this sort of claim.

14. When, for example, Marx showed how the categories "rent" and "bank capital" can be derived from the capital form, he provided an argument for seeing the latter as a more fundamental structure than the first two phenomena. This allowed him to distinguish the revolutionary overthrow of the capital form from reformist tinkering with either rent control or interest rates.

15. All translations from this work are my own. Concise statements of Hartmann's position in English can be found in his articles "Hegel: A Non-Metaphysical View" and "Towards a Systematic Reading of Hegel's *Philosophy of Right.*"

Chapter I. Hegel: Method and System

1. See Arthur's *The Dialectics of Labour: Marx and his Relation to Hegel* for a careful and detailed study of Hegel's influence on the 1844 Manuscripts. Jean Hyppolite's *Studies on Marx and Hegel* should also be mentioned in this context.

2. Dick Howard traces the parallels and the divergences between Hegel and Marx's theories of history in *From Marx to Kant*.

3. Hegel, *Philosophy of Right*, p. 11.

4. Hegel, *Lectures on the History of Philosophy III*, pp. 175-76. Consider also these statements from Hegel's *Logic*: "The point of departure for philosophy is Experience; including under that name both our immediate consciousness and the induction from it...The sciences, based on experience, exert upon the mind a stimulus...In consequence of this stimulus thought (i.e. philosophy) is dragged out of its unrealized universality and its fancied or merely possible satisfaction, and impelled onwards to a development from itself...thought incorporates the contents of science, in all their speciality of detail as submitted...Experience is the real author of *growth* and *advance* in philosophy...The reception into philosophy of these scientific materials, now that thought has removed their immediacy and made them cease to be mere data, forms at the same time a development of thought out of itself. Philosophy, then, owes its development to the empirical sciences." Hegel, *Logic*, pp. 16 ff.

5. "Thought makes the distinction between man and the lower animals... everything human is human, for the sole and simple reason that it is due to the operation of thought...Man—and that just because it is his nature to think—is the only being that possesses law, religion, and morality. In these spheres of human life, therefore, thinking...has not been inactive: its action and its productions are there present and therein contained." *Ibid.*, pp. 4-5.

6. *Ibid.*, p. 6.

7. Hegel, *Lectures on the History of Philosophy III*, pp. 176-77. Emphasis Added.

8. Elster, *Making Sense of Marx*, p. 37.

9. Popper's "What is Dialectic" contains most of the standard objections to Hegel's theory of dialectical contradictions, and most of the standard misunderstandings. A more accurate account may be found in J. N. Findlay's *The Philosophy of Hegel*, pp. 73 ff.

10. Throughout this entire study I shall be concerned solely with the dialectical contradictions that motivate transitions within a systematic theory of categories. Arguments for and against the view that dialectical contradictions provide the motor for development both in nature and in human history will not be examined here.

This topic is debated at length by Sean Sayers and Richard Norman in their *Hegel, Marx and Dialectic*, and in Milton Fisk's paper, "Dialectic and Ontology."

11. Hegel, *Science of Logic*, pp. 827-28.

12. *Ibid.*, pp. 828-29.

13. *Ibid.*, p. 829.

14. *Ibid.*, p. 830.

15. *Ibid.*, p. 831.

16. *Ibid.*, p. 835.

17. *Ibid.*, p. 835.

18. *Ibid.*, pp. 836-37.

19. *Ibid.*, p. 840.

20. *Ibid.*, p. 829.

21. *Ibid.*, p. 830.

22. A recent example of this view is found in Lucio Colletti's *Marxism and Hegel*. See the present author's "Hegelianism and Marx: A Reply to Lucio Colletti."

23. Hegel, *Philosophy of Right*, p. 233.

24. In his *Philosophy of History* Hegel speculates that the future course of world history may revolve around the Americas. But this is not presented as something that can be deduced with necessity. And he immediately adds that "as a Land of the Future, it (the New World) has no interest for us here." p. 87.

25. "Individual souls are distinguished from one another by an infinite number of contingent modifications." *The Philosophy of Mind*, p. 51.

26. "In the particularization of the content in sensation, the *contingency* and one-sided subjective form of that content is established." *Ibid.* pp. 74-5.

27. The market "subjects the permanent existence of even the entire family to dependence on itself and to contingency...Not only caprice, however, but also contingencies, physical conditions, and factors grounded in external circumstances may reduce men to poverty." *Philosophy of Right*, p. 148.

28. In positive law "there may enter the contingency of self-will and other particular circumstances." *Ibid.*, p. 136.

29. Hegel by no means includes all events within the logical ordering of historical stages that constitutes his philosophy of history. Events occuring elsewhere than at

the particular place where the specific stage of universal history is unfolding are not included in the logical ordering. On the place of contingency in Hegel's system in general, see Dieter Henrich's "Hegels Theorie über den Zufall," in *Hegel in Kontext*.

30. Hegel, *Science of Logic*, p. 28.

31. Hegel, *Logic*, p. 132. Emphasis added.

32. Hegel, *Science of Logic*, p. 50.

33. See Suchting's *Marxism and Philosophy* for a recent rejection of Hegelian dialectics on these grounds.

34. Hegel discusses the contrast between picture-thinking and categorial thought in the *Logic*, pp. 30 ff.

35. Hegel, *Logic*, p. 177. Repeated reference to the work of Klaus Hartmann will be made below. In a number of passages that will be quoted later Hartmann refers to "transcendental philosophy." For Hartmann this term characterizes any theory in which the transitions from one category to the next are intended to be immanently justified in terms of the objective content of each category.

36. Hegel, *Philosophy of Mind*, p. 26. Emphasis added.

37. Hegel, not Nietzsche, was the first philosopher to announce that "God is dead," referring to God as a metaphysical supersubject separate from the human community. See *Phenomenology of Spirit*, pp. 476 ff. (Hegel took the phrase from Luther's hymn for Good Friday.)

38. Hegel, *Philosophy of Mind*, p. 9.

39. See Hegel, *Science of Logic*, p. 799.

40. Hegel, *Philosophy of Mind*, p. 22.

41. See the collection of articles *State and Civil Society*, ed. by Pelczynski, as well as his earlier collection *Hegel's Political Philosophy*, for fuller accounts. Charles Taylor's *Hegel and Modern Society* also deserves mention.

42. Hegel assigns women to the private realm of the family. It should always be remembered that the reconciliation between universal and individual that Hegel felt characterizes both civil society and the state in principle excludes women. In the household they labor not for the social community, but for the private household headed by the husband.

43. The participation granted to citizens is more extensive in some of Hegel's remarks than in others. However, even in those works where participation in the state is more restricted, the principles justifying a more extensive participation are clearly present. See Karl Ilting's article "Hegel's Concept of the State and Marx's Early Critique."

44. It should be mentioned that Hegel did not believe that any existent state adequately embodied the principles of the modern state. He called for the reform of all existing states throughout his life. See Shlomo Avineri's *Hegel's Theory of the Modern State*, Chapter 11.

45. Of course on the existential level it is possible that a stunted personality may experience more freedom in an individual relation to a possession (categorizable in terms of a structure of being, "Abstract Right") than in intersubjective relationships on the level of ethical life (categorizable in notion terms). Such individual cases are not counterexamples to Hegel's position, for they do not provide an argument against the thesis that a structure in which relations to individual possessions are embedded within social relations *in principle* allows a greater scope of freedom than relations to individual possessions alone. The fact that some individuals fail to take advantage of this possibility does not mean that it is not present.

Chapter II. Dialectical Logic in Marx's Work

1. Karl Marx, *Grundrisse*, p. 101. (Also, see *Capital I*, p. 29.)

2. This view is widely held by non-Marxist scholars of Hegel. For instance, Michael Rosen defends what he terms "the generative reading" of Hegel in his *Hegel's Dialectic and its Criticism*. Other recent examples include William Maker's "Hegel's Critique of Marx's The Fetishism of Dialectics," and Richard Dien Winfield's "Dialectical Logic and the Conception of Truth." For other presentations of the alternative reconstructive reading defended in this and the previous chapter see *Absolute Knowledge: Hegel and the Problem of Metaphysics* by Alan White, "The Logic of Hegel's *Logic*" by Terry Pinkard, and, especially, "Hegel: A Non-Metaphysical View" by Klaus Hartmann.

3. Consider the following passage: "The sciences, based on experience, exert upon the mind a stimulus to overcome the form in which their varied contents are presented, and to elevate these contents to the rank of necessary truth...This development only means that thought incorporates the contents of science, in all their speciality and detail as submitted." *Logic*, p. 16. Or again, "The relation of speculative science to the other sciences may be stated in the following terms. It does not in the least neglect the empirical facts contained in the several sciences, but recognizes and adopts them: it appreciates and applies towards its own structure the universal element in these sciences, their laws and classifications: but besides all this, into the categories of science it introduces, and gives currency to, other categories." *Ibid.*, p. 13. These passages are compatible with the reconstructive reading of Hegel presented in the previous chapter. They are not compatible with Marx's reading of Hegel.

4. *Grundrisse*, p. 101.

5. *Poverty of Philosophy*, in *Collected Works*, Vol. 6, p. 162.

6. *Grundrisse*, p. 107.

7. This point is emphasized in Himmelweit and Mohun's excellent article, "The Anomalies of Capital".

8. See Jindřich Zeleńy, *The Logic of Marx*, *passim*.

9. *Letters on 'Capital'*, p. 8. Marx also wrote, "I too am very unwilling to impute the faults in the economic argument to M. Proudhon's philosophy. M. Proudhon does not present a false criticism of political philosophy because he is the proud propounder of a ridiculous philosophy, but rather he presents a ridiculous philosophy because he has not understood the real social conditions in their interconnection." Ibid., p. 6.

10. "Notes on Adolph Wagner" in *Karl Marx: Texts on Method*, p. 198.

11. Marx makes a similar point in his critique of Bailey's theory of value, see *Theories of Surplus Value* (henceforth "TSV") III, p. 137.

12. "Notes on Adolph Wagner", p. 201.

13. *Science of Logic*, p. 804.

14. *Ibid.*, p. 805.

15. *Collected Works*, Vol. 4, pp. 57-60.

16. *Philosophy of Mind*, p. 177. Emphasis added.

17. For this reason I cannot agree with Marx's characterization of how "movement" is generated in Hegelian philosophy. According to Marx, first general categories are abstracted from historical specificities; next a logical notion of movement is abstracted from concrete movements. Put these two abstractions together and we have transcendental philosophy a la Hegel: "Just as by dint of abstraction we have transformed everything into a logical category, so one has only to make an abstraction of every characteristic distinctive of different movements to attain movements in its abstract condition—purely formal movement, the purely logical formula of movement. If one finds in logical categories the substance of all things, one imagines one has found in the logical formula of movement the *absolute method*, which not only explains all things, but also implies the movement of things. It is of this absolute method that Hegel speaks." (*Poverty of Philosophy*, in Collected Works, Vol. 6, pp. 163-4). Given such passages it is little wonder that many commentators have insisted that Marx radically *rejected* the sort of theory we find in Hegel's *Logic*. However the movement from simple unity, through difference, to unity-in-difference is not a "purely logical formula of movement." It is a logical

"movement" that allows us to progress from one category to another; it is no more an abstraction of real movement than the transition in thought from "2+2" to "4" is based on the abstraction of real movement.

18. *Essentialism in the Thought of Karl Marx*, Scott Meikle.

19. The last category actually discussed in Volume I is "original accumulation." But as will be seen in Chapter VII this category is a digression, interrupting the ordering. From a systematic point of view "expanded accumulation" concludes Volume I.

20. Suchting, *Marx and Philosophy*, p. 96.

21. *Ibid.*, p. 100.

22. *Ibid.*, p. 100-01.

23. *Ibid.*, p. 92.

24. *Ibid.*, p. 101.

25. This is by no means only held by non-Marxists. E.P. Thompson's *The Poverty of Theory*, written almost as much against Hegel as against Althusser, makes similar points. For a recent defense of *Capital* as a purely empirical theory see Dan Little's "The Scientific Standing of Marx's *Capital*."

26. See Meek, *Economics and Ideology and Other Essays*, p. 96, and Howard & King, *The Political Economy of Marx*, pp. 46 ff. This tradition goes back to Engels, who wrote in his review of *A Contribution to the Critique of Political Economy* that "the logical method of treatment was therefore the only suitable one. This, however, is indeed nothing but the historical method, only stripped of the historical form and diverting chance occurrences." (Engels' review is given in the Progress Publishers edition of Marx's text; this passage is found on p. 225.) This topic is discussed in the present author's "The Debate Regarding Dialectical Logic in Marx's Economic Writings."

27. *Capital I*, p. 29.

28. *Ibid.*, pp. 27-9.

29. If one holds that this shift took place, it is possible to see it either as an advance in Marx's position or as a retreat. John Mepham celebrates the shift as manifestation of Marx's coming to maturity as a thinker in his "From the *Grundrisse* to *Capital*: the Making of Marx's Method." In contrast Gerhard Göhler laments the regression from the "strict dialectics" of Marx's earlier economic writings to the merely "exemplary dialectics" of *Capital*. See his *Die Reduktion der Dialektik durch Marx*.

30. See Marx's 1877 letter to Mikhailovsky, in *Selected Writings*, pp. 570-71. For

an extensive discussion of the theoretical and practical issues involved in a rejection of the theory of stages see Michael Löwy's excellent *The Politics of Combined and Uneven Development.*

31. It is interesting to note that Backhaus began his series "Materialien zur Rekonstruktion der Marxschen Werttheorie" as a defender of the systematic (Hegelian) reading of *Capital.* In his attempt to refute the orthodox logico-historical reading, however, he came to appreciate the significant textual justification for the latter reading. He therefore concluded that neither reading accounts for the methodological confusion that pervaded Marx's writings.

32. "I leafed through Hegel's *Logic* again and found much to assist me in the method of analysis." *Letters on 'Capital'*, p. 50.

33. Lenin's famous comment is that "it is impossible to completely understand Marx's *Capital*, and especially its first chapter, without having thoroughly studied and understood the *whole* of Hegel's *Logic.*" "Conspectus of Hegel's Book *The Science of Logic*," p. 180.

34. *Grundrisse*, p. 100.

35. *Ibid.*

36. *Ibid.*

37. *Ibid.*, p. 101.

38. TSV II, p. 165. This passage echoes Marx's earlier assertion that "It is not a matter of the relation which the economic relations historically occupy in the succession of different forms of society . . . Rather (it is a matter of) their articulation within modern bourgeois society." (*Grundrisse*, pp. 107-08.) Both passages are inconsistent with the logical-historical reading of Marx's theory discussed above.

39. TSV II, p. 106.

40. *Ibid.*

41. *Ibid.*, pp. 164-65.

42. *Ibid.*, p. 150.

43. TSV III, p. 163. Emphasis added.

44. The classic discussion of the need to formulate transitional goals is found in Trotsky's *The Transitional Program for Socialist Revolution.* I have argued for the compatibility of Trotsky's approach with fundamental tenets of Hegelianism in my "Hegel's Theory of the Syllogism and its Relevance to Marxism." I would like to state at this point that I am claiming only that the philosophical reading of *Capital* presented in the present study has important political implications. I am not

claiming that reading the work from this perspective captures the political dimension of *Capital* entirely. Harry Cleaver's *Reading Capital Politically* explores political concerns beyond the scope of the present study.

45. "Theses on Feuerbach", *Collected Works*, vol. 5, p. 6. See Also Ernest Mandel, *Late Capitalism*, p. 17.

46. Hegel, *Philosophy of History*, p. 18.

47. *Ibid.*, p. 416.

48. "The German Ideology", *Collected Writings*, vol. 5, p. 53.

49. On property rights cf. *Philosophy of Right, op. cit.*, Part One. (Abstract Right); on children's rights, see section 174; on freedom of speech, #319, and on various civil rights see the entire section entitled "The Administration of Justice." Recent scholarship on Hegel's political writings has emphasized these liberal elements in Hegel's thought and thoroughly refuted the view of Hegel as a precursor of totalitarianism. See the essays in Pelczynski's anthologies.

50. This statement holds only for the later-day Hegel. In his youth Hegel held much more radical positions that anticipate Marx to an astonishing degree. See "The Discovery of Hegel's Early Lectures on the Philosophy of Right" by Shlomo Avineri, p. 199 ff. On the general topic of Hegel's early radicalism, see Jacques D'Hondt's *Hegel in His Time*. When I refer to either "Hegelians" or to "orthodox Hegelians" in the course of this work this will denote those who are faithful to the later-day Hegel, after his radical impulses had been more or less expunged.

51. Material for this Postscript has been taken from my article "Hegelianism and Marx: A Reply to Lucio Colletti."

Chapter III. Hegelian Readings of "Capital"

1. Hans-Jürgen Krahl, "Bemerkungen zum Verhaltnis von Kapital und Hegelscher Wesenslogik." This view is also presented in Derek Sayer's *Marx's Method* and Patrick Murray's important study, *Marx's Theory of Scientific Knowledge.*

2. Latter from Engles to Schmidt, Nov. 1, 1981, *Letters on 'Capital'*, p. 259.

3. Rüdiger Bubner, "Logik und Kapital."

4. Richard Winfield, "The Logic of Marx's Capital." Winfield has since moved from being a Hegelian Marxist to anti-Marxist Hegelianism.

5. One example should suffice. In the *Logic* the category "ground" precedes that of "whole and parts." If Winfield's approach were on the mark, we would expect that any real embodiment of the category "ground" in the *Realphilosophie* would precede any application of the category "whole and parts." But Hegel

connects "ground" with the process of giving subjective reasons for one's acts, which falls on the level of "Morality" in the sphere of Objective Spirit. This is on a much *higher* categorial level than the relationship between bits of inorganic matter that Hegel mentions as a real embodiment of the whole/parts category. The attempt to directly map categories from the *Logic* to those in the *Realphilosophie* thus breaks down. The much more subtle relationship between the *Logic* and the *Realphilosophie* is discussed in detail by L. Bruno Puntel in his *Darstellung Methode und Struktur. Untersuchungen der systematischen Philosophie G.W.F. Hegels.*

6. Both Hegel and Marx held that it was possible in principle for a theory to assert a warranted validity claim to the effect that the categorial structures defined by a theory are isomorphic to ontological structures. This view has been rejected by Nietzschean post-structuralists, among others. This topic is beyond the scope of the present work. However it should be noted that it is extremely difficult to articulate the latter view without constructing a chaotic theory meant to match the supposed chaos of the world. And this, of course, presupposes the isomorphism of categorial and ontological structures that was to be denied.

7. See Klaus Hartmann's *Marxens 'Kapital' in transzendentalphilosophischer Sicht.*

8. "To philosophical knowledge the advance is a stream going in opposite directions, leading forward to what is other than itself, but at the same time working backwards in such a way that that which appears as the last, as founded on what precedes, shows itself rather to be the first—the foundation." Hegel, *Lectures on the Philosophy of Religion I*, p. 111. This dimension of Hegel's thought is evaluated in depth by Tom Rockmore in his *Hegel's Circular Epistemology.*

9. It must be kept in mind that the term *essence* here does not refer to "essentialism." "Essentialism" is the position that there is an "inner nature" of things, and that thought is capable of apprehending it. Both Hegel and Marx are essentialists in this sense (although—unlike other essentialists—both stress the historical dimension of both the inner nature of things and of thought). In contrast "essence" is a particular framework for apprehending the inner nature of things ("being" and "notion" are the two other basic frameworks). In order to help keep the special meaning of essence in mind I shall regularly use the German terms *Wesen* and *Wesenslogik* in place of *essence* and *logic of essence.*

10. Hegel, *Science of Logic*, p. 391.

11. Hegel, *Philosophy of Right*, p. 105.

12. Hegel, *Philosophy of Mind*, p. 254.

13. This is done in David MacGregor's *The Communist Ideal in Hegel and Marx.*

14. This complexity is reflected in Hartmann's analysis. In a few places he presents the contrast between Hegel and Marx's account of generalized commodity

production in terms of the difference between two sorts of *Wesen*-structures, with Marx employing a model of essence where the opposite pole is reduced to mere appearance and Hegel a more affirmative view in which a reflection among the various elements is present (182, 456, 458). However elsewhere he refers to "the triviality of a mere reflection determination," asserting that "the decisive matter, the reciprocal influence of both instances which are set in relation in the concept of essence (Hartmann refers here to the capital/wage labor and capital/consumer relations)...is still not presented in that concept." (459) The key point here is that "the notion of essence...cannot (capture) a categorially higher new determination—the *begriffslogische* unity, in which capital and labor would be mediated, be it socio-economically, be it in a higher whole such as the state." (457) The sharpest and most accurate way of formulating the contrast between Hegel and Marx is to oppose the former's insistence, captured in this quote from Hartmann, that a *"begriffslogische* unity" is possible on the socio-economic level with the latter's denial of that possibility. The difference in their respective views on the state, the family, and so on, stem from this contrast. Thus despite the complexity mentioned above, the debate will be formulated in these terms throughout this work.

Chapter IV. The Value Form

1. Marx wrote to Lassalle: "The work we are discussing is a Critique of Economic Categories or, if you like, the system of bourgeois economy in a critical description. It is both a description of the system and, in describing it, a critique of the same." Feb. 22, 1858, *Letters on 'Capital'*, p. 51.

2. Hartmann writes: "Against the background of benign, social, qualitative labor...the commodity is thematized as a *negative*. As such wherever it is found it explains...alienation. It is a *principle*. The negative, once introduced, explains the negative." p. 273.

3. *Ibid.*, p. 276. This view is also held by a number of Marxists. See Georg Lohmann's "'Wealth' as an Aspect of the Critique of Capital" in *Rethinking Marx* ed. by Häenninen and Paldán, p. 88, and E. M. Lange's *Das Prinzip Arbeit*, pp. 86 ff.

4. "When men are thus dependent on one another and reciprocally related to one another in their work and the satisfaction of their needs, subjective self-seeking turns into a contribution to the satisfaction of the needs of everyone else." G. W. F. Hegel, *The Philosophy of Right*, p. 129.

5. Böhm-Bawerk, *Karl Marx and the Close of his System*, *passim*.

6. Geoff Hodgson makes this a central objection to the labor theory of value in his *Capitalism, Value and Exploitation*.

7. Hegel, *Logic* p. 177.

8. *Die Marxsche Theorie*, Hartmann, p. 274. Hartmann also writes that "as an abstraction abstract labor is not suited to be a dialectical or transcendental principle...alienated, abstract labor does not allow for any affirmative synthesis." *Ibid*, p. 410 "The question is whether the reduction to value is capable of expressing economic relations correctly when the decisive aspect is removed from sight, i.e. that utility considerations must be present in order to enter into exchange." *Ibid*, p. 270.

9. *Capital I*, p. 43.

10. "The will is free, so that freedom is both the substance of right and its goal, while the system of right is the realm of freedom made actual, the world of mind brought forth out of itself like a second nature." *Philosophy of Right*, p. 20. By the "level of freedom attained" I mean the level of freedom that is structurally possible within one framework, as opposed to that structurally possible within another. The phrase does not refer to the amount of freedom that any given individual happens to attain. It is possible that a given individual attains a high degree of freedom within structures that systematically limit freedom, while conversely a given individual may not exercise liberty within a structure that allows considerale scope for free development. The comparison of the two structures ought not to rest on such contingencies.

11. *Capital I*, p. 82.

12. *Ibid*.

13. *Ibid.*, p. 713.

14. *Ibid.*, pp. 82-3. This point will be developed further in Chapter X.

15. Among the questions to be raised here two are especially important. What is the relationship between this systematic ordering of historical stages and a causal theory of historical change? And what is the precise relationship between the "sociality" component and that of "productiveness" in a causal theory of history? In more standard terminology, what is the relationship between productive forces and the relations of production? These questions are of crucial significance for Marxism. However any attempt to address them in even a provisional fashion would force us to digress too far from the task at hand, the examination of the systematic dialectic of categories in *Capital*. A discussion of these and related issues can be found in the present author's "Two Theories of Historical Materialism: G. A. Cohen and Jürgen Habermas."

16. Hegel, *Philosophy of Right*, "Introduction", pp. 14ff.

17. This point has been well put by Ernest Mandel: "The real objective of building socialism must be authentic political representation of the proletariat as a whole, which is impossible without the flourishing of political, ideological and cultural pluralism for the masses. This is the precondition for an adequate

functioning of the workers' councils, bodies of people's power or soviets. Without this sort of pluralism workers will not be able to really wield power. They will not be able to decide on the big problems of economic, social, cultural and international policy, because all these questions cannot be resolved in the workplace or on a local level. All these questions imply a choice between coherent alternatives on a national level (and even increasingly internationally). When you talk of such coherent alternatives you are dealing with different political platforms, precisely in other words about political pluralism." In *International Viewpoint*, special supplement to issue #93, Feb. 24, 1986, p. 17.

18. *Capital I*, p. 85. Of course even if it is granted that "value" and "abstract labor" characterize the "particular species of social production" Marx investigated, it could well be that there are other categories that characterize this realm as well if not better. This issue is addressed in Chapter X below. It should also be noted that the term *value* has a great number of other connotations besides that employed by Marx in his discussion of "the value form." See the interesting discussion in Sartre's *Critique of Dialectical Reason*, pp. 247-49.

19. *Capital I*, pp. 77-8.

20. The unrestrictedness of the sociality characteristic of the value form must be considered along with the productiveness of this form. Marx and Engels wrote of the system of generalized commodity exchange that it "has been the first to show what man's activity can bring about. It has accomplished wonders far surpassing Egyptian pyramids, Roman aqueducts, and Gothic cathedrals; it has conducted expeditions that put in the shade all former Exoduses of nations and crusades . . . exploitation of the world market (has) given a cosmopolitan character to production and consumption in every country. In place of the old wants, satisfied by the productions of the country, we find new wants, requiring for their satisfaction the products of distant lands and climes . . . (this) has created more massive and more colossal productive forces than have all preceding generations together. Subjection of Natures' forces to man, machinery, application of chemistry to industry and agriculture, steam-navigation, railways, electric telegraphs, clearing of whole continents for cultivation, canalization of rivers, whole populations conjured out of the ground—what earlier century had even a presentiment that such productive forces slumbered in the lap of social labour?" Unrestricted sociality is the flip side of this coin: "In place of the old local and national seclusion and self-sufficiency, we have intercourse in every direction, universal inter-dependence of nations. And as in the material, so also in intellectual production. The intellectual creations of individual nations become common property. National one-sidedness and narrow-mindedness become more and more impossible, and from the numerous national and local literatures there arises a world literature." *Communist Manifesto*, in *Collected Works*, vol. 6, p. 487-89.

21. The "private individual units of production" need not be private individuals. They could be private firms that employ a great number of individuals. This point

was missed entirely by Richard Winfield. See *The Just Economy*, pp. 64 ff. On Winfield's reading "private" means that an isolated individual interacts with nature monologically. For Marx it simply means that labor is undertaken prior to knowing whether or not it is socially necessary.

22. Of course in commodity production "socially required" does not refer to social needs *per se*. It refers only to those social needs which have sufficient purchasing power behind them; all other social needs are ignored.

23. "Hence, when we bring the products of our labour into relation with each other as values, it is not because we see in these articles the material receptacles of homogeneous human labor. Quite the contrary: whenever, by an exchange, we equate as values our different products, by that very act, we also equate, as human labour, the different kinds of labour expended upon them. We are not aware of this, nevertheless we do it." *Capital I*, p. 78-9. For a full account of how abstract labor is a real abstraction, i.e. based on a real material process, see Chris Arthur's "Dialectics and Labour."

24. Written July 11, 1968; In *Letters on 'Capital'*, p. 148. The reference to nature in this passage suggests another point. Since commodities are generally produced out of raw materials ultimately provided by nature, surely nature must play a central role in the determination of their value. Critics continually assert their astonishment that Marx missed such an obvious fact when he made abstract labor, rather than nature, the substance of value. (For a recent statement of this objection see Gerard Maarek's *An Introduction ot Karl Marx's Das Kapital*.) Marx was not unaware of this position. Nature, he stressed, is surely part of the substance of social *wealth*. But Marx insisted that "wealth" and "value" are not the same concepts. (See "Critique of the Gotha Program," in *The Marx-Engels Reader*, pp. 525-26.) There are two problems with asserting that nature is the substance of value. First, nature gives its gifts indifferently to all forms of social production. Hence it is not at all helpful in distinguishing one form from another. Second, not all of nature's gifts are relevant to social production. If sufficient amounts of carbon had not been generated, social production would have been impossible for the very good reason that the life of carbon-based producers would have been impossible. This gift of nature is a precondition for there being *any* activity; precisely because of this it is not proximately relevant to the specific activity of social production. We can take from this the clue that nature is relevant to the determination of value only in so far as it is proximately relevant to social production. This suggests that the substance of value refers to the social labor that transforms the gifts of nature in production.

25. See the works of Steedman and Shaikh for the two sides of this debate.

26. Among the few exceptions to this statement, in the English-speaking world, are the writings of Mike Roth and Michael Eldred.

27. Himmelweit and Mohun provide a compelling argument against interpreting

Marx's theory of value in terms of embodied labor in their "The Anomalies of Capital."

28. *Capital I*, p. 41. Commodities, Marx writes, "must show that they are use-values before they can be realised as values. For the labour spent upon them counts effectively, only in so far as it is spent in a form that is useful for others." *Ibid.*, p. 89. Similar passages are found on pages 35, 36, 47, 85, and 87.

29. Michio Morishima, *Marx's Economics*, p. 40.

30. It is important to remember that a "form of social production" is not to be taken as equivalent to "production" in a narrow sense. Marx explicitly included under the former term distribution, exchange, and consumption as well as production in the narrow sense. See *Grundrisse*, pp. 88 ff.

31. Hegel, *Philosophy of Mind*, p. 245.

32. *Capital I*, p. 44.

33. *Ibid.*, p. 46. One could say that "demand" also provides a principle of unity whereby two commodities can be made commensurable. But, once again, *socially necessary* abstract labor includes the concept of demand.

34. Hegel, *Philosophy of Right*. pp. 148-52.

35. Marx wrote that under exchange-value "each individual's production is dependent on the production of all others; and the transformation of his product into the necessaries of his own life is dependent on the consumption of all others...This reciprocal dependence is expressed in the constant necessity for exchange, and in exchange value as the all-sided mediation." *Grundrisse*, p. 156.

36. Hegel, *Philosophy of Right*, pp. 60-1.

37. Winfield, "Hegel's Challenge to the Modern Economy," p. 36.

38. *Ibid.*, p. 39.

39. *Ibid.*, p. 45.

40. *Grundrisse*, p. 157.

41. Winfield, "Hegel's Challenge To the Modern Economy," p. 46. The text reads "labor, power, and land" instead of "labor power and land." This is a misprint, as a comparison of this passage with similar passages in Winfield's *The Just Economy* reveals.

42. *Ibid.*, p. 47.

43. *Ibid.*, pp. 47-8.

44. *Ibid.*, p. 48.

Chapter V. The Simple Commodity Form and the Money Form

1. The other commodities are present implicitly in that the same form in principle holds for them as well. The exchange of n Commodity W for m Commodity V is just as much an instance of the elementary form. The other commodities are implicit in the elementary form in another sense as well: as a determination of a form of social production the elementary form must implicitly hold on a society-wide basis.

2. *Capital I*, p. 68.

3. "The relative expression of value is incomplete because the series representing it is interminable." *Ibid.*, p. 69. For Hegel's comments on the "spurious infinite" see *Science of Logic*, pp. 150 ff.

4. "Articles of utility become commodities, only because they are products of the labour of private individuals or groups of individuals who carry on their work independently of each other. The sum total of the labour of all these private individuals forms the aggregate labour of society. Since the producers do not come into social contact with each other until they exchange their products, the specific social character of each producer's labour does not show itself except in the act of exchange. In other words, the labour of the individual asserts itself as a part of the labour of society, only by means of the relations which the act of exchange establishes directly between the products, and indirectly, through them, between the producers. To the latter, therefore, the relations connecting the labour of one individual with that of the rest appear, not as direct social relations between individuals at work, but as what they really are, material relations between persos and social relations between things." *Capital I*, pp. 77-8.

5. *Ibid.*, p. 75. ("Equivalent form" simply means the use-value—some commodity B—in terms of which the exchange value of some other commodity A is expressed when x Commodity A is exchanged for y commodity B.)

6. TSV I, p. 205.

7. TSV II, p. 137.

8. *Ibid.*, p. 501.

9. *Ibid.*, pp. 202; 403.

10. The metaphysical question of whether contradictions really exist in the material world is beyond the scope of the present study. My own view is that dialectical contradictions do exist in the world, but that they do not involve formal contradictions in which the same predicates are affirmed and denied of the same subjects at the same time and the same respects. At least the "contradiction" between use-value and exchange-value is not of this type. These two aspects of the

commodity are "contradictory" in the sense that they involve different social goals that prove to be ultimately incompatible (the satisfaction of social wants and needs, as opposed to the private accumulation of value). In general there are two standard types of dialectical contradictions. The first occurs when something (either a category or a material reality) is asserted to be a simple unity, but upon closer inspection is seen to include implicitly a moment of difference that is not unified. The second occurs when a category or material reality is asserted to involve difference only, and then upon closer inspection an underlying unity is seen to be implicit. Both of these "contradictions" can be formulated in a manner that does not involve a denial of the law of contradiction.

11. *Grundrisse*, p. 145.

12. *Ibid.*, p. 147.

13. See Hartmann, *Die Marxsche Theorie*, pp. 288, ff.

14. *Capital I*, p. 117.

15. Hegel, *Phenomenology of Spirit*, pp. 129 ff.

16. *Capital I*, p. 115.

17. This does not imply that we have reached the ultimate stage of unity here. This unity will turn out to have its own structural tendency to fragmentation. But this fragmentation is now on a higher level, a fragmentation of a higher-level unity than the fragmentation considered thus far. The form taken by this higher-level fragmentation is that of monetary crises. See *Capital I*, pp. 137-38.

18. *Ibid.*, p.. 152.

19. *Ibid.*, p. 141.

20. "Since the theory cannot call on an ultimately true, affirmative, conclusion (as in Hegel's theory)...all weight falls on the progressive movement from (prior) grounds. The false end point cannot appear as a basis for proof." Hartmann, *Die Marxsche Theorie*, p. 300.

21. This point has been missed by Hegelians. Winfield, for example, tries to limit Marx's notion of use-value to that which satisfies natural needs: "Marx describes use value as the relation of the particular natural features of a desired object to the particular natural needs of some human being." *The Just Economy*, p. 61. The following passage is sufficient refutation of this reading of Marx: "The discovery, creation and satisfaction of new needs arising from society itself; the cultivation of all the qualities of the social human being, production of the same in a form as rich as possible in needs, because rich in qualities and relations—production of this being as the most total and universal possible social product, for, in order to take gratification in a many-sided way, he must be capable of many pleasures, hence cultivated to a high degree—is likewise a condition of production founded on

capital...The development of a constantly expanding and more comprehensive system of different kinds of labour, different kinds of production, to which a constantly expanding and constantly enriched system of needs corresponds." *Grundrisse*, p. 409. However much Hegel and Marx disagreed on other matters, they agreed that in generalized commodity production use-values satisfy conventional as well as natural needs, and that these conventional needs are capable of being multiplied indefinitely.

22. *Capital I*, pp. 152-53.

23. *Grundrisse*, p. 146.

24. Hartmann, *Die Marxsche Theorie*, p. 302.

25. Hegel interpreted the model of society presented in Plato's *Republic* as an example of this sort of essence structure. In Hegel's reading, the citizens of Plato's ideal polis are subsumed entirely under the institutions of the city-state, under the unity of the polis as a whole. See *Lectures on the History of Philosophy II*, pp. 98-9.

26. Max Weber, "Author's Introduction," *The Protestant Ethic and the Spirit of Capitalism.*

27. Jürgen Habermas, *Theorie des kommunikativen Handelns II*, pp. 499-500; 539, and *passim.*

28. *Grundrisse*, p. 776. Emphasis added.

29. TSV III, p. 253.

30. It is interesting to note that this account brings together two modes of thought that are widely viewed as incompatible, Hegelian dialectics and the search for micro-foundations of analytical Marxism. Dialectical transitions in categorial social theories are justified only when it can be shown that the structure defined by a given category necessarily has certain structural tendencies. In order to establish such tendencies one must show that within the structural parameters defined by the given category, individual agents would choose courses of action that form a certain pattern. And this, of course, means that micro-foundations must be provided for dialectical transitions.

31. See Ernest Mandel's "In Defense of Socialist Planning."

Chapter VI. The Initial Determinations of the Capital Form: Labor Power as Commodity; Exploitation

1. See Aristotle's *Politics*, Book I Chapter IX, pp. 22 ff., and John Locke's *Second Treatise on Government*, pp. 28 ff.

2. *Capital I*, pp. 152-53.

3. "Now wage-labour, however, is a *commodity*. It is even the basis on which the production of *products* as *commodities* takes place." TSV II, p. 397.

4. *Capital I*, p. 166.

5. The so-called managerial revolution in which the functions of ownership and control are separated in large firms was predicted by Marx (see *Capital III*, p. 89). However this is a matter for a much more concrete stage of the theory.

6. "The sphere...within whose boundaries the sale and purchase of labour-power goes on, is in fact a very Eden of the innate rights of man. There alone rule Freedom, Equality, Property and Bentham. Freedom, because both buyer and seller of a commodity, say of labour-power, are constrained only by their own free will. They contract as free agents, and the agreement they come to, is but the form in which they give legal expression to their common will. Equality, because each enters into relation with the other, as with a simple owner of commodities, and they exchange equivalent for equivalent." *Capital I*, p. 172.

7. "Commodities and money are transformed into capital because the worker has ceased to engage in exchange as a commodity producer and commodity owner; instead of selling commodities he is compelled to sell his labour itself (to sell directly his labour-power) as a commodity to the owner of the objective conditions of labour. This separation is the prerequisite for the relationship of capital and wage-labour in the same way as it is the prerequisite for the transformation of money (or of the commodities by which it is represented) into capital." TSV III, p. 89.

8. The English translation of *The Philosophy of Right* gives the appearance that Hegel failed to maintain the subordinate position of capital in the market economy. This is due to a mistranslation. Hegel's term *Vermögen* refers to all commodity relations, not just those of profit-making enterprises. This is missed when it is translated as "capital"; a better translation would have been "wealth." See Winfield, *The Just Economy*, pp. 139-40.

9. "Hegel's brevity (in his discussion of capital) does reflect a crucial and much misunderstood feature of capital's place in the market economy: that capital is but a component rather than the unifying structure of commodity relations...the M-C-M' scheme of capital still comprises just one form among others that commodity exchange may follow...So long as market autonomy persists, which after all is a precondition of every form of capital, commodity owners may well choose to buy and sell such that commodity circulation takes a predominantly nonprofitable form...(this) is precisely what allows nonprofit enterprises to function in the market, be they self-sustaining or not. Although Hegel barely treats the structure and dynamic of capital circulation, his conception of exchange properly takes into account the irreducibility of commodity circulation by leaving open all its possibilities without giving any one privileged hegemony." *Ibid.*, pp. 131-33.

10. "To earn their characteristic profit, the owners of capital must enter into commodity exchanges comprising the M-C-M' circuit. In doing so, they necessarily interact with members of other classes on the basis of allowing them to satisfy their own chosen needs through the buying and selling of commodities... The bearer of capital stands in an economic relation to the members of other classes only by accomodating their market autonomy." *Ibid.*, p. 143.

11. *Ibid.*, p. 121.

12. *Ibid.*, p. 125.

13. *Ibid.*, p. 110.

14. *Ibid.*, p. 111.

15. Another argument can be found in Marx regarding the move from M-C-M to M-C-M', an argument based on Hegel's *Logic*. Money is pure quantity. In the *Logic* Hegel's analysis of the category "quantity" established that it has no fixed limit. It is always already beyond any barrier that is set for it; by its inherent nature it may continue indefinitely. As pure quantity, money too has this feature. Hence the M-C-M circuit must give way to the M-C-M' circuit, in which the ability of money to increase indefinitely is explicitly posited. I do not believe that this argument is consistent with Marx's insistence that logical schemas not be imposed upon social relations. Transitions must be justified in terms specific to the ontological region being investigated; transitions in social theory thus do not map transitions in the *Logic* in any one-to-one fashion. Terrence Carver discusses Marx's own attempt to do precisely this in his discussion of money in "Marx—and Hegel's *Logic*."

16. This is no more than a provisional reply to Winfield's objection. A full reply can only come in the course of treating the determinations of the capital form as a whole. Much of the rest of the present work will be devoted to this issue. This question of capitalism and freedom is a variant of the question whether Marx was justified in interpreting the capital form in terms taken from Hegel's level of essence. If the capital form rests on autonomous choices, then notion categories would be more applicable than the essence framework Marx employed.

17. Winfield would object to this sort of reasoning: "Interdependent market autonomy... permits every owner of capital to make any market decision they choose, no matter what the 'rational' strictures of cost efficiency and profit maximization may command." *The Just Economy*, pp. 121-22. However later Winfield himself admits that those firms that do not follow these strictures will tend to be eliminated in market competition. *(Ibid.*, p. 203). This reveals that the particular form of autonomy stressed by Winfield is completely irrelevant when considering the structural tendencies that necessarily hold in economies based on generalized commodity exchange.

18. The point can be stated even more strongly. The exchange for gain of

nonproduced objects in principle cannot be an essential determination of *any* form of social production; social production only begins when found objects are transformed in some manner.

19. Winfield himself grants this tendency. He writes that all units of capital "face the market imperatives of having to reinvest and expand simply to survive in the face of advancing competition." *The Just Economy*, p. 129.

20. Although John Roemer himself ignores the dialectical dimension of Marx's theory, his work is still of relevance to the systematic ordering at this stage of *Capital*. Roemer has shown that worker cooperatives would *not* become the dominant structural tendency, given the structural parameters defined by the capital form. The capital form necessarily involves a tendency for productive resources to be distributed in an inegalitarian fashion. Roemer has established that individuals with differing initial resources optimize their positions by taking on the following five class positions: pure capitalist (only hires labor power), mixed capitalist (both hires the labor power of others and labors on his or her own means of production), petty bourgeois artisan (labors on own means of production exclusively), semiproletarian (both labors on own means of production and is hired by others), and proletarian (is hired by others only). (See *Free to Lose*, Chapter 6.) The capital/wage labor social relation is a feature of all but the third class position, making it the dominant social relation within this structure. For a tendency for workers cooperatives to become dominant factors that have not yet been introduced in the theory would be required, for instance a state that forbids private ownership of the means of production and/or extends significant amounts of credit to workers who initially lack access to productive resources. This supports the categorial transition from "capital in production" to the capital/wage labor relation captured in "labor power as commodity." In another area of Roemer's work, however, he has introduced arguments that seem to imply that this transition is *not* warranted. He has shown that the capital form may generate class relations *without* the presence of a labor market. The creditor/debtor relation is sufficient. (*Ibid.*, Chapter 7). This suggests that in the categorial progression "capital form—labor power as commodity" the latter term should be replaced with a more inclusive category, one that includes the possibility of laborers who are subordinate to the capital form through a creditor/debtor relationship without themselves selling their labor power to capital as a commodity. At first this might seem a major revision of Marx's theory. But this is not the case. Even if this amendment is accepted it would not alter the future course of Marx's systematic progression of economic determinations. For example, Roemer establishes that when the capital form is operative, labor subordinate to capital through creditor/debtor relations is just as necessarily subjected to exploitation as wage labor. "Exploitation" thus remains the next determination in the progression of economic categories. The further stages in Marx's derivation of the determinations of the capital form would remain in force as well. (Roemer has presented objections to Marx's theory that would undermine the transition to the category of "exploitation" were they accepted. See section B.4 below. Reference to Roemer's importance to later categorical stages is made in Chapter VII, section D.)

21. In Hegel's view, the family is on a categorially earlier level than civil society. The domestic labor done within the household is conceived purely as private labor, in contrast to the social labor of civil society satisfying the "system of needs." In passing over domestic labor in *Capital* Marx implicitly accepts this feature of Hegel's system. He does so at the cost of the very sort of mystification that his theory is meant to uncover; "Marx's model, in leaving the 'use-value of labour-power' as originating in a mysterious way in the process of *circulation* of the worker and of the wage-goods, recreates exactly the kind of mystification he criticises at the level of capital. In Marx's model, the 'use-value of labour-power' is a self-reproducing idea. A materialist critique, once again, shows the self-reproducing idea to be an idealogy, rooted in material processes of exploitation which sustain it. But in this case, the materialist critique is also a feminist one, showing that what was repressed in the model was female work (unpaid and for another)." Barbara Bradby, "The Remystification of Value," p. 130.

22. *Ibid.*, p. 125.

23. *Ibid.*, p. 127.

24. *Ibid.*, p. 129.

25. Consider the following passage: "*He* (the labourer) *himself* provides his costs of consumption (cooking, keeping his house clean, generally even repairs)." TSV I, p. 210; emphasis added. As a general description of the gender-based division of domestic labor, this is simply nonsense.

26. "The largest part of society, that is to say the working class, must incidentally perform this kind of labour (i.e. domestic labor, T.S.) for itself; but it is only able to perform it when it has laboured 'productively'. It can only cook meat for itself when it has produced a wage with which to pay for the meat; and it can only keep its furniture and dwellings clean, it can only polish its boots, when it has produced the value of furniture, house rent and boots. To this class of productive labourers itself, therefore, the labour which they perform for themselves appears as 'unproductive labour'. This unproductive labour never enables them to repeat the same unproductive labour a second time unless they have previously laboured productively." *Ibid.*, p. 166.

27. Referring to the proletariat Ernest Mandel writes: "Not being in a position to 'await a more propitious moment of the conjuncture', it is thus compelled to accept a wage which is not determined by the marginal productivity of labor but merely by the average subsistence needs in the given country and period...The dice are loaded." Mandel notes that for negotiation to be on an equal footing "workers should likewise possess reserves of foodstuffs, or money, that would enable them to supply their needs and those of their families, for several years," just as capitalists do now. Perhaps then wages would reflect contribution. But, Mandel concludes, "it is obvious that in a society like this there would neither exist a monopoly of capital in the hands of the bourgeoisie nor a proletariat as a class, so that it would not be capitalist society." *Marxist Economic Theory*, vol. 1, pp. 300-01.

28. *Capital I*, p. 188.

29. "Capital...remains forced labour—no matter how much it may seem to result from free contractual agreement...In the capitalist system...(surplus labor) assumes an antagonistic form." *Capital III*, p. 819.

30. "The standard for measuring exploitation is the reproduction value of labor power; the possibility of receiving a 'surplus product' in such an organization of labor is thereby bracketed out due to the premise 'the value of labor power equals the value necessary for the reproduction of labor power'." Hartmann, *Die Marxsche Theorie*, p. 311. "Laborers in principle do not participate in the expansion of capital." *Ibid.*, p. 316. Hartmann does admit that, for Marx, wages—a concrete phenomenon—can diverge from the value of labor power—an abstract determination—due to contingent fluctuations in the labor market on the level of concrete social processes. But he insists that the *value* of labor power remains fixed at a minimum level, remaining valid as a principle for the more concrete stages of the theory.

31. "Marx's formulation of surplus value theory as the theory of capital accumulation, based on that part of capital devoted to the reproduction of labour power, (is in) contrast to a theory of profit that takes both parts of capital together and relates the results to both constant capital (inclusive of fixed capital) and variable capital...It is theoretically decisive that the concept of surplus value is fixed as more basic than the concept of profit, as transcendentally prior to it." *Ibid.*, p. 314.

32. *Ibid.*, p. 321.

33. If constant capital is not set equal to zero, price, not value, is the proper category to employ even at this stage of the theory: "Precisely the demand for concretion would signify here that price must be brought in, in order to grasp the role of capital in production and productivity advances...If constant capital does not create value in terms of the labor theory of value, it is still 'value' creating from the theoretical standpoint of price." *Ibid.*, p. 318.

34. "In order to make his critique Marx intentionally overlooks the fact that variable capital without any surplus value would result in the breakdown of the work organization. This would not be due only to the capitalists' egoism. It would be bacause c, fixed capital and materials, had been overlooked." *Ibid.*, p. 319.

35. Michio Morishima, *Marx's Economics*, p. 53.

36. See Samuel Bowles and Herbert Gintis's article "Structure and Practice in the Labor Theory of Value."

37. *Capital I*, p. 168.

38. TSV II, pp. 16-71.

39. TSV III, p. 312.

40. TSV I, p. 45. Emphases added.

41. Max Weber, *Economy and Society*, Volume 2, pp. 730-31.

42. TSV III, p. 196.

43. *Ibid.*, p. 211.

44. *Capital I*, p. 206.

45. See TSV II p. 16 ff. On the other hand, the worker may be placed in a *greater* state of physical and nervous exhaustion as a result of labor in industrialized capitalist conditions: "Instead of being consumed by him as material elements of his productive activity, they consume him as the ferment necessary to their own life-process, and the life-process of capital consists only in its movement as value constantly expanding, constantly multiplying itself." *Capital I*, p. 224.

46. "A definite quantity of surplus-labor is required as insurance against accidents, and by the necessary and progressive expansion of the process of reproduction in keeping with the development of the needs and the growth of population...It is one of the civilising aspects of capital that it enforces this surplus-labour in a manner and under conditions which are more advantageous to the development of the productive forces, social relations, and the creation of the elements for a new and higher form than under the preceding forms of slavery, serfdom, etc." *Capital III*, p. 819.

47. *Selected Writings*, pp. 567. The "other purposes" include assistance to those unable to work and the provision of items of social consumption.

48. In Jon Elster's view, "This usage"—i.e. understanding exploitation in terms of lack of control over the surplus product—"is distinctly unusual" (*Making Sense of Marx*, p. 177). It is the correct usage nevertheless. Duncan K. Foley presents the point precisely: "Whether (some extraction of a surplus product) constitutes exploitation...depends on one's analysis of the mechanisms of control of the social surplus." *Understanding Capital: Marx's Economic Theory*, p. 40.

49. TSV III, p. 274. "The determinate social form of the worker's labour corresponds to the form which the conditions of labour...assume in respect of the worker. But the former is in fact merely the objective expression of the latter." TSV III, p. 415.

50. Roemer, *Free to Lose*, pp. 128-29. Roemer's contribution to the debate regarding exploitation is discussed at length in my "Roemer on Marxian Exploitation: Shortcomings of a Non-Dialectical Approach."

Chapter VII. Categories of the Production Process Proper

1. It has not often been noted that Marx's physical ailments led him to introduce so much historical material into *Capital*: "I could not make any progress with the really theoretical part. My brain was too weak for that. So I have expanded the section on the *Working Day* with historical material, which was not part of my original plan." Letter to Engels, Feb. 10, 1986, in *Letters jon 'Capital'*, p. 97.

2. See Hartmann, *Die Marxsche Theorie*, pp. 325 ff.

3. We should recall once again Marx's intent to present a systematic rather than purely historical theory. See *Grundrisse*, p. 107: "It would therefore be unfeasible and wrong to let the economic categories follow one another in the same sequence as that in which they were historically decisive."

4. However, much of Jon Elster's rejection of teleological thinking in Marxist explanations of history is well taken. See his paper "Marxism, functionalism and game theory."

5. Hartmann, *Die Marxsche Theorie*, p. 332. Hartmann has in mind passages such as the following: "As co-operators, as members of a working organism, they (workers) are but special modes of existence of capital." *Capital I*, p. 315.

6. "Marx's phenomenology of production presents matters such as the conditions of industrial production (machinery, laboring on machinery, etc.) as closely tied to capitalism. But they are what they are regardless of the question of property. The connection of a historical-factual process—the alienation of production through capitalism—and the theory of alienation would be harmless, were it not for the thesis that an acceptable capitalist (or somehow non-communist) alternative is impossible. The theory doesn't prove this, except through a quid pro quo." Hartmann, *Die Marxsche Theorie*, pp. 334-35.

7. See Marx's 1877 letter to Mikhailovsky: "(My critic) feels he absolutely must metamorphose my historical sketch of the genesis of capitalism in Western Europe into a historico-philosophic theory of the general path every people is fated to tread, whatever the historical circumstances in which it finds itself. . . But I beg his pardon. (He is both honoring me and shaming me too much.)" *Selected Writings*, p. 572.

8. "The directing motive, the end and aim of capitalist production, is to extract the greatest possible amount of surplus-value, and consequently to exploit labour-power to the greatest possible extent. As the number of co-operating labourers increases, so too does their resistance to the domination of capital, and with it, the necessity for capital to overcome this resistance by counterpressure. The control exercised by the capitalist is not only a special function, due to the nature of the social labour-process, and peculiar to that process, but it is, at the same time, a function of the exploitation of a social labour-process, and is consequently rooted in

the unavoidable antagonism between the exploiter and the living and labouring raw material he exploits." *Capital I*, p. 313.

9. Of course to some extent capitalism created the global factory when the first raw materials were plundered from the third world and shipped to Europe for processing. But today the international links of production are so much greater that we might conclude that a qualitatively new stge in the history of capitalism has been reached. For a contrasting view see David Gordon: "The Global Economy: New Edifice or Crumbling Foundations?"

10. *Capital I*, p. 386.

11. See the debate set off by Harry Braverman's *Labor and Monopoly Capital*, especially *The Degradation of Work?: Skill, Deskilling and the Labour Process*, Stephen Wood, ed.

12. As Marx writes in "Wage Labour and Capital": "capital presupposes wage labour; wage labour presupposes capital. They reciprocally condition the existence of each other; they reciprocally bring forth each other." *Selected Writings*, p. 258.

13. Despite the fact that this section of *Capital* is entitled "The Accumulation of Capital," and despite the fact that he uses the term "simple reproduction" in Volume II to discuss a quite different structure than the one now being considered, Marx also terms the structure considered here in Volume I "simple reproduction." For the sake of clarity I have used the term *simple accumulation* throughout the present stage.

14. "Original accumulation is a transition that can only be presented naturalistically, and precisely as such must ground the theory. Methodologically the transcendental theory of capital is left behind in the excursus on original accumulation in favor of a socio-historical and picture-thinking point of view, which is supposed to incorporate a presupposition that hasn't been included." Hartmann, *Die Marxsche Theorie*, p. 342.

15. *Ibid.*, p. 343.

16. "The conflation of transcendental and historical viewpoints makes us believe that a form of capital untainted by history, or at least one that compensates for this, is impossible." *Ibid.*, p. 344.

17. Note how the very ordering of categories in *Capital* undermines the attempt to read Marx as a technological determinist. The social form that defines capital is systematically prior to constant capital, the embodiment of technical advance. Our discussion of the systematic ordering of categories in *Capital* thus provides independent confirmation for the argument against reading Marx as a technological determinist provided in Richard Miller's *Analysing Marx*.

18. "It took both time and experience before the workpeople learnt to

distinguish between machinery and its employment by capital, and to direct their attacks, not against the material instruments of production, but against the mode in which they are used.," *Capital I*, p. 404.

19. *Ibid.*, p. 415.

20. TSV III, p. 265.

21. "These two descriptions are far from being identical. In one, the collective labourer, or social body of labour, appears as the dominant subject, and the mechanical automaton as the object; in the other, the automaton itself is the subject, and the workmen are merely conscious organs, co-ordinate with the unconscious organs of the automaton, and together with them, subordinated to the central moving-power. *The first description is applicable to every possible employment of machinery on a large scale*, the second is characteristic of its uses by capital, and therefore of the modern factory system." *Capital I*, pp. 395-96. Emphasis added.

22. "It is true that the particular social form of these things in relation to labour and their real determinateness as factors of the labour process are as confused and inseparably interwoven with one another in the minds of the economists as they are in the mind of the capitalist. Nevertheless, as soon as they analyse the labour process they are compelled to abandon the term capital completely and to speak of material of labour, means of labour, and means of subsistence. But the determinate form of the product as material, instrument and means of subsistence of the worker expresses nothing but the relationship of these *objective* conditions to labour; labour itself appears as the activity which dominates them. It says nothing at all about (the relationship of) labour and capital, only about the relationship of the purposeful activity of men to their own products in the process of reproduction. They neither cease to be products of labour nor mere objects which are at the disposal of labour. They merely express the relationship in which labour appropriates the objective world which it has created itself, at any rate in this form; but they do not by any means express *any other domination of these things over labour*, apart from the fact that activity must be appropriate to the material, otherwise it would not be purposeful activity, labour." TSV III, pp. 264-65.

23. "Developed capitalist production can approach the case of simple reproduction due to v. ages being so high." Hartmann, *Die Marxsche Theorie*, p. 339.

24. See *Explaining Technical Change*, Jon Elster, Chapter 7.

25. The full passage reads: "It is possible that, owing to an increase of productiveness, both the labourer and the capitalist may simultaneously be able to appropriate a greater quantity of these necessaries, without any change in the price of labour-power or in surplus-value...If the productiveness of labour were doubled without altering the ratio of necessary labour to surplus-labour, there would be no change of the magnitude in surplus-value and price of labour-power. The only result

would be that each of them would represent twice as many use-values as before; these use-values being twice as cheap as before. . . It is possible with an increasing productiveness of labour, for the price of labour-power to keep on falling, and yet this fall to be accompanied by a constant growth in the mass of the labourer's means of subsistence." *Capital I*, pp. 489-90.

26. *Ibid.*, pp. 579-80.

27. "The division of labour develops the *social* productive power of labour or the productive power of *social* labour, but at the expense of the *general productive ability* of the worker. This increase in *Social productive power* confronts the worker therefore as an increased productive power, *not of his labour*, but of *capital*, the force that dominates his labour." TSV II, p. 234.

28. "*Accumulation* by means of the reconversion of profit, or surplus product, into capital now becomes a continuous process as a result of which the increased products of labour which are at the same time its objective conditions, conditions of reproduction, continuously confront labour as *capital*, i.e., as forces—personified in the capitalist—which are alienated from labour and dominate it." TSV III, p. 272.

29. *Ibid*, pp. 352-53.

30. Even when increased real wages accompany capital accumulation, "the value of capital relative to the share of labour has risen. The division of social wealth between capital and labour has become still more unequal. With the same capital, the capitalist commands a greater quantity of labour. The power of the capitalist class over the working class has grown, the social position of the worker has deteriorated, has been depressed one step further below that of the capitalist." "Wage Labour and Capital," in *Selected Writings*, p. 261.

31. *Capital I.*, pp. 581-82.

32. "Machinery not only acts as a competitor who gets the better of the workman, and is constantly on the point of making him superfluous. It is also a power inimical to him, and as such capital proclaims it from the roof tops and as such makes use of it. It is the most powerful weapon for repressing strikes, those periodical revolts of the working-class against the autocracy of capuital. . . It would be possible to write quite a history of the inventions, made since 1830, for the sole purpose of supplying capital with weapons against the revolts of the working-class." *Capital I*, pp. 410-11.

33. Under this heading fall phenomena such as giant agribusiness firms subcontracting with "independent" producers, multinational manufacturing firms subcontracting with small family shops, and so on. In this manner capital is able to get the benefits of real subsumption of the labor process while simultaneously displacing risk, fragmenting its labor force, and reducing its costs (e.g. the costs of the various benefits it must provide for its own wage laborers).

Chapter VIII. The Categories of Circulation

1. If this argument is correct, it provides a further case against those who propose a historical or "logico-historical" reading of the progression in *Capital*. There is no historical stage of capitalism in which the strictures Marx imposed on the two departments hold. There are no historical examples of a period in which, for example, capital accumulated in industries producing means of production could not be invested in industries producing means of consumption. The present level of categories is a step in the systematic reconstruction of the capital form, not an ideal type of a historical period. Rosa Luxemburg was one of the few representatives of classical Marxism to emphasize the schemes of reproduction presented in Volume II of *Capital*. However she criticized them on the grounds that they abstract from concrete historical reality, especially the dynamic between capitalist societies and their environment of precapitalist formations. (See Luxemburg, *The Accumulation of Capital, passim.*) She thus entirely missed the methodological architectonic of *Capital*. Volume II is not meant to be a depiction of concrete historical reality. It instead presents stages that are still fairly abstract in the categorial progression reconstructing that reality. See Rosdolsky's excellent discussion of Luxemburg in *The Making of Marx's 'Capital'*, pp. 66 ff.

2. *Capital II.*, p. 477.

3. Hartmann, *Die Marxsche Theorie*, p. 347. For another formulation of this Hegelian criticism of Marx, see also Winfield, *The Just Economy*, p. 121.

4. "As personified capital he produces for the sake of production, he wants to accumulate wealth for the sake of the accumulation of wealth. In so far as he is a mere functionary of capital, that is, an agent of capitalist production, what matters to him is exchange-value and the increase of exchange-value, not use-value and its increase. What he is concerned with is the increase of abstract wealth... the production of the normal capitalist, of the industrial capitalist as he ought to be, is *production for the sake of production.*" TSV I, p. 282.

5. *Capital I*, pp. 536-37. "It could indeed be said that the labourer sells a commodity (labour-power) for money, spends this money on commodities, and then sells his labour-power again, so that for him too the movement is M - C - M; and since the money is constantly fluctuating between him and the capitalist, it could equally be said, depending on whether one considers it from the standpoint of the one or of the other, that for him as well as for the capitalist the movement is M - C - M. The capitalist, however, is the buyer. The renewal of the process starts from him, not from the labourer, while the return flow of the money is compulsory, since the labourer must buy means of subsistence." TSV I, pp. 321-22.

6. "Now there are only two points of departure: the capitalist and the labourer. All third categories of persons must either receive money for their services from these two classes or, to the extent that they receive it without any services in return,

they are joint owners of the surplus-value in the form of rent, interest, etc." *Capital II*, p. 338.

7. *Ibid.*

8. *Ibid.*, p. 385.

9. Hartmann, *Die Marxsche Theorie*, p. 352.

10. *Ibid.*

11. Various forms of this disproportionality are described by Marx as follows: "Formation of virtual additional money-capital in class I (hence underconsumption from the view-point of II); piling up of commodity-supplies in class II which cannot be reconverted into productive capital (hence relative over-production in II); surplus of money-capital in I and reproduction deficit in II." *Capital II*, p. 507.

12. This follows only if we add a further premise to the effect that the capital form continually forces the need to accumulate upon capitalists, thereby limiting the amount of accumulated surplus that can be set aside for their consumption.

13. *Capital II*, p. 320.

14. *Ibid.*, p. 144.

15. Hartmann, *Die Marxsche Theorie*, p. 352.

16. *Ibid.*, pp. 352-53.

17. *Capital II*, p. 147.

18. Hartmann, *op. cit.*, p. 356.

19. *Capital II*, pp. 414-15.

Chapter IX. The Categories of Concretion

1. As a result the exploitation of wage labor is covered over: whenever this concrete level is not considered within the categorial reconstruction of capitalism as a whole: "We see only finished and existing values—the portions of the value of the advanced capital which go into the making of the value of the product—but not the element creating new values. the distinction between constant and variable capital has disappeared." *Capital III*, p. 32.

2. "The price of production of a commodity is equal to its cost-price plus the profit, allotted to it in per cent, in accordance with the general rate of profit, or, in other words, to its cost-price plus the average profit." *Ibid.*, p. 157.

3. It is important to stress that this unity is a class unity, uniting the units of

industrial capital over against the working class, even if the process establishing this unity is as unconscious to the former as it is to the latter: "At a given degree of exploitation, the mass of surplus-value produced in a particular sphere of production is then more important for the aggregate average profit of social capital, and thus for the capitalist class in general, than for the individual capitalist in any specific branch of production." *Ibid.*, p. 167.

4. Böhm-Bawerk's *Karl Marx and the Close of His System* first proposed this objection. It has been repeated more recently by Paul Samuelson in his "Understanding the Marxian Notion of Exploitation: A Summary of the so-Called Transformation Problem Between Marxian Values and Competitive Prices."

5. It is important to stress that the transformation process that redistributes value and surplus value is logical, not temporal. See Himmelweit & Mohun's "The Anomalies of Capital."

6. A representative example of this position is developed in Ian Steedman's *Marx After Sraffa.*

7. Hartmann, *Die Marxsche Theorie*, p. 370.

8. "In order to arrive at the equalisation of profit rates from the theory of profit based upon surplus value Marx must set all factors except profit as unchanged. Otherwise the competition which is made responsible for the equalisation would explain nothing and any sort of conception of the profit rate would be possible. It is precisely a matter of presenting the immanent movement of the profit rate over against the surplus value rate, and for this the surplus value rate must be held fixed. And precisely this supposition—made in the interest of a linear explanation—is contradictory." Hartmann, *Ibid.*, p. 367.

9. Ernest Mandel, "Gold, Money and the Transformation Problem," in *Ricardo, Marx, Sraffa.* See also G. Carchedi's "The Logic of Prices as Values." We should always be wary of transposing Marx's perspective into a static equilibrium framework. Marx insisted that "the general rate of profit is never anything more than a tendency, a movement to equalize specific rates of profit. The competition between capitalists—which is itself this movement toward equilibrium—consists here of their gradually withdrawing capital from spheres in which profit is for an appreciable length of time below average, and gradually investing capital into spheres in which profit is above average. Or it may also consist in additional capital distributing itself gradually and in varying proportions among these spheres. It is continual variation in supply and withdrawal of capital in regard to these different spheres, and never a simultaneous mass effect." *Capital III*, p. 366.

10. Anwar Shaikh, "The Transformation from Marx to Sraffa," in *Ricardo, Marx, Sraffa.*

11. "Should...quantity be smaller or greater, however, than the demand for them, there will be deviations of the market-price from the market-value." *Capital*

III, p. 185. This too is part of the law of value: "There exists an accidental rather than a necessary connection between the total amount of social labour applied to a social article, i.e., between the aliquot part of society's total labour-power allocated to producing this article, or between the volume which the production of this article occupies in total production, on the one hand, and the volume whereby society seeks to satisfy the want gratified by the article in question, on the other. Every individual article, or every definite quantity of a commodity may, indeed, contain no more than the social labour required for its production, and from this point of view the market-value of this entire commodity represents only necessary labour, but if this commodity has been produced in excess of the existing social needs, then so much of the social labour-time is squandered and the mass of the commodity comes to represent a much smaller quantity of social labour in the market than is actually incorporated in it. (It is only where production is under the actual, predetermining control of society that the latter establishes a relation between the volume of social labour-time applied in producing definite articles, and the volume of the social want to be satisfied by these articles.) For this reason, these commodities must be sold below their market-value, and a portion of them may even be altogether unsaleable. The reverse applies if the quantity of social labour employed in the production of a certain kind of commodity is too small to meet the social demand for that commodity." *Ibid.*, p. 187.

12. Richard Dien Winfield, "Hegel's Challenge To the Modern Economy," p. 45.

13. *Ibid.*, p. 47.

14. *Ibid.*, p. 48.

15. See Winfield, *the Just Economy*, p. 132, and Hartmann's comment, "Capital must be oriented to demand, to the purchasing power of the workers; there is an interdependence between production and purchasing power, which thus is in the interest of capital...Raising purchasing power (a reflection of capital not only on itself, but on its counter-instance, its partner on the other side) (is) required for capital's own continuance. Marx's analysis is one-sided in that it proceeds from the supposed interests of capital, from its inner nature, instead of from its interests properly understood...It is conceivable that production and wages can be indefinitely high." Hartmann, *Die Marxsche Theorie*, pp. 394-95.

16. "It would seem, then, that there is on the side of demand a certain magnitude of definite social wants which require for their satisfaction a definite quantity of a commodity on the market. But quantitatively, the definite social wants are very elastic and changing. Their fixedness is only apparent. If the means of subsistence were cheaper, or money-wages higher, the labourers would buy more of them. And a greater "social need" would arise for them, leaving aside the paupers, etc., whose "demand" is even below the narrowest limits of their physical wants. On the other hand, if cotton were cheaper, for example, the capitalists' demand for it would

increase, more additional capital would be thrown into the cotton industry, etc."
Capital III, p. 188.

17. These themes are discussed at length in Ernest Mandel's *Late Capitalism*.

18. This example is found in Joan Robinson's *An Essay on Marxian Economies*, pp. 36-7.

19. This point is seen quite clearly by Jürgen Habermas. See Habermas, "Between Philosophy and Science: Marxism as Critique," in *Theory and Practice*, pp. 195 ff. Unfortunately Habermas goes on to assert that this involves an alternative to Marx's position. Habermas holds that we must now grant that scientific-technical labor is a second source of surplus value, one which in principle allows the rate of profit to avoid falling indefinitely. Marx himself was well aware of the contribution made by scientific-technical labor. He insisted, however, that scientific-technical labor be categorized in the same terms as other forms of labor; it is part of the collective laborer that collectively creates value. "The characteristic feature of this kind of saving of constant capital arising from the progressible development of industry is that the rise in the rate of profit in *one* line of industry depends on the development of the productive power of labour in *another*. Whatever falls to the capitalist's advantage in this case is once more a gain produced by social labour, if not a product of the labourers he himself exploits. Such a development of productive power is again traceable in the final analysis to the social nature of the labour engaged in production; to the division of labour in society; and to the development of intellectual labour, especially in the natural sciences. What the capitalist thus utilizes are the advantages of the entire system of the social division of labour. It is the development of the productive power of labour in its exterior department, in that department which supplies it with means of production, whereby the value of the constant capital employed by the capitalist is relatively lowered and consequently the rate of profit is raised." *Capital III*, p. 81-2. See also *Grundrisse*, p. 325, and *Capital I*, p. 47.

20. Hartmann, *Die Marxsche Theorie*, p. 383.

21. A. Bhaduri has constructed a simple and elegant proof that the marginal productivity of capital does not in general equal the rate of profit. Let Y be the net national income, K the value of capital, L the number of employed workers, r the rate of profit, and w the real wage per worker unit of time, with Y, K, and w measured in terms of a homogeneous consumption good (say corn). Then assume that $Y = Kr + Lw$; i.e. the net national income is distributed between profits and wages. If we normalize this equation by setting $L = 1$ (which can be done without loss of generality), then $y = kr + w$ (with "k" = "K" measured in terms of work time). If this equation is totally differentiated, we arrive at the equation $dy = r\, dk + k\, dr + dw$. From this it follows that the marginal productivity of capital (dy/dk) equals the rate of profit (r) only if $k\, dr + dw = 0$ (or only if $-dw/dr = k$). This is a special case that can only occur by chance. Therefore in general the neoclassical thesis that the

marginal productivity of capital determines the rewards capital receives does not hold. See Bhaduri's "On the Significance of Recent Controversies in Capital Theory: A Marxian View" and Brian Burkett's discussion in *Radical Political Economy*, Chapter 10.

22. "The real barrier of capitalist production is capital itself. It is that capital and its self-expansion appear as the starting and the closing point, the motive and the purpose of production; that production is only production for capital and not vice versa, the means of production are not mere means for a constant expansion of the living process of the society of producers. The limits within which the preservation and self-expansion of the value of capital resting on the expropriation and pauperisation of the great mass of producers can alone move—these limits come continually into conflict with the methods of production employed by capital for its purposes, which drive towards unlimited extension of production, towards production as an end in itself, towards unconditional development of the social productivity of labour. The means—unconditional development of the social productive forces of society—comes continually into conflict with the limited purpose, the self-expansion of the existing capital. The capitalist mode of production is, for this reason, a historical means of developing the material forces of production and creating an appropriate world-market and is, at the same time, a continual conflict between this its historical task and its own corresponding relations of social production." *Capital III*, p. 250.

23. Hartmann, *Die Marxsche Theorie*, p. 384.

24. "The contradiction of the capitalist mode of production, however, lies precisely in its tendency towards an absolute development of the productive forces, which continually come into conflict with the specific *conditions* of production in which capital moves, and alone can move. There are not too many necessities of life produced, in proportion to the existing population. Quite the reverse. Too little is produced to decently and humanely satisfy the wants of the great mass. There are not too many means of production produced to employ the able-bodied portion of the population. Quite the reverse." *Capital III*, p. 257.

25. The reader will note that I have not mentioned the most famous refutation of Marx's law of the tendency of the rate of profit to fall, that found in Nubuo Okishio's "Technical Change and the Rate of Profit" and later repeated by Elster, Roemer, and many others. This is because "Okishio's theorem" rests on a fundamental error regarding the systematic progression of economic categories in *Capital*. Okishio supposes that the same profit rate holds for all units of capital. If a new technology is introduced that happens to lower this rate, then capitalists will simply abandon it and return to the older technology. Hence it is impossible for the rate of profit to fall. (This is a very simplified presentation of his argument, but it is sufficient for present purposes.) It is true that on the categorial level of prices of production Marx did introduce the idea that the rate of profit is identical for all units of capital. But this was a simplifying abstraction introduced in order to explicate the

transition from cost prices to prices of production. The level of market prices, the categorial level where the law is located, is on a more concrete stage of the theory. On this level the simplifying abstraction of an identical rate of profit is dropped. The many units of capital, each competing for market share, are each trying to attain higher rates of profit than their competitors. The structure defined on this categorial level could in principle introduce the following prisoner's dilemma. Suppose that there is a new technology that will increase the rate of profit for the firm that introduces it, as long as other firms do not employ it. If the use of this technology is generalized, then the rate of profit falls for all firms. From the standpoint of collective rationality the capitalists would be better off not introducing the technology. But from the individual standpoint of a particular capitalist it may be rational to introduce the technology, enjoy an increase in the rate of profit until the technology becomes generalized, and then hope that some new technology will be available that will allow the process to be repeated. In this manner the individually rational pursuit of higher profits may lead to the collectively irrational result of a lower rate of profit for capital as a whole. Okishio's theorem illegitimately rules out this possibility by assuming that all units of capital always enjoy the identical rate of profit. In other words, the theorem is based upon the systematic confusion between the abstract stage of prices of production (where rates of profit are assumed by Marx to be identical) and the more concrete stage of market prices (where rates of profit are not assumed to be identical). Since the law of the tendency of the rate of profit is formulated on the latter, more concrete, level, this systematic confusion makes Okishio's theorem completely irrelevant.

26. "The contradiction, to put it in a very general way, consists in that the capitalist mode of production involves a tendency towards absolute development of the productive forces . . . while, on the other hand, its aim is to preserve the value of the existing capital and promote its self-expansion to the highest limit (i.e., to promote an ever more rapid growth of this value). The specific feature about it is that it uses the existing value of capital as a means of increasing this value to the utmost. The methods by which it accomplishes this include the fall of the rate of profit, depreciation of existing capital, and development of the productive forces of labour at the expense of already created productive forces. The periodical depreciation of existing capital—one of the means immanent in capitalist production to check the fall of the rate of profit and hasten accumulation of capital-value through formation of new capital—disturbs the given conditions, within which the process of circulation and reproduction of capital takes place, and is therefore accompanied by sudden stoppages and crises in the production process." *Capital III*, p. 249.

27. "This confusion and stagnation paralyses the function of money as a medium of payment, whose development is geared to the development of capital and is based on those presupposed price relations. The chain of payment obligations due at specific dates is broken in a hundred places. The confusion is augmented by the attendant collapse of the credit system, which develops simultaneously with capital, and leads to violent and acute crises, to sudden and forcible depreciations, to the

actual stagnation and disruption of the process of reproduction, and thus to a real falling off in reproduction." *Ibid.*, p. 254.

28. "Since the aim of capital is not to minister to certain wants, but to produce profit, and since it accomplishes this purpose by methods which adapt the mass of production to the scale of production, not vice versa, a rift must continually ensue between the limited dimensions of consumption under capitalism and a production which forever tends to exceed this immanent barrier." *Ibid.*, p. 256. "The tendency to accumulate, the drive to expand capital and produce surplus-value on an extended scale . . . is law for capitalist production, imposed by incessant revolutions in the methods of production themselves, by the depreciation of existing capital always bound up with them, by the general competitive struggle and the need to improve production and expand its scale merely as a means of self-preservation and under penalty of ruin. The market must, therefore, be continually extended, so that its interrelations and the conditions regulating them assume more and more the form of a natural law working independently of the producer, and become more and more uncontrollable. This internal contradiction seeks to resolve itself through expansion of the outlying field of production. But the more productiveness develops, the more it finds itself at variance with the narrow basis on which the conditions of consumption rest." *Ibid.*, pp. 244-5.

29. "From time to time the conflict of antagonistic agencies finds vent in *crises.* The crises are always but momentary and forcible solutions of the existing contradictions. They are violent eruptions which for a time restore the disturbed equilibrium." *Ibid.*, p. 249.

30. "Alongside the fall in the rate of profit mass of capitals grows, and hand in hand with this there occurs a depreciation of existing capitals which checks the fall and gives an accelerating motion to the accumulation of capital-values." *Ibid.*, p. 249.

31. "How is this conflict settled and the conditions restored which correspond to the 'sound' operation of capitalist production? The mode of settlement is already indicated in the very emergence of the conflict whose settlement is under discussion. It implies the withdrawal and even the partial destruction of capital amounting to the full value of additional capital delta C, or at least a part of it. Although, as the description of this conflict shows, the loss is by no means equally distributed among individual capitals, its distribution being rather decided through a competitive struggle in which the loss is distributed in very different proportions and forms, depending on special advantages or previously captured positions, so that one capital is left unused, another is destroyed, and a third suffers but a relative loss, or is just temporarily depreciated, etc." *Ibid.*, p. 253. "The fall in prices and the competitive struggle would have driven every capitalist to lower the individual value of his total product below its general value by means of new machines, new and improved working methods, new combinations, i.e., to increase the productivity of a given quantity of labour, to lower the proportion of variable to constant capital,

247

and thereby to release some labourers; in short, to create an artificial over-population. Ultimately, the depreciation of the elements of constant capital would itself tend to raise the rate of profit. The mass of employed constant capital would have increased in relation to variable, but its value could have fallen. The ensuing stagnation of production would have prepared—within capitalistic limits—a subsequent expansion of production. And thus the cycle would run its course anew. Part of the capital, depreciated by its functional stagnation, would recover its old value. For the rest, the same vicious circle would be described once more under expanded conditions of production, with an expanded market and increased productive forces." *Ibid.*, p. 255.

32. "The stagnation of production would have laid off a part of the working-class and would thereby have placed the employed part in a situation, where it would have to submit to a reduction of wages even below the average. This has the very same effect on capital as an increase of the relative or absolute surplus-value at average wages would have had." *Ibid.*, p. 254.

33. Hartmann, *Die Marxsche Theorie*, p. 435.

34. *Chapter III*, p. 253.

35. Hartmann, *Die Marxsche Theorie*, p. 389.

36. "The conversion of commodities (products) into money, and of money into commodities (means of production) is a necessary function of industrial capital and, therefore, a necessary operation of the capitalist." *Capital III*, p. 289.

37. "It is, therefore, the metamorphosis of commodities that is here promoted by credit; not merely C-M, but also M-C and the actual production process. A large quantity of credit within the reproductive circuit (banker's credit excepted) does not signify a large quantity of idle capital, which is being offered for loan and is seeking profitable investment. It means rather a large employment of capital in the reproduction process. . . The maximum of credit is here identical with the fullest employment of industrial capital, that is, the utmost exertion of its reproductive power without regard to the limits of consumption. These limits of consumption are extended by the exertions of the reproduction process itself." *Ibid.*, p. 482.

38. "Just as industrial capital makes profit by selling labour embodied and realised in commodities, for which it has not paid any equivalent, so merchant's capital derives profit from not paying in full to productive capital for all the unpaid labour contained in the commodities. . . and by demanding payment for this unpaid portion still contained in the commodities when making a sale. The relation of merchant's capital to surplus-value is different from that of industrial capital. The latter produces surplus-value by directly appropriating the unpaid labour of others. The former appropriates a portion of this surplus-value by having this portion transferred from industrial capital itself. *Ibid.*, p. 293.

39. "Landownership. . . constitutes a limitation to the investment of capital and

the free expansion of capital in the land...Differential rent presupposes the existence of a monopoly in landownership, landed property as a limitation to capital, for without it surplus-profit would not be transformed into ground-rent nor fall to the share of the landlord instead of the the farmer. And landed property as a limitation continues to exist even when rent in the form of differential rent disappears." *Ibid.*, pp. 750-51.

40. *Ibid.*, pp. 761-62.

41. Hartmann, *Die Marxsche Theorie*, p. 399.

42. "It is clear that the normal condition of capital does not go back to the original sin of expropriation, but to abstinence (saving) on the one side and credit on the other, which is paid back with interest out of the profits of a production process or other sort of profit generating process. What is to be understood is this systematic circle of capital that is always already present as presupposition and new capital, not the finding of a place for credit and other conditions of capital at the tail end of the economic theory of categories...The transcendental-linear schema, in which interest appears late as the (determination) furthest from labor value, makes a theoretical grasp of capital impossible in the last analysis." *Ibid.*, p. 400.

43. *Ibid.*

44. "The stock market is the reflection of effective demand on the price of capital and the psychological power of the expectation of effective demand reflected in the price of capital. It explains the inclination to the greater instability of economic occurences. In contrast, for Marx this instability is already based on an earlier phase (of the theory), so that the stock market is only a late consequence of capital in the sector of money transactions. It thus cannot be understood as a determining factor of the reproduction of capital." *Ibid.*, p. 400-01.

45. "Land, like capital, is loaned only to capitalists. Of course, means of production in kind, such as machines and business offices, can also be loaned instead of money. But they then represent a definite sum of money, and the fact that in addition to interest a part is paid for wear and tear is due to their use-value, i.e., the specific natural form of these elements of capital. The decisive factor here is again whether they are loaned to direct producers, which would presuppose the non-existence of the capitalist mode of production—at least in the sphere in which this occurs—or whether they are loaned to industrial capitalists, which is precisely the assumption based upon the capitalist mode of production. It is still more irrelevant and meaningless to drag the lending of houses, etc., for individual use into this discussion. That the working-class is also swindled in this form, and to an enormous extent, is self-evident; but this is also done by the retail dealer, who sells means of subsistence to the worker. This is secondary exploitation, which runs parallel to the primary exploitation taking place in the production process itself. The distinction between selling and loaning is quite immaterial in this case and merely formal, and, as already indicated, cannot appear as essential to anyone, unless he be wholly unfamiliar with the actual nature of the problem." *Capital III*, p. 609.

46. "Credit, through shareholding, combines in one magnitude of capital a large number of individual capitals. It makes available to each capitalist the use of other capitalists' money—in the form of industrial credits. As commercial credit it accelerates the exchange of commodities and therefore the return of capital into production, and thus aids the entire cycle of the process of production. The manner in which these two principle functions of credit influence the formation of crises is quite obvious. If it is true that crises appear as a result of the contradiction existing between the capacity of extension, the tendency of production to increase and the restricted consumption capacity of the market, credit is precisely, in view of what was stated above, the specific means that makes this contradiction break out as often as possible. To begin with, it increases disproportionately the capacity of the extension of production and thus constitutes an inner motive force that is constantly pushing production to exceed the limits of the market. But credit strikes from two sides. After having (as a factor of the process of production) provoked over-production, credit (as a factor of exchange) destroys, during the crisis, the very productive forces it itself created. At the first symptom of the crisis, credit melts away. It abandons exchange where it would still be found indispensible, and appearing instead ineffective and useless, there where some exchange still continues, it reduces to a minimum the consumption capacity of the market. Besides having these two principle results, credit also influences the formation of crises in the following ways. It constitutes the technical means of making available to an entrepreneur the capital of other owners. It stimulates at the same time the bold and unscrupulous utilization of the property of others. That is, it leads to speculation. Credit not only aggravates the crisis in its capacity as a dissembled means of exchange, it also helps to bring and extend the crisis by transforming all exchange into an extremely complex and artificial mechanism that...is easily disarranged at the slightest occasion." Rosa, Luxemburg, "Reform or Revolution," p. 42.

47. *Capital III*, p. 441.

48. *Ibid.*, pp. 606-07.

49. *Ibid.*, p. 819.

50. The reversal is complete and fetishism attains its ultimate form when wage labor is itself treated as a type of capital to which interest is due. "We shall now consider labour-power in contrast to the capital of the national debt, where a negative quantity appears as capital—just as interest-bearing capital, in general, is the fountain-head of all manner of insane forms, so that debts, for instance, can appear to the banker as commodities. Wages are conceived here as interest, and therefore labour-power as the capital yielding this interest. For example, if the wage for one year amounts to 50 and the rate of interest is 5%, the annual labour-power is equal to a capital of 1,000. The insanity of the capitalist mode of conception reaches its climax here, for instead of explaining the expansion of capital on the basis of the exploitation of labour-power, the matter is reversed and the productivity of labour-power is explained by attributing this mystical quality of interest-bearing capital to labour-power itself." *Ibid.*, p. 465.

51. *Ibid.*, p. 491.

52. "Interest is, therefore, the expression of the fact that value in general—materialised labour in its general social form—value which assumes the form of means of production in the actual process of production, confronts living labour-power as an independent power, and is a means of appropriating unpaid labour; and that it is such a power because it confronts the labourer as the property of another. But on the other hand, this antithesis to wage-labour is obliterated in the form of interest, because interest-bearing capital as such has not wage-labour, but productive capital for its opposite. The lending capitalist as such faces the capitalist performing his actual function in the process of reproduction, not the wage-worker, who, precisely under capitalist production, is expropriated of the means of production. Interest-bearing capital is capital as property as distinct from capital as a function. But so long as capital does not perform its function, it does not exploit labourers and does not come into opposition to labour." *Ibid.*, p. 379.

53. Often the "enhanced value of money-capital corresponds directly on the other hand to the depreciated money-value of real capital (commodity-capital and productive capital). The value of capital in the one form rose because the value of capital in the other fell." *Ibid.*, p. 421.

54. "This social existence of wealth therefore assumes the aspect of a world beyond, of a thing, matter, commodity, alongside of and external to the real elements of social wealth. So long as production is in a state of flux this is forgotten. Credit, likewise a social form of wealth, crowds out money and usurps its place. It is faith in the social character of production which allows the money-form of products to assume the aspect of something that is only evanescent and ideal, something merely imaginative. But as soon as credit is shaken—and this phase of necessity always appears in the modern industrial cycle—all the real wealth is to be actually and suddenly transformed into money, into gold and silver—a mad demand, which, however, grows necessarily out of the system itself. And all the gold and silver which is supposed to satisfy these enormous demands amounts to but a few millions in the vaults of the Bank. Among the effects of the gold drain, then, the fact that production as social production is not really subject to social control, is strikingly emphasized by the existence of the social form of wealth as a thing external to it." *Ibid.*, p. 573-74.

Chapter X. Conclusion

1. Value theory, of course, also comes into play in areas of Marx's theory that do not have to do with systematic considerations. These dimensions of value theory will not be discussed here.

2. Max Weber, *General Economic History*, p. 209. Emphasis added.

3. Ian Steedman, *Marx After Sraffa*, p. 173.

4. But see the writings of Anwar Shaikh for a strong rebuttal of the Sraffian position on this point.

5. Steedman, *op. cit.*, p. 16.

6. *Ibid.*, p. 19.

7. Steedman does not capture all of Marx's concept of abstract labor with this definition. For Marx abstract labor is labor that has proven its social necessity in successful sale.

8. See Rosdolsky's *The Making of Marx's Capital*, Chapter Two.

9. Even then, however, civil society and the state remain categorizable in essence terms in so far as they are on the level of objective spirit as opposed to absolute spirit.

10. See Shlomo Avineri's *The Social and Political Thought of Karl Marx*, pp. 202 ff.

11. For a discussion of the role of opportunity costs in social change, see Elster's *Making Sense of Marx*, p. 420.

12. A recent contribution is Norman Geras' "Post-Marxism," especially pp. 48 ff.

13. On this complex of issues see G. William Domhoff's *The Powers That Be*.

14. See "Media Monotony," by the editors of *Dollars and Sense*.

15. All units of capital "face the market imperative of having to reinvest and expand simply to survive in the face of advancing competition." *The Just Economy*, p. 129.

16. This argument is found in "Theses on the Theory of the State," by Claus Offe and Volker Ronge.

17. "By what is the accrual of state property to high finance conditioned? By the constantly growing indebtedness of the state. And the indebtedness of the state? By the constant excess of its expenditure over its income, a disproportion which is simultaneously the cause and effect of the system of state loans." Karl Marx, "The Class Struggles in France," in *Collected Works*, Volume 10, p. 115.

18. For further discussion of the structural limits on the state, see my paper "John Rawls and the Structural Contradictions of the Capitalist State."

19. Marx and Engels, "The Manifesto of the Communist Party," in *Collected Works*, Volume 6, p. 497.

20. This position is developed in Ernest Mandel's *Revolutionary Marxism Today*, Cahpter 3.

21. "(The Commune's) true secret was this. It was essentially a working-class government, the product of the struggle of the producing against the appropriating class, the political form at last discovered under which to work out the economic emancipation of labour." "The Civil War in France," in *Selected Writings*, p. 544. The three features mentioned in the main text are discussed by Marx on pp. 541-42.

22. "Even the best of revolutionary parties will never be but one fraction of the proletariat (certainly it will try to be the majority party but that is scarcely guaranteed in advance once and for all). This same party, far from being infallible, will make a lot of errors. It will never be perfectly democratic but will experience the beginnings of bureaucratization and will regularly be tempted to manipulate the masses in a paternalist way. In these real conditions...the real objective must therefore be authentic political representation of the proletariat as a whole, which is impossible without the flourishing of political, ideological and cultural pluralism for the masses... Without this sort of pluralism workers will not be able to really wield power....Far from being some sort of concession to the bourgeoisie, petty bourgeoisie, or to Social Democracy, it (pluralist socialist democracy) corresponds to the interests of the proletariat. It facilitates a better knowledge of the real aspirations and opinions of different layers of workers. The authentic needs of the masses and their different fractions can be determined. It enables the better planning of production, bringing closer together working people's genuine preferences in the field of productive effort and consumption. It helps as much as possible to avoid political errors and, once these errors have been made (which is inevitable), they can be corrected as quickly as possible." Ernest Mandel, "In Defence of the Fourth International," p. 17.

23. Marx and Engels, "The German Ideology," in *Collected Works* Volume 5, p. 78. I argue for the superiority of Marx's notion of socialism over the normative models defended by Kant and Habermas in "Kant's Political Philosophy: *Rechtsstaat* or Council Democracy?" and "Habermas and History: The Institutionalization of Discourse as Historical Projects" respectively.

Bibliography

Albrecht, Reinhardt. *Hegel und die Demokratie.* Bonn: Bouvier, 1978.

Aristotle. *The Politics.* Oxford: Oxford Univ. Press, 1959.

Arthur, Chris. "Dialectics and Labour." In Mepham & Ruben.

_____. *The Dialectics of Labour: Marx and his Relation to Hegel.* N.Y.: Basil Blackwell, 1984.

Avineri, Shlomo. *The Social and Political Thought of Karl Marx.* Cambridge: Cambridge Univ. Press, 1971.

_____. *Hegel's Theory of the Modern State.* Cambridge: Cambridge Univ. Press, 1972.

_____. "The Discovery of Hegel's Early Lectures on the Philosophy of Right." *The Owl of Minerva* 16, no. 2, 1985.

Backhaus, Hans-Georg. "Zur Dialektik der Wertform." In Schmidt, 1970.

_____. "Materialien zur Rekonstruktion der Marxschen Werttheorie." In *Gesellschaft. Beiträge zur Marxschen Theorie,* Numbers 1, 3, 11, 1974, 1975, 1978, respectively.

Bhaduri, A. "On the Significance of Recent Controversies in Capital Theory: A Marxian View." *Economic Journal,* 1969.

Böhm-Bawerk, E. von. *Karl Marx and the Close of His System.* ed. Paul Sweezy. N.Y.: Augustus M. Kelly, 1949.

Bowles, Samuel, and Herbert Gintis. "Structure and Practice in the Labor Theory of Value." *Review of Radical Political Economy* 12, no. 4, 1981.

Bradby, Barbara. "The Remystification of Value." *Capital and Class* 17, Summer, 1982.

Braverman, Harry. *Labor and Monopoly Capital.* N.Y.: Monthly Review Press, 1974.

Brenner, Robert. "The Social Bases of Economic Development." In Roemer, ed. *Analytical Marxism.*

Bubner, Rüdinger. "Logik and Kapital," In *Dialektik und Wissenschaft.* Frankfurt: Suhrkamp, 1973.

Burkett, Brian. *Radical Political Economy.* Brighton: Wheatsheaf Books, 1985.

Carchedi, Guglielmo. "The Logic of Prices as Values." In Fine.

Carver, Terrence. "Marx—and Hegel's *Logic.*" *Political Studies* 24, 1976.

Cleaver, Harry. *Reading Capital Politically.* Austin: Univ. of Texas Press, 1979.

Colletti, Lucio. *Marxism and Hegel.* London: New Left Review Books, 1973.

D'Hondt, Jacques. *Hegel in His Time: Berlin, 1818-1831.* Lewiston, N.Y.: Broadview Press, 1988.

Desmond, William, ed. *Hegel and His Critics: Philosophy in the Aftermath of Hegel.* Albany: S.U.N.Y. Press, 1988.

Dollars and Sense, editors. "Media Monotony: Corporate Media Support Status Quo." *Dollars and Sense,* Nov., 1984.

Domhoff, G. Willian. *The Powers That Be: Processes of Ruling Class Domination in America.* N.Y.: Vintage Press, 1978.

Eldred, Michael. *Critique of Competitive Freedom and the Bourgeois-Democratic State: Outline of a Form-Analytic Extension of Marx's Uncompleted System.* Copenhagen: Kurasje, 1984.

Eldred, Michael, and M. Hanlon. "Reconstructuring Value-Form Analysis." *Capital and Class* 13, 1981.

Elson, Diane, ed. *Value: the Representation of Labour in Capitalism.* Atlantic Highlands, N.J.: Humanities Press, 1979.

Elster, Jon. "Marxism, functionalism and game theory." *Theory and Society* 11, 1982.

———. *Explaining Technical Change.* Cambridge: Cambridge Univ. Press, 1983.

———. *Making Sense of Marx.* Cambridge: Cambridge Univ. Press, 1985.

Engels, Frederick. "Karl Marx: A Contribution to the Critique of Political Economy." In Marx, 1970.

Findlay, J. N. The Philosophy of Hegel. N.Y.: Collier Books, 1966.

Fine, Ben. ed. The Value Dimension. London: Routledge and Kegan Paul, 1986.

Fisk, Milton. "Dialectic and Ontology." In Mepham & Ruben.

Foley, Duncan. Understanding Capital: Marx's Economic Theory. Cambridge, Mass.: Harvard Univ. Press, 1986.

Geras, Norman. "Post-Marxism." New Left Review 163, 1987.

Göhler, Gerhard. Die Reduktion der Dialektik durch Marx. Strukturveränderungen der dialektischen Entwicklung in der Kritik der politischen Öknomie. Stuttgart, 1980.

Gordon, David. "The Global Economy: New Edifice or Crubling Foundations?" In New Left Review 168, May-June 1988.

Habermas, Jürgen. Theory and Practice. Boston: Beacon Press, 1974.

_____. Theorie des kommunikativen Handelns Band 2: Zur Kritik der funktionalischen Vernuft. Frankfurt: Suhrkamp, 1981.

Hänninen, S. and L. Paldán, ed. Rethinking Marx. N.Y.: International General, 1984.

Hartmann, Klaus. Die Marxsche Theorie. Bonn: Walter de Gruyer & Co., 1970.

_____. Marxens "Kapital" in transzendentalphilosophischer Sicht. Bonn: H. Bouvier, 1971.

_____. "Hegel: A Non-Metaphysical View." In MacIntyre.

_____. "Towards a New Systematic Reading of Hegel's Philosophy of Right." In State and Civil Society, Pelczynski, ed.

Hegel, G. W. F. Philosophy of Right. Oxford: Oxford Univ. Press, 1942.

_____. Lectures on the History of Philosophy. 3 vol. London: Routledge & Kegan Paul, 1955.

_____. The Philosophy of History. N.Y.: Dover, 1956.

_____. Science of Logic. New York: Humanities Press, 1969.

_____. The Philosophy of Mind. N.Y.: Oxford Univ. Press, 1971.

257

————. *Lectures on the Philosophy of Religion*. 3 vol. N.Y.: Humanities Press, 1974)

————. *Logic: Being Part One of the Encyclopaedia of the Philosophical Sciences*. London: Oxford Univ. Press, 1975.

————. *The Phenomenology of Spirit*. N.Y.: Oxford Univ. Press, 1979.

Henrich, Dieter, "Hegels Theorie über den Zufall." In *Hegel im Kontext*. Frankfurt: Suhrkamp, 1971.

Himmelweit, S. and S. Mohun, "The Anomalies of Capital." *Capital and Class* 6, 1978.

Hodgson, Geoff. *Capitalism, Value and Exploitation*. Oxford: Martin Robertson, 1982.

Howard, Dick. *From Marx to Kant*. Albany: S.U.N.Y. Press, 1985.

Howard, M. C., and J. E. King. *The Political Economy of Marx* London: Longman, 1975.

Hyppolite, Jean. *Studies on Marx and Hegel*. London: Heinemann, 1969.

Ilting, Karl. "Hegel's Concept of the State and Marx's Early Critique." In *State and Civil Society*, Pelczynski ed.

Inwood, Michael, ed. *Hegel*. N.Y.: Oxford. Univ. Press, 1985.

Kojéve, A. *Introduction to the Reading of Hegel; Lectures on the Phenomenology of Spirit*. New York: Basic Books, 1969.

Krahl, Hans-Jürgen. "Bermerkungen zum Verhältnis von Kapital und Hegelscher Wesenslogik." In Negt.

Lange, E. M. *Das Prinzip Arbeit*. Berlin, 1980.

Lenin, V. I., "Conspectus of Hegel's Book *The Science of Logic*." In *Collected Works*, Vol. 38. London: Lawrence & Wishart, 1976.

Little, Dan. "The Scientific Standing of Marx's *Capital*." *Review of Radical Political Economics* 17, no. 4, 1985.

Locke, John. *The Second Treatise on Government*. Indianapolis: Bobbs Merrill, 1952.

Lohmann, Georg. "'Wealth' as an Aspect of the Critique of Capital." In Hänninen and Paldán.

Löwy, Michael. *The Politics of Combined and Uneven Development*. London: Verso, 1981.

Luxemburg, Rosa. "Reform or Revolution." In *Rosa Luxemburg Speaks*. N.Y.: Pathfinder Press, 1970.

_____. *The Accumulation of Capital-An Anti-Critique*. N.Y.: Monthly Review Press, 1972.

Maarek, Gerard. *An Introduction to Karl Marx's Das Kapital* London: Martin Robertson, 1979.

MacGregor, David. *The Communist Ideal in Hegel and Marx*. Toronto: Univ. of Toronto Press, 1984.

MacIntyre, Alasdair, ed. *Hegel*. N.Y.: Anchor Books, 1972.

Maker, William. "Hegel's Critique of Marx's Fetishism of Dialectics." In Desmond.

_____. ed. *Hegel on Freedom and Economics*. Mercer Univ. Press, 1987.

Mandel, Ernest. *Marxist Economic Theory*. 2 vol. N.Y.: Monthly Review Press, 1968.

_____. *Late Capitalism*. London: Verso, 1975.

_____. *Revolutionary Marxism Today*. London: Verso, 1979.

_____. "Gold, Money, and the Transformation Problem." In Mandel and Freeman.

_____. "In Defense of the Fourth International." *International Viewpoint*, supplement to No. 93, Feb. 24, 1986.

_____. "In Defense of Socialist Planning." *New Left Review* 159, 1986.

Mandel, Ernest, and Alan Freeman. *Ricardo, Marx, Sraffa*. London: Verso, 1984.

Marx, Karl. *Theories of Surplus Value* Part I Moscow: Progress Pub., 1963.

_____. *Theories of Surplus Value* Part II Moscow: Progress Pub., 1968.

_____. *A Contribution to the Critique of Political Economy*. Moscow: Progress Publishers, 1970.

_____. *Theories of Surplus Value* Part III Moscow: Progress Pub., 1971.

_____. *Grundrisse*. New York: Vintage Press, 1973.

_____. *Karl Marx: Texts on Method*. ed. T. Carver. Oxford: Basil Blackwell, 1974.

_____. *Capital* Volume I. Moscow: Progress Pub., 1978.

————. *Capital* Volume II. Moscow: Progress Pub., 1978.

————. *Capital* Volume III. Moscow: Progress Pub., 1978.

Marx, Karl, and Frederick Engels. *Selected Writings.* ed. McLellan. Oxford: Oxford Univ. Press, 1977.

————. *The Marx-Engels Reader.* ed. Tucker. N.Y.: Norton Press, 1978.

————. *Collected Works.* N.Y.: International Publishers, various dates.

————. *Letters on 'Capital'.* London: New Park, 1983.

McBride, William. *The Philosophy of Marx.* London: Hutchinson, 1977.

McCarney, Joe. *The Real World of Ideology.* Atlantic Highlands: Humanities Press, 1980.

Meek, R. L. *Economics and Ideology and Other Essays.* London: Chapman and Hall, 1967.

Meikle, Scott. *Essentialism in the Thought of Karl Marx.* LaSalle, Il.: Open Court, 1985.

Meiners, Reinhard. *Methoden Probleme bei Marx und ihr Bezug zur Hegelsche Philosophie.* Munich: Minereva-Publikation, 1980.

Mepham, John. "From the *Grundrisse* to *Capital:* The Making of Marx's Method." In Mepham and Ruben.

Mepham, John & D-H. Ruben. *Issues in Marxist Philosophy Volume One: Dialectics and Method.* Atlantic Highlands, N.J.: Humanities Press, 1979.

Mészàvos, Istvan. *Marx's Theory of Alienation.* London: Merlin Press, 1975.

Miller, Richard. *Analysing Marx.* Princeton: Princeton Univ. Press, 1984.

Morishima, Michio. *Marx's Economics: A Dual Theory of Value and Growth.* Cambridge: Cambridge Univ. Press, 1973.

Murray, Patrick. *Marx's Theory of Scientific Knowledge.* Atlantic Highlands, N.J.: Humanities Press, 1988.

Negt, Oskar. *Aktualität und Folgen der Philosophie Hegels.* Frankfurt: Suhrkamp, 1970.

Norman, Richard, and Sean Sayers. *Hegel, Marx and Dialectic: A Debate.* Atlantic Highlands, N.J.: Humanities Press, 1980.

Nove, Alex. "Markets and Socialism." *New Left Review* 161, 1987.

Offe, Klaus and Volker Ronge. "Theses on the Theory of the State." *New German Critique* 6, 1975.

Okishio, Nubuo. "Technical Change and the Rate of Profit." *Kobe University Economic Review*, 1961.

Ollman, Bertell. *Alienation*. N.Y.: Cambridge Univ. Press, 1971.

Pelczynski, Z. A. ed. *Hegel's Political Philosophy* Cambridge: Cambridge Univ. Press, 1971.

_____. *State and Civil Society: Studies in Hegel's Political Philosophy*. Cambridge: Cambridge Univ. Press, 1984.

Pilling, Geoffrey. *Marx's 'Capital': Philosophy and Political Economy*. London: Routledge & Kegan Paul, 1980.

Pinkard, Terry. "The Logic of Hegel's *Logic*." In Inwood.

Plant, Raymond. *Hegel*. N.Y.: Basil Blackwell, 1983.

Popper, Karl. "What is Dialectic?" *Mind* 49, 1940.

Prokopczyk, Czeslaw. *Truth and Reality in Marx and Hegel*. Amherst: Univ. of Massachusetts Press, 1980.

Puntel, L. Bruno. *Darstellung, Methode und Strukture. Untersuchungen der systematischen Philosophie G. W.F. Hegels. Hegel-Studien*. Beiheft 10. Bonn: Bouvier, 1973.

Robinson, Joan. *An Essay on Marxian Economics*. N.Y.: St. Martin's Press, 1942.

Rockmore, Tom. *Hegel's Circular Epistemology*. Bloomington: Indiana University Press, 1986.

Roemer, John. ed. *Analytical Marxism*. Cambridge: Cambridge Univ. Press, 1986.

_____. *Free to Lose*. Cambridge Ma.: Harvard Univ. Press, 1988.

Rosdolsky, Roman. *The Making of Marx's 'Capital'*. London: Pluto Press, 1977.

Rosen, Michael. *Hegel's Dialectic and its Criticism*. Cambridge: Cambridge Univ. Press, 1982.

Roth, Mike, and Michael Eldred. *Guide to Marx's Capital*. London: CSE Books, 1978.

Samuelson, Paul. "Understanding the Marxian Notion of Exploitation: A Summary of the So-Called Transformation Problem Between Marxian Values and Competitive Prices." *Journal of Economic Literature*, vol. ix, no. 2, June 1971.

Sartre, Jean Paul. *Critique of Dialectical Reason*. London: Verso, 1982.

Sayer, Derek. *Marx's Method: Ideology, Science, and Criticism in 'Capital'*. New Jersey: Humanities Press, 1979.

Schmidt, Alfred. *Beiträge zur marxistischen Erkenntnistheorie*. Frankfurt, Suhrkamp, 1970.

Shaikh, Anwar. "The Transformation from Marx to Sraffa." In Mandel & Freeman.

Smith, Tony. "Robert Nozick's Critique of Marxian Economics." *Social Theory and Practice*, vol. 8, no. 2, 1982.

————. "Two Theories of Historical Materialism: G. A. Cohen and Jürgen Habermas." *Theory and Society*, vol. 13, no. 4, 1984.

————. "Kant's Political Philosophy: *Rechtsstaat* or Council Democracy?" *The Review of Politics*, Vol. 47, no. 2, 1985.

————. "Hegelianism and Marx: A Reply to Lucio Colletti." *Science and Society*, 50, no. 2, 1986.

————. "Habermas and History: The Institutionalization, of Discourse as Historical Project." In *At the Nexus of Philosophy and History*, Univ. of Georgia Press, 1987.

————. "Hegel's Theory of the Syllogism and its Relevance to Marxism." *Radical Philosophy* 48, Spring, 1988.

————. "Rawls and the Structural Contradictions of the Capitalist State. In *Ideals of a Good Society: Problems in Social Philosophy Today*. Lewiston, N.Y.: Edwin Mellen Press, 1989.

————. "Roemer on Marxian Exploitation." *Science and Society* 53, no. 3, 1989.

————. "The Debate Regarding Dialectical Logic in Marx's Economic Writings." To appear in *International Philosophical Quarterly*, 1990.

————. "Analytical Marxism and Marx's Systematic Dialectical Theory." To appear in *Man and World*.

Steedman, Ian. *Marx after Sraffa*. London: New Left Review Books, 1977.

Suchting, William. *Marxism and Philosophy*. N.Y.: New York Univ. Press, 1986.

Taylor, Charles. *Hegel and Modern Society*. N.Y.: Cambridge Univ. Press, 1979.

Thompson, E.P. *The Poverty of Theory*. N.Y.: Monthly Review Press, 1978.

Trotsky, Leon. *The Transitional Program for Socialist Revolution*. N.Y.: Pathfinder Press, 1977.

Weber, Max. *The Protestant Ethic and the Spirit of Capitalism*. N.Y.: Scribner's, 1958.

_____. *General Economic History*. New York: Collier Books, 1961.

_____. *Economy and Society*. 2 vol. N.Y. Bedminster Press, 1968.

White, Alan. *Absolute Knowledge: Hegel and the Problem of Metaphysics*. Athens, Ohio: Ohio Univ. Press, 1983.

Winfield, Richard Dien. "The Logic of Marx's *Capital*." *Telos* 27, Spring 1976.

_____. "Dialectical Logic and the Conception of Truth." *Journal of the British Society for Phenomenology*, 18, No. 2, 1987.

_____. "Is Hegel's Logic a Transcendental Ontology?" *Man and World* 20, 1987.

_____. "Hegel's Challenge to the Modern Economy." In Maker, ed.

_____. *The Just Economy*. N.Y.: Routledge, Chapman & Hall, 1988.

Wolff, Robert Paul. *Understanding Marx: A Reconstruction and Critique of Capital*. Princeton: Princeton Univ. Press, 1984.

Wood, Steven, ed. *The Degradation of Work: Skill, Deskilling, and the Labor Process*. London: Hutchinson, 1983.

Zeleńy, Jindřich. *The Logic of Marx*. N.Y.: Rowman & Littlefield, 1980.

Index

Absolute, 6, 10-12, 25, 32, 215n.37
Abstinence, 135, 138
Abstract labor: manifested in
  commodities, 53, 60, 67-71, 81; and
  money, 95; negative social form,
  58-59, 223n.8; social necessity in,
  72, 75, 252n.7; and value, 80. *See
  also* Alienation; Labor theory of
  value; Socially necessary labor
Abstract right, 16, 17, 18, 26, 62, 200
Abstraction, 67, 69
Accumulation, 133-46, 155, 174-5,
  203, 237n.13; expanded, 27-28,
  133-6, 141, 171; original, 133-5,
  137, 218n.19; simple, 27-28, 133,
  134-6, 141
Alienation, 67, 79, 187, 194, 251n.52;
  in abstract labor, 58-9; in
  accumulation, 140, 141, 142-4,
  239nn.27, 28; in commodity form,
  75; of consumers, 77; from means
  of production, 120, 181; in
  production process, 125, 126, 128-
  9, 130, 131-3, 236n.6; in technical
  change, 64
Aristotle, 98
Arthur, Chris, 225n.23
Artisan Production, 63
Autonomy. *See* Freedom

Backhaus, Hans-Georg, 32, 219n.33
Bad infinite, 81

Being *(Sein)*, xi, 17, 73, 75, 211n.11;
  in category of "abstract right," 16,
  in Hegel's *Logic*, 13, in Marx, 205
Big industry, 127, 129
Bradby, Barbara, 109, 233n.21
Bubner, Rüdiger, 44

Capital: bank, 188-9, 192, 194; in
  circulation, 99, 106, 148-63;
  concentration of, 187, 194; different
  species of, 107-8; in distribution,
  99, 164-78, 188-92; divisions of,
  150-4; as essence structure, 44, 53-
  54; form of, 99; industrial, 170,
  194, 248nn.37, 38; in general
  (versus many capitals) 164, 168,
  170-1, 173, 174-5, 179-81, 183;
  investment, 131-2; marginal
  productivity of, 244n.21; merchant
  capital, 107, 108, 188, 189,
  248n.38; non-industrial, 189-94; as
  notion structure, 53-54; organic
  composition of, 166, 168, 183-4; as
  principle of organization of
  production, 124-6, 136, 146; as
  principle of transformation of
  production, 127-33, 136, 146; in
  production, 99, 100-47; strike
  threat of, 118, 204-5; technical
  composition of, 183-4
Categories: connections among, 5,
  11-12, 30, 35, 46, 96-97; as

265

reproduction process, 155

Winfield, Richard, xi, 98, 224n.21; on commodity exchange, 74-8; critique of Marx, 102-9; early analysis of capital, 44-5; on market prices, 173-4; on state, 202

Women, 109-12, 215n.42. *See also* Domestic labor

Workers cooperatives, 103, 108, 232n.20